The

VATICAN COUNCIL

LONGMANS, GREEN AND CO. Ltd.
39 PATERNOSTER ROW, LONDON, E.C. 4
6 OLD COURT HOUSE STREET, CALCUTTA
53 NICOL ROAD, BOMBAY
MOUNT ROAD, MADRAS

LONGMANS, GREEN AND CO.
55 FIFTH AVENUE, NEW YORK
221 EAST 20TH STREET, CHICAGO
TREMONT TEMPLE, BOSTON
128-132 UNIVERSITY AVENUE, TORONTO

BY THE SAME AUTHOR

BENEDICTINE
MONACHISM

8vo   10s. 6d. net

Pio Nono

The VATICAN COUNCIL

THE STORY TOLD FROM INSIDE IN BISHOP ULLATHORNE'S LETTERS

BY

Dom CUTHBERT BUTLER

MONK OF DOWNSIDE ABBEY

VOLUME I

WITH PORTRAITS

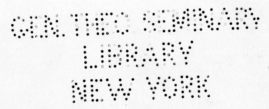

LONGMANS, GREEN AND CO.
LONDON ♦ NEW YORK ♦ TORONTO
1930

Nibil obstat.

GEORGIUS D. SMITH, D.D.,
Censor deputatus.

Imprimatur.

EDM. CAN. SURMONT,
Vic. Gen.

WESTMONASTERII,
die 14 *Octobris,* 1929.

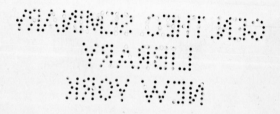
Made in Great Britain

INTRODUCTION

THE series of Bishop Ullathorne's letters suggested to me this History of the Vatican Council, and they are its backbone. But I have gone much further afield, and have laid myself out, by a survey of the documents and literature of the Council, to present a history, authentic and adequate, and of a size that may reasonably be offered to the public likely to be interested in the subject. So far as I know, no such story of the Council exists in any language : the two histories, of Friedrich and of Granderath, are of great length, running each to over two thousand pages.

Dr. Ullathorne, Bishop of Birmingham, was a letter-writer of the old school, who loved writing letters, and wrote them well. Week by week he wrote to friends in England, telling them what news of the Council and of Rome he was at liberty to impart. In these letters we have his impressions, almost from day to day, of the course of events, his estimations of men and movements, his hopes and fears at every turn, told with great actuality : in all, a living picture of the Council from inside, such as, to the best of my knowledge, has nowhere else been given us.

Readers of the *Life of Bishop Ullathorne* will know him as a plain straightforward Yorkshire man, of high character, with wide experience of men and affairs, shrewd and intelligent. At the Council he took up and maintained a 'moderate' or middle position, holding aloof from all movements, all intrigues outside the Council Chamber, refusing to act with any party, or to sign any petition, protest, or other document whatsoever; yet closely in touch with leading bishops on both sides. Thus we have in him probably a witness as well informed, and as independent, impartial, and objective, as could well be found.

No pains have been spared in the endeavour to make the framework in which these letters are set a comprehensive, living, and (as I hope) faithful account of the Council itself, of the controversies waged at it and round it, and of the men that waged them.

There is no need to stress the religious importance of the Vatican Council; it is universally recognized as being, with Trent, an outstanding landmark in the modern history of the Catholic Church, with repercussions on all religious Bodies claiming the name of Christian. This is its first substantive history in English not by the hand of an enemy. I believe that the impression left, as the outcome of it all, is one at which the Catholic Church has no cause to blush.

My thanks are due to Mr. Leslie Toke for kind help in making the Index.

I have to thank also Mr. H. N. Gladstone for the permission to print Mr. Gladstone's letter in c. XVII.

Above all, thanks are due to the Superioress of the Dominican Convent at Stone, for placing at my disposal the dossier of Dr. Ullathorne's letters.

I also desire to acknowledge my indebtedness to the following for permission to reprint certain extracts from copyright works :—

The Art & Book Co., Ltd., for extracts from the 'Memoir of Francis Kerril Amherst'.

Messrs. Burns, Oates & Washbourne, Ltd., for extracts from the English translation of Fessler's

'True and False Infallibility' and extracts from Abbot Butler's 'Life of Bishop Ullathorne'.

Messrs. Chapman & Hall, Ltd., for an extract from the English translation of 'The Life of Dupanloup'.

Messrs. Constable & Co., Ltd., for an extract from an article by Abbot Butler in 'The Hibbert Journal' of April, 1906.

Messrs. Hodder & Stoughton, Ltd., and Messrs. Richard R. Smith, Inc., for an extract from Dr. Foakes-Jackson's 'Peter, Prince of the Apostles'.

Messrs. Macmillan & Co., Ltd., for extracts from Purcell's 'Life of Manning'.

Messrs. Sheed & Ward for extracts from Fr. Vincent McNabb's 'Infallibility'.

The Society for Promoting Christian Knowledge for extracts from articles by Prof. Turner in 'Theology'.

CUTHBERT BUTLER.

EALING PRIORY
March, 1930

CONTENTS OF VOL. I

ix

ILLUSTRATIONS OF VOL. I

SOURCES

THE literature of the Vatican Council is immense, and no attempt is made here to draw up anything of the nature of a Bibliography. Only certain outstanding works are named that are fundamental : just collections of Acts and documents, and the standard histories of the Council. The chief controversial literature it called forth is dealt with currently in these pages ; it all is fully recorded and summarized in Granderath's History of the Council.

A.—PRIMARY SOURCES

Collections of Acts and Documents

1. MANSI.—The complete *Acta* are printed in the five concluding volumes of the Continuation of Mansi's *Collectio Conciliorum*, tomes 49-53, 1923-27. Here is printed in full everything official or semi-official relating to the Council : public Acts, documents, reports, petitions, minutes of congregations and committees, and the stenographers' reports in full of all the speeches at the debates—everything. It all fills 6000 folio columns. The various volumes in the Vatican Archives in which this mass of material is preserved are enumerated in the opening chapter of Granderath's History.

In the references these five volumes are numbered I to V, the Mansi number being added in brackets : thus : Mansi I (49).

2. CECCONI.—Shortly after the Council Eugenio Cecconi, Canon of Florence, was commissioned to write the official History, fully documented. He produced one volume in 1873 ; and another, in 3 parts, in 1879 ; the work was not continued, he having become Archbishop of Florence. The volumes published contain only the ' Antecedente del Concilio '. The chief feature of the work is the collection of documents, cccviii in number, most miscellaneous in character, dealing with the pre-history of the Council in all its aspects. They are the basis

of all the history up to the actual opening, December 8, 1869. The work has been translated into French by Bonhomme, Paris, 1887, 4 vols.

3. *Collectio Lacensis Conciliorum recentiorum*, tome vii : Acta et Decreta S. Concilii Vaticani, cum permultis aliis documentis ad Concilium eiusque historiam spectantibus, 1892. A large 4° volume of 2000 columns. The first 1000 columns is the pith of Mansi's 6000 : viz.,

1-500 *Acta et Decreta.*
500-1000 *Documenta Synodalia.*

This portion is superseded by Mansi, where all is given much more fully : e.g. the reports of the speeches are not given in *Lac.* The other portion contains material not found in Mansi : viz.,

1000-2000 *Documenta Historica.*

The documents number 585, and they are fundamental as sources for the external history, reproducing the principal documents, before and during the Council, of movements among Catholics and on the part of the Governments. This collection is indispensable ; as also are the two excellent and exhaustive Indexes of Persons and of Things, which are an invaluable help to students working at the Council.

Two minor collections should be named, though now superseded :

Friedrich : *Documenta ad illustrandum Concilium Vaticanum*, 1871.

Friedberg : *Sammlung der Aktenstücke zum Vat. Konzil*, 1872.

A word should be said on the work of V. Frond : *Actes et Histoire du Concile de Rome*, Paris, 1871. The title is a misnomer ; though the work is in eight great folio volumes *de luxe*, there is nothing in it to justify the title—no acts, no history of the Council. It gives biographies of all the cardinals and bishops, and its interest lies in the fact that it gives portraits and facsimile signatures of most of them.

B.—SUBSIDIARY SOURCES

Collections of Letters, Diaries, etc.

1. The best-known series of Letters are those of 'Quirinus'. They are dealt with in c. XIV, and what is said there need not be repeated here. They are hostile to the Council, and everything

they say needs to be controlled. An English translation, 800 pages, was published in 1870.

2. Thomas Mozley : *Letters from Rome*, London, 1891, 2 vols. He was the correspondent of *The Times* so severely handled by Ullathorne (I, 178). It is hard to imagine how these letters could have been thought worth reprinting after twenty years. They are not good, even as literature ; they contain hardly anything of value, and not much of interest. This is not surprising, seeing that Mozley frankly confesses he could speak neither Italian nor French, and so had to rely on what English gossip he could pick up. The general tone is unsympathetic and frivolous.

3. Louis Veuillot : *Rome pendant le Concile*, Paris, 1872, 2 vols. The redoubtable editor of the *Univers* was in Rome all through the Council, and these are his letters to his paper. They are disappointing ; there is not much in them about the Council itself, only outside gossip ; there is more of Paris and its religious and political controversies than of Rome. But as ' pièces justificatives ' are printed documents of high importance.

4. Bishop Ullathorne's Letters, printed here for the first time ; the only letters that give any consecutive information of the workings of the Council from the inside. They were written, some to his Vicar General, some to his secretary, some to Dr. Northcote, President of Oscott College, some to Newman ; but most to his great and intimate friend Mother Imelda Poole, Superioress of the Dominican Convent at Stone : to her successor we are beholden for placing at my disposal the dossier of Dr. Ullathorne's letters. The letters range over a wide field : antiquities of Rome, Christian and Pagan ; churches, functions ecclesiastical and social, festivals—there is a lively description of the old Carnival and the horse-race in the Corso. A selection is printed in the volume *Letters of Archbishop Ullathorne*. Here only those letters or portions of letters concerned with the Council are reproduced.

5. Diary of M. Icard, Superior of Saint-Sulpice, theologian at the Council of the Archbishop of Sens. The Diary has not been printed, but it is used in Mourret's book, see below, under C. On Icard see c. XIV. If this Diary, which is of considerable length, were printed in full, it would give an intimate picture of

the inner working of the Council and of the persons that would be quite unique.

6. Diary of Cardinal Gibbons : *Retrospect of Fifty Years*, 1916. The first section, of 185 pages, contains extracts from his Diary with reminiscences. It gives interesting sketches of prominent figures, but tells little of the Council itself.

7. Friedrich's *Tagebuch während des Vatikan Konzils*, or Diary during the Council, 1871, ed. 2, 1873. It is to some extent the raw material of Quirinus' letters, and is entirely hostile to the Council.

8. A great number of Biographies of the Council bishops have chapters on the Council, often embodying letters or extracts from diaries. The Lives of Manning and of Dupanloup stand out as of special interest.

C.—HISTORIES

1. Friedrich : *Geschichte des Vatikanischen Konzils*, 3 vols., 1877-87 ; 2500 pages in all. This History is written in defence of the Old Catholic position, and like all Friedrich's writings on the Council, is strongly prejudiced. Without doubt a great deal of the information it gives is authentic ; but the work is animated by the spirit of Quirinus, and is tendentious, abounding in exaggerations and distortions, every incident receiving the worst interpretation.

2. Granderath : Fr. Theodore Granderath, S.J., the editor of the Lacensis volume of *Acta*, produced an extended History of the Council. The German, *Geschichte des Vatikanischen Konzils*, in 3 vols., appeared in 1903-6 ; a French translation, in 6 vols., in 1908-19. The scale of the work may be gauged from the fact that the German covers 2000 closely printed pages, the French 2500. Everything at Rome was placed at his disposal, all archives thrown open. Thus he was able to refute not a few of Friedrich's misstatements, and the work is in great measure a rectification of Friedrich. But though no doubt on the whole Granderath is more right, and his account substantially true, he shows himself almost as decided a partisan : for him the Majority always were right, and the Minority wrong, always and in everything ; and in the summaries of the debates and speeches he frequently intervenes personally, arguing and scolding, in a way that spoils his book as a piece of mere history.

For all that, it is, and is likely to remain, the standard work on the Council ; and, needless to say, the present book is greatly indebted to it.

The divisions and subdivisions are complicated : each volume is divided into Books and each Book into Chapters ; but the numbering is not continuous, restarting in each volume and each book. The references will be given in the form

II, Bk. iii, c. 2,

and are applicable equally to the German and the French. When necessary to name a page, the number in the German is given, being recorded in the lower margin of the French.

3. Campana. An Italian history, *Il Concilio Vaticano*, is in course of publication by Dr. Emilio Campana, canon of Lugano, Switzerland. It promises to be on a still larger scale than Granderath ; the only volume so far published, 1926, in two parts, 'the atmosphere of the Council,' dealing with the preliminary stages and the controversies up to the actual opening, runs to 900 pages, just double the corresponding portion of Granderath. In this volume are to be found interesting biographical character sketches of the foremost actors at the Council. The position is of course definitely Ultramontane ; but the appreciations make the impression of being written with fairness and understanding. There are good grounds for hoping that Campana's work, when accomplished, will provide not only an exhaustive and fully documented history of the Council, but one that is impartial, well balanced, and objective. He tells me, however, that he has had to lay aside the work for the time being.

4. Pomponio Leto : *Otto Mesi a Roma durante il Concilio*, 1873 : English translation, *Eight Months at Rome during the Council ; Impressions of a Contemporary*, 1876.

Friedrich was responsible for starting the report that the author was Cardinal Nobili Vitelleschi, who had taken part in the Council. This canard got currency in the English press, and in spite of denials was persisted in, as by the *Saturday*, the *Contemporary*, and the *Guardian* (see Manning, *True Story*, p. 161). The idea was as absurd as it was injurious : Vitelleschi's votes, speeches, written memoranda, are all to be seen in Mansi, and show him to have acted consistently with the Majority. The British Museum Catalogue gives the author correctly as ' the Marquis Francesco Nobili Vitelleschi ', a brother of the Cardinal, a man of strong Italian liberal tendencies. The book is of the same colour as Quirinus, abounding in apocryphal incidents, and is altogether antagonistic to the Council.

Two works, not exactly histories, but historical accounts of the Council, must be named :

5. Émile Ollivier : *L'Église et l'État au Concile du Vatican*, 2 vols. 1877 ; 4th ed. 1884. Ollivier and his book are spoken of in c. VI. It is by far the best book on the outside aspects of the Council—the political and religious currents, especially in France, and the proceedings of the Governments in regard to the Council. It may almost be called a philosophical history ; all the great principles at issue, political and religious, are expounded with much learning, ability, understanding, and moderation. Ollivier was not a Catholic, but as a leading French statesman he knew the French bishops and other French actors in the affairs of the Council. His character sketches of Pio Nono, Antonelli, Montalembert, Darboy, Dupanloup, Pie, and others, all of whom he knew personally, are eloquent pieces of writing, marked by sympathetic insight. The book may be recommended as an eminently sane and sensible presentation of the story of the Council, told by an independent and understanding onlooker.

Ollivier returned to the Council in vol. xiii of his work, *L'Empire libéral*, 1908. But this is mostly made up of extracts from the earlier book. In a note at the beginning he tells how some one had sent that earlier work to Rome, to be placed on the Index, and how Leo XIII read it himself, and handed it on to the official, with the note ' Dimittatur ',—surely rightly, for it is the best apologia of the Council.

6. Fernand Mourret : *Le Concile du Vatican*, 1919, 340 pp.

The abbé Mourret is a Sulpitian, now Director or Superior of Saint-Sulpice, Paris. He has produced a general History of the Church in 9 vols. His book is based largely on the Diary of M. Icard (see c. XIV), and on the large and rich collection of letters stored in the archives of Saint-Sulpice. This is the best short book to read on the Council, especially on the French side of it. After fifty years the bitternesses of the 'sixties had died down, and Mourret was able to apportion praise and blame with even-handed justice, and with generous recognition for good. There is one blemish : a French post-war mentality appears now and then—all evils of Church and society come from Germany.

SOURCES

It was unfortunate that the writings hostile to the Council and the Church—Quirinus, Pomponio Leto, Friedrich—were allowed to run for thirty years without effective refutation. The small tracts of Fessler, *Das Vatikanische Konzilium*, 1871, and of Manning, *The True Story of the Vatican Council*, 1877, were quite inadequate to meet the massive and circumstantial writings on the other side. Thus the account of the enemies of the Council and the Papacy got the start, and held the field practically uncontradicted for so long a time, up to the publication of Granderath, that the case for the Council, it may almost be said, was allowed to go by default. Ollivier, it is true, raised his voice for the Council; but his book had no general circulation out of France. In England, educated public opinion has hitherto been formed wholly on Janus, Quirinus, Pomponio Leto, all promptly translated into English, and on the letters of Acton and of Mozley, the correspondent of *The Times*. The present work is the first attempt in English to present an account of the Vatican Council based on the Acta and other authentic documents, interpreted, it is hoped, with such objectivity and impartiality as may be possible in one who has clear and strong convictions.

BACKGROUND OF THE COUNCIL

VOL. I.—I

CHAPTER I

THE PAPAL QUESTION: TEMPORAL POWER: DEPOSING POWER

ALTHOUGH the Vatican Council was convoked to deal with issues of widest import, the errors and calamities of the times, the matter with which in fact it principally dealt was the Papacy; and the outcome of the Council was the settlement of long-standing controversies concerning the position and authority of the Pope in the Church. These questions it was that set going the storm of hostility to the Council throughout the world, and not least in governmental circles in the Catholic countries, as Austria and Bavaria, and in a lesser degree France. But the statesmen and politicians were not greatly interested in such purely theological questions as papal infallibility: it was the question of relations of Church and State that interested them, and their fears were stirred up by the idea that in some way the acts of the Council were going to issue in a reassertion of the claims to temporal power associated with the names of Gregory VII, Innocent III, Boniface VIII. This temporal power was a thing quite different from that understood by the term in modern times, when it has been used for that far lesser thing, the Pope's civil princedom or sovereignty over the portions of Italy known for a thousand years as the States of the Church. This latter question was acutely alive at the time of the Council, but it did not come up during its course. Neither did that other greater temporal power, of which the statesmen were in fear; though aspects of it, relations of Church and State, were all the time simmering beneath the surface and threatening to emerge. And in fact after the Council many did suppose that the old claims had been in some way revived: witness the great English statesman, W. E. Gladstone, who in 1874 could write that at the Council 'Rome had refurbished and paraded anew every rusty tool she was fondly thought to have disused.' In order to understand the Council it is necessary to understand the atmosphere of suspicion and hostility in which it sat; and to understand this, it is necessary to go back a long way, to the roots of the Papal Question on the temporal side.

The dual system set up in A.D. 800 with the crowning of Charlemagne by Pope Leo III as Emperor of the Holy Roman Empire of the West, whereby Pope and Emperor should rule together over Western Christendom, governing in mutual accord the spiritual and temporal domains, had broken down by the end of the century in the practical extinction of the family of Charles, and Empire and Papacy alike fell on evil days. For eighty years there was no fixed successor in the Empire, and at most times not even a nominal Emperor; while the Papacy became the plaything of rival factions of Roman nobles, probably the most turbulent and vicious of all European history, who for more than a century forcibly intruded into the papal chair Popes according to their will—licentious youths, feeble old men, worldly sycophants. In the hundred years 870-970 twenty-five Popes reigned, many of them violently done to death. It was a period of unparalleled disorder, violence, depravity in all ranks of Church and State alike. The Empire

4

was the first to recover itself in the person of the first Saxon Emperor, Otho the Great, crowned Emperor in Rome, 964, the founder of the line of Saxon Emperors, with whom the Empire became definitely German, attached to that one of themselves chosen King of Germany by the princes and dukes of the great German tribes.

In 1044 the scandal of the condition of the Papacy reached such a pitch that the Emperor Henry III intervened. As the only means of freeing the Papacy from the domination of the Roman nobles, the Emperor was given by the electors of the Roman Church the right of practically nominating to the Papacy, and he now used this right to appoint a series of German Popes, among them his cousin, the Bishop of Toul, known as Pope St. Leo IX, 1049-54. There is no more wonderful phenomenon in history than the resilience of the Papacy at this critical moment; the immediate resurgence of its position and prestige at the middle of the eleventh century, out of the state of prostration and degradation in which it had lain for wellnigh two hundred years.

The name associated with this resurrection is Hildebrand the monk. For a quarter of a century he was of five Popes the adviser, inspirer, strengthener; their legate and plenipotentiary in all difficult affairs, with a courage, perseverance and clear-sighted vision that overbore all opposition. Then in 1073 he mounted the apostolic throne as Gregory VII, to hold it during twelve of the most fateful years in the life-history of the Church and of the whole of Western Christendom. He was faced with gigantic evils in Church and State. It was a time of violence, of confusion, of the break-up of the bonds of society. Those whose historical outlook has been cramped and confined to the regulation school course of

5

History of England are not equipped with the knowledge necessary for judging the actions of Popes or Emperors in the eleventh, twelfth, and thirteenth centuries. Hildebrand at once took in hand the Herculean labour of stemming the flood of evils that threatened to engulf Western Europe, of purifying the Church, and freeing the spiritual power from its thraldom to the secular powers. His first concern was to strike at the tap-root of the evil, simony, which was rife and rampant on all sides: emperors, kings, bishops unblushingly trafficked in bishoprics, abbeys, benefices, often with great possessions and incomes.

With the winning for the spiritual power of freedom from the trammels of state authority was bound up the securing of freedom of election to bishoprics and to the Papacy itself, and the abolishing of the practice of investiture, whereby bishops and abbots received from emperor or king the ring and pastoral staff, the symbols of spiritual authority. Even after the just compromise was found in England by St. Anselm and Henry I, whereby bishops and abbots did homage to the king for their temporal feudal possessions, but did not receive from him ring and staff, a compromise eventually adopted on the Continent, the temporal sovereigns sought with pertinacity to cling to this right of investiture.

Modern historians are for the most part able to admire Hildebrand in the stand he made for the betterment of things in an evil day. They can recognize that he and the Popes that came after him stood, on the whole, for religion, for the assertion of spiritual interests, for justice, and for freedom, not only for Church but for Society at large. It has to be remembered that of all the States of modern Europe, England alone, and after the Conquest, was under the actual effective rule of the monarch.

The other countries — German Empire, France, Spain—were long partitioned into feudal territories under rulers recognizing only a dubious and often disputed suzerainty in the sovereign. Thus the eleventh and twelfth centuries were the time when the European States were in process of formation, when the sovereigns were asserting their claims, bringing the feudal territories under control, and gradually fusing all into the great compact nations we know to-day. The process was one of force and violence, of intrigue, of perpetual wars waged with ruthless savagery, of rebellions and feuds, of widespread evils of all kinds, and a consequent loosening of the bonds of morality.

In face of such political and social chaos, it may safely be said—and it is agreed by standard modern historians—that the chief hope not only for the Church and religion, but for Society, lay in a strong Papacy. The Papacy was the one power in Western Europe of sufficient weight and authority to make a firm stand against the evils of the time.

Though the exercise of the Popes' spiritual authority by excommunication or interdict might be defied or ignored, the spiritual authority itself was not questioned in Western Christendom. Even the most recalcitrant emperor or king or feudal prince took it as axiomatic that the Pope, as successor of St. Peter, was the Vicar of Christ and God's supreme representative, invested with His authority to rule in things spiritual. In times of strain the Pope's spiritual authority was not disputed, but an Antipope was set up—Antipopes were an almost constantly recurring feature of the period. That which was contested by temporal rulers was what they held to be invasions of their rightful authority in the government of their countries. It was the problem of Church and State : the adjusting in practice of the

7

command to give to Caesar the things that are Caesar's, and to God the things that are God's. The temporal rulers ever strove to bring the spiritual order under their control—to appoint bishops and abbots, to invest them with ring and staff, thus claiming to be the source of spiritual authority as well as temporal : though the claim of exclusive supremacy in the spiritual order, as made by Henry VIII in England, was not ever so nakedly put forward in the Middle Ages.

The invasions of the spiritual order by temporal rulers led, by an inevitable reaction, to a vast claim by the Popes of authority in the secular order ; and the union—the mixing up—of the two orders by the Popes must seem to us an extraordinary, and to our modern minds an almost unthinkable thing. The organizing of wars by the Popes for purposes hardly or not at all religious ; their leading forth military expeditions to subdue to their authority rebellious cities or castles in the States of the Church ; the ruthless use of the spiritual weapons of excommunication and interdict on issues often purely political and secular ; the launching of crusades against cities, as Venice in 1309, when no issue of heresy or religion was at stake : it all makes bewildering reading, which even in an unfolding of the story on the whole so sympathetic as the late Mgr. Mann's *Popes in the Middle Ages*, teems with episodes that must distress those who are accustomed to look on the Holy Father as standing for the Kingdom of God on earth. Yet must it be recognized, and it is recognized by the most independent modern historians, that this side of the Papacy was a necessary factor in the formation of modern Europe. The great German Emperors of the Franconian and Suabian Houses, who confronted the Popes during two centuries, were terrific men : powerful, able, determined, ruthless, resourceful, often un-

scrupulous and faithless, sometimes openly licentious.
And not unlike them were Kings of France and of
England. In the contest for the independence of the
Church against such rulers, the modern Pope, interested
only in the welfare of religion, wielding only spiritual
authority, would not have counted, would have had
no power for good, in those times of brute force and
turbulence. Only that union of spiritual and temporal
force that seems so strange to us, could have with-
stood the evils and achieved the great work for
Western Christendom, which the medieval Papacy
would seem to have been providentially raised up to
achieve in the transitional period while the Teutonic
principalities were being welded into the nations of
modern Europe.

That which probably causes to us the greatest
surprise is that single-minded men, as confessedly
Gregory VII was, whose one care was the purifying
of the Church and the raising of the level of religion,
should have been so keenly desirous to extend the
temporal dominions of the Pope, whether direct, as
over the States of the Church, or indirect, by way of
feudal suzerainty exercised over many of the kingdoms
and principalities of Western Europe. With alterna-
tions of shrinkage and increase the States of the
Church, as fixed by Pepin and Charles the Great in
800, remained practically the same during a thousand
years, until the annexation of most of them by the
Italian Kingdom in 1860. But they were a perpetual
thorn in the side of Hildebrand and his successors.
These Popes cannot have thought that their dominions
were well-governed : Rome itself was the centre-
spot of turbulence for all Europe. Seldom did the
Popes rule effectively in their own City, but were
at the mercy of the most riotous and fickle populace
and the most violent nobles of Europe,—hunted out
again and again, and forced to call in Emperors or

Norman Dukes of Sicily to quell disorder. The Popes had to organize and lead out in person military expeditions to reduce rebellious towns and fortresses by the methods of ruthlessness usual in those times. Yet do we find Gregory VII and his successors for more than a century striving to add to their possessions the vast territories bequeathed to the Church by the Countess Matilda of Tuscany, embracing Tuscany and Modena, up to Mantua. As South Italy and Sicily was effectively recognized as a fief of the Holy See, and was held as such by Norman Dukes and later by Kings of the Two Sicilies or Naples, the entire Italian Peninsula south of the Po, south of Genoa, would thus have fallen under the temporal sway of the Popes.

And not only an increase of sovereignty, but still more an increase of suzerainty was aimed at by these Popes. Naples and Sicily were recognized fiefs of the Holy See; the first Christian King of Hungary, St. Stephen, had made his country a fief, and he and his successors held it by feudal law from the Pope. Gregory VII tried to get William the Conqueror to take the oath of fealty to him, and thus acknowledge that he held England from the Holy See: he urged that the Peter's Pence which William paid was a tribute and a sign of suzerainty. William replied that he had ascertained his predecessors the Saxon Kings had sent Peter's Pence but had never taken an oath of fealty; he would do as they had done. Gregory replied he did not much care for the money without the oath; but he did not press the thing to an issue, recognizing in William the best sovereign of the time.

In the century after Hildebrand the Popes came to be suzerains over a great part of Western Europe. By no means always was it of their own seeking. Confronted with a doubtful succession rulers knew that the most effective way of making sure their crown was to obtain the recognition of the Pope : thus our English King Stephen obtained practical recognition of himself as King of England, but on the condition that his son should not succeed him, and that the crown should pass to the rightful heir, Henry II, at the time too young to reign. On the gradual expulsion of the Moors from Spain, the Kings of the Christian kingdoms of Aragon, Leon, Castile, all sought for recognition from the Pope ; similarly the rulers of the Balkan States. Many countries were made fiefs of the Holy See as the surest way of safeguarding their independence : the independence of Scotland was preserved for a long time owing to the Scottish kings holding as feudatories of the Holy See. Gradually, in one way or another, the whole of Western Europe, it may be said, save only France, had come under the overlordship of Innocent III.

The grounds on which this, to us incomprehensible, state of things came about were manifold. In part it was the culmination of the feudal system, the root idea of which was that every possessor of landed property held it from an overlord. And the supreme overlords, Emperor, Kings of France or of England, of whom did they hold? Of God ; but mediately through God's representative, the Pope. This idea received colour from the circumstance that the Emperor, recognized as holding a unique position, with precedence and authority above all other temporal rulers, did in fact receive his status, not as King of Germany, but as Roman Emperor, from the Pope, and could not be invested in his imperial position save by receiving his consecration and crowning at the hands of the Pope. If the Emperor, much more other sovereigns. Thus though England was always independent of the Empire, still even before the act of King John, English Kings, as Henry II and Richard Cœur de Lion, did in a way recognize the idea of a certain suzerainty of the Pope.

Then there was the Donation of Constantine, accepted without question throughout the Middle Ages, whereby it was believed that the first Christian Emperor had, in the plenitude of his power, handed over to the Pope, when he himself transferred the imperial residence to Constantinople, the New Rome, the power to rule over Italy and 'the Islands', and in a vague way all the West. It was on the strength of the Donation that the Popes gave authority for the Norman invasions of England and of Ireland, and many similar assignments of territory.

Added to these secular considerations were various theological considerations enunciated with great force by Hildebrand and his successors. Thus he cited, in order to establish his right to decide between rival claimants of the Empire, the texts of St. Paul, 'If we shall judge angels, how much more the things of this world,' and 'the spiritual man judgeth all things.' Similarly, 'the greater light to rule the day' signified the spiritual power, and 'the lesser light to rule the night' the temporal power, which receives its authority from the spiritual. Also the 'two swords' of Luke xxii, 38, were constantly interpreted as meaning the spiritual sword wielded by the Church by excommunication and interdict, and the temporal sword to be wielded by the State at the behest of the Church, in defence of its interests spiritual and religious, but in practice often secular.

Such claims were formulated in their most extreme form by Boniface VIII in the bull 'Unam Sanctam'. They came nearest to realization with Innocent III, who claimed to exercise, and did exercise, a guidance and effective control of the higher politics of Western Christendom. But the two volumes of Mgr. Mann's

Popes devoted to Innocent III, make the impression
that the task was superhuman, beyond the powers
of man, and that his high policies were for the most
part failures. Much more was it beyond the powers
of the lesser men who followed him in the Papal
Chair.

The idea of the Papal Monarchy, to use Dr.
William Barry's term,[1] culminated and broke in the
hands of Boniface VIII. Philip of France, to avert
a pending excommunication, had recourse to physical
force which brought about the death of Boniface,
1303. The fact was that the medieval system had
passed away. France, England, Spain, Scandinavia,
were now strong kingdoms without any vestige of
the idea of subordination to the Empire. The
Empire had changed its character, had expired with
Frederick II in 1250; he was the last real Roman
Emperor of the West after the old idea. The death
of Boniface VIII was followed by the seventy years
of the Avignon residence of the Popes; and that
again by the thirty years of the Great Schism. This
century of depression of the Papacy ended the
medieval conception of the Pope's Temporal Power
and reduced it to the limits of the Civil Sovereignty
over the hereditary States of the Church. Instead of
being the general arbiter and director of the affairs of
Western Christendom, the Pope, on the temporal side,
became one of the Italian Princes.

It is worth recording that a great change of
mentality has come over the modern historical schools
in regard to the persons, characters, objects, policies,
actions of the great Popes of the Middle Ages, notably
Gregory VII and Innocent III. They are now commonly written about with much understanding and
even sympathetic appreciation.

[1] See his book, so entitled.

The Deposing Power

It has just been said that the Temporal Power of the Popes in its greater sense ended with Boniface VIII, 1303 ; but the most formidable feature of that power continued in action for a longer time ; namely, the Deposing Power : the power claimed and often exercised by the Popes of excommunicating a temporal ruler—emperor, king, or prince—declaring him deposed, absolving his subjects from their allegiance, and assigning the crown to another chosen by the Pope. The outstanding and best-known case, and the first, was the deposition of the Emperor Henry IV by Hildebrand, which ended in Canossa. The quarrel was over investiture and simony, over Henry's imprisoning of Saxon bishops after crushing the Saxon revolt, over his invasions of Church liberties, rights, and property, and over his notoriously licentious life. It may be said that Gregory was only hitting back ; for Henry had held a synod of German and Lombard bishops and princes who had declared the Pope excommunicate and deposed. Once established in this test case, the deposing power was brought into play a surprising number of times during the next two centuries. Often the mere threat was enough : the greatest Emperors, Frederick Barbarossa and Frederick II, Kings of France, Dukes and Princes, our own King John, were thus brought to submission. That the Pope had the power to excommunicate anyone fallen into heresy, or leading an openly scandalous life, or invading Church property, or setting at defiance the laws of the Church—and emperors or kings no less than smaller folk—was not questioned in those days, at any rate after its effective assertion in the case of Henry IV. And it was unquestioned, a part of the ' ius publicum ' or law of nations, and an accepted law of the Empire, that ' if

14

a man were not absolved from a sentence of excommunication within a year and a day, he was to be deprived of every dignity.'[1] Thus sentences of excommunication of monarchs and consequent deposition were generally accepted by all concerned : Henry IV found his supporters, princes and bishops, falling away from him as the year was running out, and preparing to elect another King of Germany ; this it was that took him to Canossa. There was no questioning of the power, even when it was resisted ; no theorizing about it ; it was part of the Pope's prerogative as Successor of St. Peter and Vicar of Christ, exercising His authority. It was founded on an amalgam of political and civil, and of religious and spiritual ideas, that were not analysed out into their component parts, and lived on in the minds of Popes and Roman authorities and theologians and canonists long after the medieval polity of Europe had broken up.

It is necessary to go into this matter of the deposing power, because it arose in connexion with the Vatican Council ; and in particular the bull ' Unam Sanctam ' of Boniface VIII came up, as one of the four difficulties from history, recognized as having substance in them, standing in the way of the definition of papal infallibility. Over these questions of the temporal power there has been running in the *Irish Ecclesiastical Record* in 1928 and 1929 a series of articles by Fr. R. Hull, S.J., one of the staff of the Jesuit theological college at Heythrop, near Oxford. He says : ' The Popes had long been acting as masters of the world,' before any theory was formulated of the principle on which such action was based. This was done, among others, by one Jacobus de Viterbio, who at the height of the conflict between Boniface VIII

---

[1] References given by Mann, *Popes*, VII, 104.

and Philip of France wrote in 1302 a defence of Boniface's claims : *De Regimine Christiano*. Fr. Hull gives an instructive analysis of the contents of this politico-theological tractate, and the following summary of its thesis :[1]

> According to it, in its broad outlines, the Pope was the supreme ruler of the Christian Commonwealth ; and, in particular, from him all temporal power was derived. All Christian princes owed the full possession of their authority to the spiritual power ; there was in fact really only one *regia potestas*, which was in the hands of Christ's Vicar. The temporal rulers were instituted, could be judged, and even deposed, by the Pope.

This is the high theory of the ' direct power ' of the Pope over temporals. In the article on the ' Unam Sanctam ' (March 1929) Fr. Hull sees in that famous bull an assertion of the direct power—rightly, I cannot but think : ' That this was the personal view of Boniface, and that this was the teaching of the bull, can hardly be questioned.' He points out of course that only the formal definition at the end, and not the body of the bull, is, according to received principles, to be taken as an *ex cathedra* pronouncement ; and the definition does not assert the theory of the direct power : many theologians see in it no more than a vigorous assertion of the Pope's universal spiritual authority.

Less extreme theories were held by other authorities, and the whole question was in vigorous controversy among theologians and canonists for wellnigh three centuries. It fell to Cardinal Bellarmine to treat the question systematically in his great work on ' Controversies ' against the Reformers (1586). He was in the presence of a school of theologians and canon lawyers who maintained that the Pope, as Vicar of Christ, was Lord of the entire

[1] L.c. May and September 1928.

earth, with supreme power over temporals no less
than spirituals. There was a curious theological
controversy as to whether Jesus Christ had exercised
as Man jurisdiction over temporals, a jurisdiction
handed on to St. Peter and inherited by the Popes.
Bellarmine maintained that He had not; and in regard
to the temporal authority of the Pope he formulated
what was in those days looked on as a middle and
moderate position.[1] He laid down that the Pope
is not the Lord of the whole world, nor even of
all Christendom; nor has he any merely temporal
jurisdiction directly by divine right. But though he
has no direct or immediate power in the temporal
order, still when spiritual and religious interests are
involved, he has an indirect power that is supreme:
' he possesses in order to spiritual good supreme
power of disposing the temporal affairs of all Christians.'
Hence, though he cannot ordinarily make civil laws,
nor confirm or abrogate the laws of civil princes,
he can do all this, if any civil law be necessary for the
salvation of souls, and kings are not willing to enact
it; or if a law be harmful to the salvation of souls,
and kings are not willing to abrogate it. Similarly,
though he cannot as Pope ordinarily depose temporal
sovereigns as he may depose bishops, as the supreme
spiritual ruler he can change kingdoms, take them
from one and confer them on another, if it be necessary
for the salvation of souls. This indirect deposing
power, when necessary for the spiritual good of the
people, Bellarmine stoutly maintained, above all in
cases wherein a ruler should try to lead his people
into heresy. This doctrine seems strong enough to
us; but in those days it was looked on by the ' direct '
school as a giving away of the Catholic position;

[1] The whole subject is fully dealt with in Fr. J. Brodrick's
Life and Work of Blessed Robert Bellarmine, I, cc. xii, xiii.

and Pope Sixtus V—that terrible old man, of whom
Queen Elizabeth is reported to have said that he was
the only man in Europe fit to be her husband,—
ordered the first volume of the 'Controversies' to be
put on the Index, for its denial of the Pope's direct
power in temporals. Only his death prevented the
actual publication, and his successor hastened to
revoke the decree and to give his approval to
Bellarmine's doctrine.

The last case, I believe, of the exercise of the
deposing power was the deposition of Queen Elizabeth
by Pius V in 1570 by the bull 'Regnans in excelsis'.
For her propagation of heresy she and her abettors
are declared excommunicate ; she is deprived of her
pretended right to be Queen of England ; all her
subjects are released from their oath of allegiance
and from all obedience to her ; and all who obey her
are declared to be implicated in the same excommunication. This last clause created an impossible
position for the English Catholics ; consequently the
operation of the deposition was suspended until such
time as it should become possible.

This matter of the deposing power was, for the
two centuries of penal times, the outstanding political
difficulty of the English and Irish Catholics. A repudiation of it was insisted on by successive British
Governments as the condition of any mitigation of
the penal laws, or any measure of relief or emancipation. At the middle of the eighteenth century, 1757,
a body of representative Irish Catholics, lay and
clerical, drew up a Declaration contradicting certain 'misrepresentations and calumnies' popularly
alleged against the Catholic religion. Among such
calumnies they disavow the principle that no faith
is to be kept with heretics, or that it is lawful to
murder heretics, and other equally monstrous doctrines.
Furthermore,

18

they abjure, disavow, and condemn the opinion that princes excommunicated by the Pope and Council, or by any ecclesiastical authority whatsoever, may therefore be deposed or murdered by their subjects, or any other persons :
. . . or that the Pope or Council or any other ecclesiastical power whatsoever, can absolve the subjects of this kingdom, or any of them, from their allegiance to His Majesty King George. We do further declare that we do not believe that the Pope of Rome, or any other prince, prelate, state, or potentate, hath, or ought to have, any temporal or civil jurisdiction, power, superiority, or pre-eminence, directly or indirectly, within this realm.[1]

The Declaration is given by Sir Henry Parnell, *History of the Penal Laws* (p. 49). He says it was proposed by the Bishop of Kildare and was ' signed by many clergymen and gentlemen of rank and property, and sent to Rome as the act and deed of the Irish Catholics.' [2] What Rome thought or said —if anything—is not recorded. But presumably there was no formal condemnation, for the Declaration was the basis of the Oaths of Allegiance imposed by the Relief Acts from 1774 to 1829, and considered

[1] It is worth noting that the language of the Declaration is, with a few necessary modifications, that of the Oath taken by Protestant office-holders at that date : ' I do swear that I do from my heart abhor, detest, and abjure, as impious and heretical, that damnable doctrine and position that princes excommuni-cated, etc. (this is the oath of 1606). And I do declare that no foreign prince, person, prelate, state, or potentate, hath, or ought to have, any jurisdiction, etc., ecclesiastical or spiritual, within this realm.' The terms ' heretical ', ' damnable ', have been eliminated in the Catholic form, and for ' ecclesiastical or spiritual' has been substituted ' temporal or civil '. Protestants had to make the declaration against mental reservations, thought to be particularly insulting to Catholics.

[2] See article ' The Oaths ' in *Rambler*, Jan. 1862 (p. 250). The ' Declaration ' is there printed in full. Though clearly the origin of the series of relief and emancipation oaths, 1774 to 1829, it seems to have escaped those who in recent years have dealt with these oaths.

by the Irish and English bishops, including Milner, lawful for Catholics to take with safe conscience.[1] The whole course of negotiations over Emancipation had at every turn been submitted to Rome, and it is morally certain that the form of the oaths was known there, and at least tacitly tolerated. And there is definite evidence that such was the case. Dr. Gradwell, Rector of the English College at Rome, wrote to Lingard in 1827: 'Rome would never approve, but only tolerate, the Oath which English Catholics take at present.' But even toleration of a denial of the deposing power marks a change in theological opinion since the early years of the seventeenth century, when for such standard theologians as Bellarmine and Suarez the deposing power was an integral part of the Catholic system, next door to an article of Faith.

Not only in England, but in France also, the deposing power was one of the questions exercising men's minds in the sixteenth and seventeenth centuries, and the first of the four famous Gallican Articles of 1682 was a repudiation of it, and of any right on the part of the ecclesiastical power to intervene directly or indirectly in purely civil and political affairs.

The deposing power fell into desuetude after the failure in the case of Elizabeth ; even the excommunication of a sovereign was no longer held to imply or lead to deposition : thus when Napoleon was excommunicated by Pius VII he was not deposed. It certainly is strange that this bogey of the deposing power should have been resuscitated at the time of the Vatican Council. Yet so it was. The 'Old Catholic' professor Dr. Schulte, in a tractate of 1871 against the Definitions of the Council,[2] sought to

[1] For these oaths see Bishop Ward, *Dawn of Catholic Revival*, App. E, and *Eve of Emancipation*, App. O.
[2] See below, Chapter XXVI.

discredit them by treating as infallible pronouncements
the series of bulls of excommunication and deposition
of sovereigns.   On this Pius IX made a noteworthy
declaration, July 1871 :

There are many errors regarding infallibility, but the
most malicious of all is that which would include in the
doctrine the right of deposing sovereigns and declaring
the people free from their duty of allegiance.   This right
was, indeed, exercised at times by Popes in extreme cases ;
but neither the claim to it nor the use of it have anything
to do with papal infallibility.   Its source was not papal
infallibility, but papal authority.   That authority, according
to the public law then in force and by the agreement
of Christian nations, which revered in the Pope the supreme
judge of Christendom, included the judging, even in temporal matters, of princes and states.

But present conditions are altogether different from
this, and only malice could confuse things and times so
different ; as if an infallible judgement concerning a principle of revealed truth had any affinity with a right which
the Popes, solicited by the desire of the peoples, had to
exercise when the common good demanded it.   It is very
clear why currency is now being given to such an absurd
idea, that no one any more thinks of, and least of all the
Supreme Pontiff.   They seek for pretexts, even the most
frivolous and the most untrue, to stir up Princes against
the Church.[1]

The direct purpose of Pius IX in this pronouncement was to assert, as against Schulte and others,
that the exercise of the deposing power had nothing
to do with infallibility.   But it would be incorrect to
say that this is all he said.   He explicitly based the
right, not on theological grounds, as a right *jure
divino* inherent in the papacy ; but on an authority
derived from the public law of the Christian Common-
wealth of the Middle Ages, and by the agreement of

---

[1] Text in *Civiltà Cattolica*, August 1871, p. 485.

the Christian nations, in conditions altogether different from those now existing. It is not too much to say that herein is an endorsement of the theory associated with the name of Fénelon, and developed by abbé Gosselin, Director of St. Sulpice, Paris; according to which the deposing power was not exercised *jure divino*, and is not an article of Catholic Faith; but was exercised *jure humano*, as part of the common public law (*jus publicum*) of Europe in the Catholic centuries.[1]

The deposing power was the logical issue and the culmination of Bellarmine's theory of the 'indirect power'; lesser aspects of the theory will come up for consideration in a later place (Chapter XVII).

[1] See Gosselin's work, translated 1853, *Power of the Pope during the Middle Ages*, II, 7 ff.

CHAPTER II

GALLICANISM

GALLICANISM may be defined in general as the tendency, while accepting the Papacy as of divine institution, to oppose or minimize the papal claims as they have been made in history. It has been of two kinds: political and theological. Political Gallicanism contested the claims to authority in the temporal order as asserted and exercised by Gregory VII, Innocent III, and Boniface VIII; theological Gallicanism contested certain claims of the Papacy in the spiritual and religious order. These tendencies of course manifested themselves in other countries than France; they have received the name 'Gallican' because all through history it has been in France that they have found their chief expression.

Political Gallicanism reached its culminating point in the contest of Philip the Fair with Boniface VIII, whereby was practically broken what Dr. William Barry has named 'The Papal Monarchy', the temporal power as it had been asserted and exercised by the Popes during two centuries. These claims were formulated in Boniface's famous bull 'Unam Sanctam'; he protested, indeed, that he claimed no direct authority in things temporal and secular; but his actual claims were very far-reaching, and as we shall see, the 'Unam Sanctam' was one of the four things finally sorted out at the Vatican Council as presenting real difficulty to the definition of papal infallibility. Philip opposed physical force to

Boniface's spiritual force, and in such wise that the Pope's death ensued. This, and the transference of the papal residence to Avignon, where the Popes fell more and more under French influence, followed by the Great Schism, in reality an attempt to perpetuate French domination over Pope and Church, brought about a century of impotence for the Papacy, and broke for ever, in fact if not in theory, the medieval conception of the temporal predominance of the Popes.

Of greater interest for us is theological Gallicanism, for the practical work of the Council was to rule it out of the Catholic Church as a permissible theological opinion. After various earlier adumbrations, it received its first formulation at the Council of Constance, held 1414-17, to bring to an end the Great Schism. Here was raised the question of the relations between General Council and Pope. The situation was abnormal, unique. The question uppermost in the minds of all was the ending of the Schism, which for five and thirty years had devastated the Church and produced a state of unparalleled confusion. There were three Popes in the field, and all men saw that the only way of achieving the so necessary result was by bringing about the withdrawal or retirement of all three claimants, and the electing of a new Pope acknowledged by all. As for a long time the rival Popes refused to abdicate, the question was mooted of the power of the Council to depose them, and this in turn led on to the question of theory as to the relations between General Council and Pope. At the fourth and fifth sessions, 1415, decrees were adopted declaring that a General Council, as representing the Universal Church, held its power immediately from Jesus Christ; that it could not be dissolved nor prorogued without its own consent; and that every one, even the Pope, was bound to obey the Council in matters concerning the Faith, the extinction of the Schism, and the reform of the Church in its head and members; and that the Council had authority over the Pope as well as over all Christians. It followed that when a General Council was in session the supreme authority of the Church was vested in it, not in the Pope.

As a matter of fact, the three Popes were induced to withdraw, he of the Roman line, wherein as is now recognized the lawful succession lay, regularizing the Council from the Roman point of view, before formally abdicating. The view has ever been held at Rome, that it was by virtue of this act of the real Pope that the Council was made properly œcumenical, and the approval of its acts was given with the reservation 'saving the rights, dignity, and pre-eminence of the Apostolic See' (so Eugenius IV, 1439).

The chief protagonists of the theory of the supremacy of the Council had been the two great Frenchmen, Peter d'Ailly, Archbishop of Cambrai, and John Gerson, Chancellor of the University of Paris. After Constance these questions of the theoretical constitution of the Church—monarchical or constitutional—continued to be debated, and during the long period that the Council of Basle dragged out its chequered course, 1430-47, they were discussed and contested among the theologians, canonists and lawyers, the Popes steadily resisting the attempts of the Council and its adherents to encroach on the monarchical status of the Papacy, as the one established by Christ. On the whole the renaissance Popes were successful in maintaining their position substantively, though there existed through the fifteenth and sixteenth centuries theological schools, especially in France, hostile to the full Roman claims.

The Gallican position was quite different from that of the Protestant Reformers, and from that of

Henry VIII and Elizabeth in England : these threw off entirely papal authority even in things spiritual, and rejected the Pope's position as Vicar of Christ and Head on earth of the Church. The Gallicans accepted these fundamental positions, while contesting some of the conclusions and applications drawn from them. They accepted also fully the Catholic teaching on the Church, one, visible, infallible. Bossuet is the classical exponent of theological Gallicanism. We find him laying down such propositions as these :[1]

> The Son of God, since He willed that His Church should be one, . . . instituted the primacy of St. Peter to maintain and cement it.
>
> The Chair of St. Peter is the common centre of all Catholic unity.
>
> The Catholic Church from her birth has had for a mark of her Unity her communion with the Chair of Peter, so that remaining in it, as we do, without letting anything separate us from it, we are the body which has seen those who have severed themselves fall on the right hand and on the left.
>
> We grant that in Church law there is nothing the Pope cannot do, when need requires it. The canons prescribe the mode of the exercise of this power ; they do not touch the power itself, but its use (*Defensio*, lib. XI, c. 20).
>
> There is one chief bishop, there is one Peter appointed to guide all the flock, there is one Mother Church established to teach all the others ; and the Church of Jesus Christ founded on that unity, as on an immovable rock, cannot be shaken.

And on the Petrine texts :

> Peter by his confession of Christ's Godhead attracts to himself that inviolable promise which makes him the

---

[1] I owe these pieces from Bossuet to the *Catholic Dictionary* of Addis and Arnold, art. ' Pope ' ; I have, however, verified them.

foundation of the Church. And Peter will live in his successors; Peter will ever speak in his Chair.

'Confirm thy brethren.' Christ does not merely give a commandment to Peter individually : Peter receives an office which Christ founds and institutes in His Church for ever. There was always to be a Peter in the Church to confirm his brethren in the faith ; it was the most fitting means of establishing that unity of sentiments which the Saviour desired above everything ; and that authority was so much the more necessary for the successors of the Apostles, inasmuch as their faith was less stable than that of those from whom they sprang [i.e. the Apostles].[1]

The Gallican position was practically French only ; Pascal says that scarcely anywhere except in France is it permissible in these days to say that the Council is above the Pope.[2] The official formulation of the Gallican position was made in the famous 'Four Articles' of 1682 :

1. Rejects the deposing power and the right, direct or indirect, of the Pope or the ecclesiastical power to interfere in civil and temporal affairs.

2. Asserts the full validity of the decrees of the fourth and fifth sessions of Constance on the authority of General Councils over the Pope.

3. Declares that the exercise of the Apostolic power is to be regulated by the canons of the Church, and in France by the laws and customs of the Gallican Church.

4. 'In questions of faith the Pope has the chief part,

---

[1] Anyone wishing to know Bossuet's mind, should read the sermon on the 'Unity of the Church', preached at the Opening of the General Assembly of the Clergy of France, Nov. 1681 (Œuvres de Bossuet, Paris, 1748, tom. V ; 1862, tom. XI).

[2] Il n'y a presque plus que la France où il soit permis de dire que le concile est au-dessus du pape (*Pensées*, art. XXIV, No. 85, édition Lahure, Paris, 1858). In some editions this sentence is omitted. It stands in the latest edition by Chevalier, 1925, p. 528. In the same place Pascal rejects the personal infallibility of the Pope, while affirming that of the Church.

and his decrees apply to all the churches and each church in particular ; yet his judgement is not irreformable unless the consent of the Church be given to it.'

These articles were in 1690 declared by the Pope to be null and void, but without theological censure ; so that they could be, and were, taught in Catholic schools in France and elsewhere, up to the Revolution.

The standard assertion of Gallicanism was Bossuet's *Defensio Declarationis Conventus Cleri Gallicani.* It is a big work, immensely learned, teeming with citations from Fathers, Councils, theologians, historians. To attempt to extract from it an account of the Gallican theory would be a labour of great difficulty and of prolonged study. Fortunately a simpler and more satisfactory course lies at hand for setting forth the practical Gallican teaching as held in France during the eighteenth century. In 1768 Dom Jamin, a Maurist Benedictine, published a volume, *Pensées Theologiques relatives aux Erreurs du Temps,* which had a great vogue, a seventh edition appearing in 1792. It is a popular manual of Christian and Catholic doctrine intended for the educated laity, treating of God, Religion, the Church, and so on ; and it contains a clear and sober statement of the Gallican theory. An attempt will be made to set out the principal heads of this teaching.

In the first place it should be made clear that the author was no Jansenist, nor had he any sympathy with the attitude of the later Jansenists. He utterly reprobates the famous distinction ' de droit et de fait ':

The Church exacts from all her children an interior submission to the judgements she passes on ecclesiastical books and their authors. How can we reconcile this true submission which every faithful man owes to the Church with the distinction ' de droit et de fait ' which a proud subtlety has often imagined, only to elude the apostolic decisions ? It is deceiving ourselves to pretend to obey by keeping silence in regard to the fact, without making the submission of our minds (p. 233 ; cf. p. 235).

Jamin lays down as basis of his theological position the full Catholic doctrine of the Church as a visible society, the depository of religion (121).

The Roman Church, that which recognizes the See of Rome as its centre of unity, alone possesses the Marks of the Church of Christ, one, holy, catholic, apostolic (124).

Jesus Christ is the supreme Head, and the Roman Pontiff is the ministerial Head, in his quality of successor of St. Peter (125).

The form of ecclesiastical government is not a democracy ; it is not an aristocracy—those who govern are not equal in authority. Nor is it a monarchy, because the authority does not reside in one single person. What then ? It is a monarchy tempered by aristocracy, which recognizes one Head whose power is limited (liée) by the canons (170, see 3rd Gallican article).

The Church must have a visible Head because she is one, and her unity cannot be preserved without a common centre. But this Head is the Roman Pontiff, who in his quality of successor of St. Peter has by divine right, above the other bishops, the primacy of honour and of jurisdiction. It appertains to him to secure the observance of the canons of the Church by the whole Christian world, to convoke General Councils, to excommunicate those who will not attend. As the common Father of Christians he can make new laws and propose them to the Church ; but they have not the force of general laws except by the acceptance of his colleagues in the episcopate (170).

The bishops are bishops by divine right : they hold their power immediately from Jesus Christ, and not from the Sovereign Pontiff whose equals they are, except in the primacy, which was established by Christ only to show forth unity (Cyprian). They judge with him in matters of faith and of discipline ; but their jurisdiction is limited by their diocese : whereas that of the Pope has no limits other than those of the Christian world (171).

The complete mutual independence of the spiritual and temporal powers, of Church and State, is very strongly laid down :

The union of the two powers can never be on the principle of the subjection of the one or the other. Each is sovereign, independent, absolute, in that which concerns it. They owe one another a mutual assistance, but by way of concert, not by way of subordination and dependence (188).

To attribute to sovereigns the primacy in matters purely ecclesiastical is to reverse the order which God has established (194).

To subordinate the power of the pastors in its exercise and its functions to the temporal power is to misunderstand it (197).

The King in the civil and temporal order has no superior on earth (204).

To attribute to the Popes a power direct, or even indirect, over the temporals of Kings, is a doctrine unknown to the Fathers of the first centuries, and of which we find no trace in the Gospels (210).

The deposing power is rejected (212, 213).

It is not for Popes to give Kings to the earth, nor for Kings to give Bishops to the Church : if they enjoy the right of nominating those to be raised to prelacies, this is not a primitive right, but a concession from the Church (214).

Jamin speaks at some length on the infallible teaching authority of the Church and its exercise :

We must recognize in the Church an infallible authority which terminates disputes that arise concerning the faith. If there is not in the Church a living infallible oracle, then believe what you please. But if there is in the Church a living oracle, an infallible authority, there is no liberty of choice : one must hold without questioning to the teaching of the Church (216).

Infallibility in dogmatic judgements has been given only to the body of bishops. No particular bishop, not even the Bishop of Rome, may attribute to himself this glorious privilege. Jesus Christ spoke to all the Apostles in common, and in their persons to all the bishops, the promise, 'I am with you, etc.' (218).

To maintain that the right of judging causes which concern the faith appertains only to the Pope or the Holy See, and that they ought to be carried there in the first instance, is a pretension unknown to all antiquity and contrary to the practice of the Church (219).

The Church pronounces on the Faith in many ways : (1) by General Council ; (2) by particular Council, when she approves the decision ; (3) by the Sovereign Pontiff, when the moral unanimity of the body of bishops accepts his judgement ; (4) by the diocesan bishop who condemns an error that arises in his flock, if the censure becomes known and is not blamed by the bishops (220).

A General Council lawfully assembled and held according to canonical rules, represents the universal Church, and in this quality holds its authority immediately from God. All should be subject to it, from the tiara to the lowest clerk, from the throne to the last layman, not only in what regards faith, but also in what regards morals. It is the organ of the Holy Ghost, and its decisions are to be respected as the Gospel itself (St. Gregory Great) (220).

It is not the acceptance which the Church dispersed makes of a General Council that gives certitude and infallibility to its decisions (221).

General Councils are of great utility, and in certain circumstances they may be called necessary ; but to pretend that no controversy can be ended except by their means is an error (222).

The Church in order to decide has not the need to be assembled. Dispersed, but united in the condemnation of new opinions, she merits from her children a submission without reserve. To think that she enjoys the privilege of infallibility only in General Councils is to limit unduly the promises of Jesus Christ and is an error in faith (223).

The dogmatic constitutions of the Sovereign Pontiffs, although they are not irreformable except by the consent of the body of the bishops, are for all that of great authority, and merit on the part of the faithful great respect. If the presumption ought to be in favour of the superior, it is especially in favour of the common Father of Christians : it is therefore criminal insolence to take occasion of his fallibility to despise his decrees (224).

It is permitted without doubt, in certain cases, to appeal from the Roman Pontiff to a General Council, as from a lower to a higher tribunal : but to do so when his decrees are received by all the dispersed churches, is to cloak one's disobedience and to seek to prolong disputes : it is to appeal from the Church to herself (225).

To propose to the faithful a bull of a Pope as having by itself and of its own nature the force to subject to it all minds ; or, to propose it as conformable to the doctrine of the Church, are two very different things. In the first case it is to profess openly the dogma of the infallibility of the Popes, unknown to the ancient Fathers, and to destroy the rights of the episcopate, reducing the bishops to the simple rôle of executors of the decrees of Rome. In the second case it is to recognize that one does not owe to the Pope's judgements a submission entire and without reserve, save in so far as they are in the analogy of faith ; and this can be proved only by the acquiescence of the bishops scattered throughout the Christian world. It is in this latter sense that the Church of France exacts from the faithful submission to the constitutions of the Sovereign Pontiffs (225).

The Pope condemns a number of propositions extracted from a book in determinate terms : the bishops dispersed in the Catholic world know the decision and applaud : I say, ' The Cause is finished '. I recognize the voice of Peter in his successor ; I submit, I obey (226).

One cannot without temerity refuse to the Church the power of judging the meaning of books that concern religion. This right necessarily implies on the part of the faithful the obligation of submitting to its decisions (232, 233).

The belief that the Church exacts on dogmatic facts is not a divine faith, which is due only to revealed facts ; but a human faith, or to speak more correctly, an ecclesiastical faith, inasmuch as it is founded on the authority of the Church, which has the right to regulate our sentiments on everything that has relation with religion (235).

It is a dogma universally accepted that the Church is infallible in the exposition of tradition. But this infallibility can only subsist by supposing it no less in the discussion and examination of ecclesiastical books ; because it is by this examination that the Church makes her discernment of true tradition, and a means liable to error could not lead surely to the knowledge of the truth (236).

Such is an authentic presentment of Gallicanism in the terms of one who held the Gallican theory as it was popularly held in France during the eighteenth century. It seemed worth while stating it at some length, because Gallicanism is a thing often much misunderstood ; and a right understanding of it is necessary for any just estimation of the Vatican Council.

The doctrine of the Four Gallican Articles of 1682 had to be taught in all theological schools in France. In 1766 a decree was issued that the Statutes and Constitutions of all Religious Orders and Institutes domiciled in France should be registered at the High Court of the Realm. In compliance with this decree the Constitutions of the English Benedictines, three of whose houses were in France, were presented, and the Letter of Registration contains the clause, as a condition of authorization, that the Superiors undertake that the doctrine of the Gallican Declaration of 1682 be taught to all theological students in the houses of the Congregation, and be defended in all public theses and disputations.[1] And so it was everywhere in France.

It would be a mistake, however, to suppose that even in those days the Gallican tenets were held

[1] *Constitutiones*, 1784, p. 266.

universally in France. In 1724 a Benedictine abbot, Matthieu Petit-Didier, published a *Traité de l'Infaillibilité du Pape*, wherein he said :[1]

When it is asserted that the doctrine of papal *fallibility* in matters of faith is the opinion of France, at least one-half of the assertion ought to be retrenched. For a very considerable number of bishops and doctors, of pastors and churchmen of every rank, is found throughout the kingdom, who hold the infallibility of the Roman Pontiffs, and their authority and pre-eminence over Councils, to be undoubted truths.

As a case in illustration of this St. Francis de Sales may be mentioned. In his book *Les Controverses* he teaches quite unequivocally the doctrine of papal infallibility.[2]

To anyone desirous of understanding the Gallican position may be recommended the section in Ollivier's book, *L'Église et l'État au Concile du Vatican*, ' Système des Gallicans ' (I, iii, § 2). In the following section he traces the gradual decline of Gallicanism in France even before the Revolution. The stiffest upholders of it were the State lawyers and jurisconsults, not the bishops, and still less the clergy, whose Gallicanism tended ever to grow more attenuated. The whole presentation of the subject is made with great knowledge and understanding.

[1] I owe this citation to a note in the *Month*, Jan. 1929, p. 64. Of abbot Petit-Didier and his book I have no knowledge.

[2] Annecy edition of the *Œuvres* of St. Francis, Vol. I, p. 305 (1892).

CHAPTER III

ULTRAMONTANISM

OVER against the Gallican conception of the Papacy
stood what was called the Ultramontane, the conception held ' over the mountains ', beyond the Alps,
in Italy and Rome.   It is but natural that the chief
upholders of the prerogatives of the Roman See and
of the Papacy should have been the Popes : the chief
upholders of prerogatives of all kinds are commonly
those most intimately concerned.   And so it is well
recognized that the Popes from early times, and the
greatest and best among them the most vigorously—as
Leo the Great and Gregory the Great—have asserted
the claims and vindicated the prerogatives of their See.
And from the time that their position was first
definitely challenged in the West at Constance and
the Gallican theory formulated ; and still more when
the Protestant Reformers went much further and
denied the very basis of that position in its entirety,
the Popes right up to the Vatican Council went on
asserting their claims unflinchingly.

It was in face of the Reformers' denials that the
Catholic theory of Church and of Pope was drawn
out in scientific theological form, and the treatise
' de Ecclesia Christi ' added to the body of dogmatic
theology.   The first systematic, and in many ways
the most remarkable, presentation of Catholic teaching
as against the Protestant Reformers over the whole
field of theology, was Cardinal Bellarmine's great

work, *Controversies against the Heretics of our Times* (Vol. I, 1586). It is to this day a masterpiece of controversial theology, marked by great knowledge, great thoroughness, great acumen.[1] Its statement of the Ultramontane, that is Roman, theory of the Papacy may be taken as representative, and may be set forth thus :

[What follows is a mere statement of the theory as held, and is in no way argumentative.]

Bellarmine's fundamental thesis is that the government of the Church is not a democracy, nor an aristocracy, but a monarchy. The implications of the Petrine texts are that Christ made St. Peter the monarchical ruler of His Church : and the Roman Bishop has succeeded not only to the See, but to the primacy and the prerogatives of Peter, and this by divine ordinance—' iure divino ', not merely ' iure ecclesiastico '. Christ is the supreme Head of the Church ; the Roman Pontiff the ministerial Head under Him on earth. The Keys signify supreme power over the whole Church ; so the Pope has absolute power to rule the Church, and can promulgate laws binding in conscience.

So much on his universal jurisdiction ; the power of dogmatic definition will be dealt with presently, after the relation between Pope and General Council. On this Bellarmine lays down :

It belongs to the Pope to convoke a General Council ; or to sanction its being convoked by another, as the Emperor ; or, it suffices if he afterwards gives his confirmation to what has been done. But if it neither be convoked, nor approved, nor its acts confirmed by him, it is no true

[1] Ollivier's tribute to Bellarmine is worth recording : ' His books are not unworthy of the old Roman jurisconsults, in their precision of language, force of dialectic, range of ideas, abundance of knowledge, loyalty in discussion ' (*L'Église et l'État au Concile du Vatican*, I, 266).

General Council, but a conciliabulum. It belongs to the Pope to preside, in person or by a delegate.

The Pope simply and absolutely is above the Universal Church, in that he is the Head of the whole Church on earth ; and so he is above a General Council, and can recognize no judge upon earth above himself. He cannot be judged, punished, or deposed by a General Council, or by any human authority. But should a Pope become a formal heretic he would by the very fact cease to be Pope, and could be judged and declared deposed by the Church.

Bellarmine's treatment of the question of infallibility is of special interest. Of course the infallibility of the Church is the background of his exposition :

The Pope is supreme judge in deciding controversies on faith and morals. When he teaches the whole Church in things pertaining to faith, he cannot err. Nor can he err in moral precepts prescribed for the whole Church, and relating to things necessary for salvation, or in themselves good or evil.

More than once the actual term ' de cathedra docens ' is used (see Index, ' Pontifex Romanus ') :

It is the Pope's confirmation that gives to decrees of General Councils their authority and authentication as free from error in faith and morals. General Councils may err before the Pope's confirmation has been given, unless in defining they have followed his instructions. The decrees of particular Councils, if confirmed by the Pope, are thereby stamped as free from error.

Of special interest is the answer to the objection : If the Pope can by himself infallibly define dogmas of faith, Councils are useless, or at least unnecessary. Bellarmine replies :

This does not follow. For even though infallibility be in the Pope, for all that he ought not to neglect the human and ordinary means of arriving at a true knowledge of the matter in question: but the ordinary means is a Council, greater or smaller, according to the relative magnitude of the matter in question. Besides, definitions *de Fide* depend principally on the apostolic tradition and the consent of the churches.[1] But in order that, when a question arises, it may be known what is the mind of the whole Church, there is no better way than that the bishops should come together from all provinces, and each one state the custom of his own Church.

This is strikingly like the preamble to the Vatican definition of Infallibility. And it will be seen that the definitions of the Vatican Council on the Pope hardly go beyond Bellarmine's formulation of the Ultramontane doctrine, and indeed are practically the same as it; so that there has been, it may almost be said, no advance in the three hundred years.

A word should be said concerning the term 'Ultramontane', as designating what was in reality the Roman doctrine. Since the Vatican Council there is no longer place for the term 'Ultramontanism'; because that doctrine of the Papacy has, for all in communion with the Holy See, been stamped as Catholicism, much as at Nicea what had been 'Athanasianism' was stamped as Catholicism. But up to the Council, strictly speaking, it was not so; for the Gallican position was still permissible within the pale of the Catholic Church. It is true that 'Ultramontanism' was in its origin a nickname, like many theological names. But at the time of the

---

[1] 'Ex consensu ecclesiarum.' In sound this is like the Gallican formula; but its meaning is other. The Gallican formula: 'Nisi Ecclesiae consensus accesserit', means a subsequent endorsement on the part of the Church, i.e. the bishops, after the definition has been promulgated. Bellarmine's means an enquiry beforehand, to ascertain the mind of the Church, as the basis of the definition. Perhaps 'ex sensu' would have been clearer than 'ex consensu'.

Council it was freely used even by its defenders, though sometimes under protest.

It is convenient, indeed necessary, when writing of the Vatican Council, to have some name for the school opposed to Gallicanism; and none other than Ultramontanism is to hand. The upshot of the Council was to identify the Ultramontanism of the Roman theological schools, as formulated by Bellarmine, with Catholicism, Gallicanism being ruled out.

Any controversial discussion of the Ultramontane or Roman theory, or any presentation of the line of proof put forward by Catholic theologians, would be out of place here.[1]

But there can be no question that many readers will come to this story of the Vatican Council prepossessed with the idea that the doctrine of the Papacy defined at it was a theological theory in defiance of sound exegesis and of all history, the offspring of worldly ambitions, and so on. Therefore, in order that the general reader may not approach the subject with the conviction that the theory defined at the Council is wholly devoid of justification in history or theology, it may be allowable, and it will be in place, to cite certain words of highly credited ecclesiastical historians of recent times, English and foreign, not of the Roman Communion, who are recognized on all hands as among the foremost critical scholars

[1] Anyone desiring a good concise statement of the Catholic theological position will find it in the article 'Infaillibilité du Pape', in *Dictionnaire de Théologie Catholique*, VII (1923).

M. Ollivier's presentation of the 'Système des Romains', in *L'Église et l'État au Concile du Vatican* (I, iii, § 1), is very clear and good, and has the advantage of being by a writer detached from all theological bias.

of our day. In this way it may be hoped to prepare an unprejudiced mental atmosphere for the reading of this book.

For instance, no scholar stands in higher estimation than Bishop Lightfoot for sobriety and surety of his judgements. He wrote:

> Even a cursory glance at the history of the Apostles, so far as it appears in the Gospel records, reveals a certain primacy of St. Peter among the Twelve.

This primacy is seen in action throughout the first twelve chapters of the Acts. Lightfoot recognizes that this 'primacy', 'pre-eminence', was conferred on St. Peter by our Lord in the Petrine texts, and that in virtue of them he 'received from Christ special pastoral charges.'[1]

Similarly Bishop Westcott:

> The representative official precedence of St. Peter underlies the whole narrative of the Fourth Gospel: he takes the precedence, and occupies exactly the same place with regard to the Christian Society in the Fourth Gospel as in the other three.[2]

To complete the great Cambridge trio, it may be noted that for Dr. Hort also St. Peter was 'the leading Apostle', 'the foremost of the Twelve', holding an 'absolutely exceptional position, in the early days at Jerusalem.'[3]

These eminent English scholars discuss, as they needs must, the Petrine texts, especially Matthew xvi, 18, 19. Lightfoot (op. cit.) holds that the words of these verses 'are directed with all the force which repetition can give them to the person addressed'; yet not Peter himself was the Rock, but his constancy,

---

[1] *Clement of Rome*, II, ' St. Peter in Rome.'
[2] *Gospel according to St. John*, ed. 1908, Introd. p. xxiii.
[3] *Ecclesia*, pp. 79, 232.

his firmness, his confession of faith. Curiously enough Hort reverses these two positions, declaring, 'I believe the most obvious interpretation of this famous phrase is the true one. St. Peter himself, yet not exclusively St. Peter but the other disciples of whom he was the spokesman, was the Rock which Christ had in view.'[1]

The basis of the Ultramontane exegesis of the text is (1) that the promise was to St. Peter individually, and (2) that he himself, and not his profession of faith, is the Rock. It thus appears that each half has the support of one of the two most learned Anglican divines of our day, while each of them limits the import of the text by rejecting the half of the exegesis accepted by the other.

It is therefore worthy of note that one of the chief pupils of the Cambridge trio, the late Dr. Chase, Bishop of Ely, himself no mean scholar, rules out both limitations as inadmissible, saying :[2]

Our Lord's words as reported by St. Matthew could not be more personal. To suppose that the Lord addresses St. Peter here as a type of his fellow apostles, is in effect to imply that no words could be personal unless a typical reference were explicitly excluded. St. Peter's confession, or his faith, would have been wholly inadequate as the Rock. The Rock is the Apostle who has just made the confession that Jesus is the Messiah. Almost certainly the Rock does not signify the foundation stone, but the soil or rock on which the first stones are laid.

It is worth citing on the other elements of this famous text yet another Cambridge pupil of the great trio, the late Dr. A. J. Mason. In article 'Power of the Keys ',[3] he says :

[1] *Ecclesia*, p. 16.
[2] Hastings' *Dict. of the Bible*, III, 759, art. ' Peter.'
[3] *Ibid.*, IV, 30.

The Kingdom of Heaven is likened to a house or palace of which our Lord promises that St. Peter shall be the chief steward or major-domo, who is entrusted with full authority over everything which the house contains. . . . As the house is at the same time the kingdom, it is evident that the authority is of very wide range. . . .

[On the 'binding' and 'loosing']: to bind is to forbid, to loose is to permit. . . . It is the power of laying down the law for his fellow disciples which is thus bestowed upon St. Peter. Or perhaps it is more exact to say that it is the power of determining in detailed application the law which God has laid down in general terms. Authority is given him to say what the law of God allows, and what it forbids; and the promise is added that his ruling shall be upheld in heaven,—and is consequently to be regarded as binding upon the consciences of Christians. The power of binding and loosing is in fact the power of legislation for the Church. . . . The whole of Peter's chief-stewardship was included in the promise; and both in his appointment of other Christians to sacred offices, in the administration of the Christian sacraments at large, and in his expositions of Christian truth, he was exercising the power of the Keys.

When we turn to Oxford we may confine ourselves to two recent articles in *Theology* (1826, Aug. and Oct.), by Mr. C. H. Turner, Ireland Professor of Exegesis. On St. Peter he says:

What impresses me is the convergence of the testimony of the four gospels in the prerogative position allotted to St. Peter: they must in this be taken to represent the common attitude of all parts and sections of the Christian society in its earliest stages.

[On Matt. xvi, 17-19.] No words could well be more startling than these. In the Palestinian surroundings where the first gospel was put into shape no sort of doubt can have existed as to the unique position believed to have been conferred by Christ on His chief Apostle.

[On Luke xxii, 31, 32.] Here St. Luke comes into line with St. Matthew and St. John (xxi, 15-17) in assigning to our Lord a solemn commission of leadership—we might almost say of authority—to His chief Apostle.

Thus Matthew, Luke, and John are at one in recording some definite saying of our Lord which raises St. Peter to a unique position among and above the other Apostles. The constant tradition of the primitive Church, so far as we have it positively expressed, asserted the unique prerogative of St. Peter.

[He sums it up as] the commission to Peter, by express words of Christ, of a place of unique authority, whether in relation to the other Apostles or to the Christian community as a whole.

Most of the Anglican writers who accept St. Peter's primacy hold that it was purely personal, temporary, transient. Thus Bishop Lightfoot said it was ' a primacy of historical inauguration ', which lapsed of itself on the reception of the Gentiles into the Church ; and Bishop Chase, after declaring that the Rock was Peter himself and that it signified the soil or rock on which the first stones of the building were laid, goes on :

The parable itself limits the application. When the foundation has been laid, the Apostle's function as described by the metaphor will have ceased. He will support the first stones of the ecclesia.[1]

So much on St. Peter and his Primacy. But the continuance of this Primacy in his successors, the Bishops of Rome, is vital to the Ultramontane and to the Gallican positions alike. Let us now see how this matter is dealt with by the English scholars.

For Bishop Lightfoot the Roman Church was at the end of the first century ' the most prominent ', ' the most important church of Christendom.' It held ' a pre-eminence of rank ', ' a primacy ' among

---

[1] It is hardly possible to forbear remarking that the function of the ' soil or rock on which the first stones are laid ' does not cease when the building has been erected.

the churches.[1] Speaking of the Epistle of Clement he calls attention to ' the urgent and almost imperious tone ' it uses in addressing another apostolic church, that of Corinth ; he says : ' It may perhaps seem strange to describe this noble remonstrance as the first step towards papal domination, and yet undoubtedly this is the case.' [2] A century later, *c.* 200, occurred the controversy over the date for keeping Easter, in which Pope Victor ' cut off from the common unity ' the Churches of Asia Minor for clinging to their own custom. Of him Lightfoot says : ' He was the first who advanced those claims to universal dominion which his successors in later ages have always consistently and often successfully maintained.' [3]

Thus, for Lightfoot, the first articulate voice that issues from the mouth of a Roman Bishop, *c.* 100, ' was the first step towards papal domination ' ; the second, a century later, was ' the first claim to universal dominion.' During the course of another half-century (*c.* 250) these ' pretensions ' had made such way that Rome was now ' the most powerful Church in Christendom.'

Lightfoot's view is that the supremacy originally was the supremacy of the Roman Church, not of the Roman Bishop, and that the later clear supremacy of the Roman Bishop was derived from that of the Roman Church, not *vice versa*.

But by the middle of the third century there stands out, as in possession, the idea that the primacy of the Roman Church lies in the fact that it is ' the See of Peter '—' Cathedra Petri '. This conception first finds

---

[1] Most of Lightfoot's utterances are from the essay ' St. Peter in Rome ' (*Clem. Rom.*, II) ; all references are fully given in two articles, ' Bp. Lightfoot and the Early Roman See ', by the present writer (*Dublin Review*, 1893).

[2] *Clem. Rom.*, I, 69, 70.

[3] *Dissertations on the Apostolic Age*, 186.

expression explicitly in Cyprian, who, however, uses it in such a way as to suggest that it was an idea currently accepted : certain schismatics have appealed ' to the chair of Peter and to the principal church, whence the unity of the priesthood (i.e. episcopate) took its rise ' (*Ep.* lix, 14). Similarly he speaks of the Roman See as ' the place of Peter ', ' locus Petri ' (*Ep.* lv). This conception of the Roman See as ' Chair of Peter ', ' See of Peter ', ' Apostolic See ' *par excellence*, became a commonplace of Christian thought : Council of Sardica, 343, Hilary, Optatus, Ambrose, Jerome, Augustine, and the Eastern Œcumenical Councils of Ephesus and Chalcedon.[1]

Prof. Turner's remarks on St. Cyprian are of interest :

Cyprian's whole mind was riveted on the problem of church organization and on the doctrinal basis of the episcopate, and he was the first writer to attempt to arrive at a definite theory. . . . He was the first who made the Petrine primacy in relation to the Roman Church an integral element of a theory of the episcopate. History has tended to single out St. Cyprian as the special upholder of the rights of other bishops, and of the episcopate at large, against the autocratic claims of the Pope ; but we must not forget what a decisive share he had in the formulation of the theory which saw a continuance of the primacy of Peter in the primacy of the Bishop of Rome. . . . He had a clear-cut theory of which the first element is the essential identity of the episcopal and apostolic office, and the second is the essential identity of the position of Peter and of his successors at Rome. What Peter was among the Apostles that his successor was among Catholic bishops, the symbol and source of unity. What Peter had not among the Apostles, that is, any difference in dignity or authority, that the Pope had not in regard to

[1] On Ephesus, see Rev. S. H. Scott, *General Councils (Ephesus),* 1927 : at Chalcedon, the famous acclamation of the bishops, ' It is Peter who has spoken by Leo.'

other members of the episcopate. In each case there was, so to say, a college and a head. But the head could not act apart from his colleagues ; moreover, though the Bishop of Rome was successor of St. Peter and inherited all the prerogatives that Peter had in relation to the other Apostles, there was of course one thing that he could not inherit. Peter was the original foundation on which Christ built His Church. Cyprian would never have said that the Church was built on Peter and his successors.

The rapidly succeeding stages in the growth of the papal claims during the first six centuries, as marked by Anglican authorities, is worthy of note. Thus a writer in the *Church Quarterly Review* (April 1903) : ' It was in the first six Christian centuries that the foundations of the papal theory were established, and the ground which the Papacy had won before the time of Gregory the Great was never called in question by any national Church before the Reformation.' It has long been a commonplace to say that the full formulation and assertion of the papal claims to universal jurisdiction, and even to control General Councils, was made by Leo the Great (450). But Mr. Scott, in the little tract already mentioned, has shown from the Acts of the Council of Ephesus that twenty years earlier Pope Celestine took up and exercised without opposition a like attitude. While for Prof. Turner, half a century earlier, ' under the pontificate of Damasus (366-84), a long step forward was taken in formulating the claim of the Roman Church to be the exclusive inheritor of all, and more than all, that the New Testament tells us of the prerogative of St. Peter.'

Thus, as seen by the eyes of the best modern Anglican scholarship, the course of steady consistent growth and successful assertion of the position of the Roman Bishop is marked as by a series of milestones : Clement (100), Victor (200), Stephen (250),

Damasus (375), Celestine (430), Leo (450), Gregory (600)—whose position was maintained unchallenged throughout Western Europe up to the Reformation.

After these Church of England writers, who all in divers ways and measures accept the idea of Church, episcopate, Catholic tradition, authority, it will be of interest to turn our attention to a writer who views things from the opposite pole of extreme French liberal Protestantism, rationalistic and pietistic. The late Auguste Sabatier, who died a quarter of a century ago, was Dean of the Faculty of Protestant theology at the Sorbonne. For him the whole Catholic movement—the idea of church, ministry, episcopacy, sacraments, ritual, creed, dogma—was all from first to last progressive corruption of the pure gospel delivered by Christ, even though the Catholic current began to flow at the very beginning, and received its first great impetus from St. Paul. Though one differs profoundly from the anti-ecclesiastical standpoint of Sabatier, still he was a foremost representative of a great school of modern critical scientific Church historians, of whom another protagonist is Prof. Adolf Harnack ; and it must be of interest to see how a scholar of such strong liberalistic tendencies views the course of early church history in regard to the Papacy : [1]

We must recognize in St. Paul's Epistles the idea of the Church of God or of Christ, one and universal, the great idea which was to preside over the evolution of the Christian communities and make it issue in the constitution of the Catholic Church. In the opening years of the second century monarchical episcopacy was practically established

[1] The following sketch is derived from the book *Les Religions d'Autorité et la Religion de l'Esprit* (1904 ; also in English). The fragments extracted in what follows may be found, with the references, in an article of the present writer, *Hibbert Journal*, April 1906.

in the great centres. The episcopate came to be regarded as the continuation of the apostolate—it is so in the Letter of Clement of Rome. In Irenaeus, Hippolytus, Tertullian, we have before us the Catholic bishop. Cyprian pushed the idea to its utmost consequences : in the body of bishops the apostolic college is perpetuated, and the bishops inherit the authority, the inspiration, and the powers of the Apostles.

[Now for the Papacy.] In Cyprian's system the bishops were all equal, and there was no place for an *episcopus episcoporum*. Yet such is the interior logic of the system, that Cyprian himself posited the germ of a new evolution which was to produce from the body of bishops that head of the episcopate, that bishop of bishops, against whom he tried to guard himself. Cyprian gave the body a head. The unity of the bishops has a central point ; as Peter was the beginning of the unity of the Church, and as his see was fixed at Rome, the Roman Church is the principal church whence arises the unity of the episcopate. Cyprian regarded this primacy as purely honorific and symbolic. But his protests against Stephen were but as wisps of straw thrown across a torrent that nothing ever again could stem : he was swept along by the irresistible logic of the move-ment he had himself created. The same law which had produced the bishop in the parishes of the time of Ignatius, was to produce the universal bishop in the œcumenical Church.

But the beginnings of the Papacy were before Cyprian : the future centre of the Catholic Church appeared from the commencement of the second century, and in the year 194 —when for the first time a Bishop of Rome speaks as master to the other bishops, presents himself as inter-preter and arbiter of the universal Church, acts as universal bishop, and proclaims heretical the churches that would resist his authority—must be placed the true birthday of the Papacy.

In the growth of the power of the Roman Church and her Bishop, there was no ambition or other unworthy motive,—it was all only natural, inevitable. The Popes claimed their prerogative as the successors of St. Peter ;

as no one called in question the fact of this succession, nothing was more natural than that they should draw from it the practical conclusions that flowed from it. Their exegesis and their history had neither more nor less value than those which Cyprian used to establish his theory of the episcopate. They used it with more logic, but not with less sincerity.

Finally, once the Roman primacy was recognized, all later developments of the papal powers and prerogatives, up to and including the Vatican decrees, are but the logical issue and the conclusion of the Catholic conception of the Church. The infallibility which was the attribute of the universal Church gradually was concentrated in the Roman Church, and thence passed to the Roman Bishop; when the Pope was held to be the head and mouth of the Church, could the infallibility of the latter express itself by another head or another mouth? Thus it is not difficult for Catholic apologists to show that the dogma of papal infallibility is the logical conclusion of the premises of Catholicism.

Here we are brought to the question of the papal infallibility. And returning to the Anglican scholars, we may cite words of another English Church historian, the late Dr. Bigg, Professor of Ecclesiastical History at Oxford:

Every abuse of the medieval and even of the later Roman Church—papal infallibility (and others)—can be not unreasonably defended from the usage of the sixth, the fifth, the fourth, and even of the third century.[1]

Dr. William Bright saw that the Roman Church was trusted for its 'traditional immunity from heretical speculations.'[2] So also Harnack: 'The Roman Church was recognized as being able, with special precision, to discriminate between the true and the false.'[3]

[1] Letter in *The Times*, March 2, 1905.
[2] *Roman Claims*, p. 3.
[3] Excursus, 'Catholic and Roman' (see below).

So also Bossuet : ' The Roman Church, taught by St. Peter and his successors, knew no heresy. All the heresies received there their death-blow. And so the Roman Church is ever virgin ; the Roman faith is ever the faith of the Church.'[1]

The infallibility first appears not as a formulated doctrine but as a principle in work : it seems to have been instinctively felt throughout Christendom that when some new teaching arose, or some dispute on points of theology, Rome was the place to which the question should be referred for judgement. Thus heretics and orthodox alike had recourse to Rome for a verdict on matters in controversy.

In the second and early third centuries Caspari enumerates fifteen heretics who came to Rome seeking recognition.[2] In the story of Pelagianism this recourse to Rome stands out with especial clearness, both on the part of Pelagius and on that of Augustine. It was felt, consciously, or perhaps subconsciously, that the Roman Church was endowed with a charisma, peculiar to herself, for the discernment of truth and falsehood in matters of Christian Faith. And in all such cases, inevitably, it was the Bishop of Rome who was spokesman of his Church, and whose the decisions were. Bishop Lightfoot recognizes that already in the second century ' the succession of the Bishops of Rome is with Hegesippus and Irenaeus the chief guarantee of the transmission of the orthodox doctrine.' And at Chalcedon the assembled bishops, all Easterns, received the Tome of St. Leo with the acclamation ' Peter has spoken by the mouth of Leo ';—

[1] Sermon on ' the Unity of the Church ' (Œuvres, Paris, 1748, tom. V ; 1862, tom. XI).

[2] *Quellen zur Geschichte des Tauf-Symbols*, III, 309-48. Similarly Harnack : ' The teachers and founders of the sects always betook themselves to Rome, in order to push their cause ' (*Expansion*, II, 445).

they attributed the doctrinal charisma of the Roman Church to the Bishop, in that he, as successor of St. Peter, spoke with Peter's authority in solemnly defining the Catholic Faith.

To assign, as Bright and Harnack do, this unique doctrinal charisma of the Roman Church as an explanation of its predominance in the first ages, is to offer as an explanation the very thing itself most clamorously calling for explanation.

It will be, perhaps, not without instruction to cast a hasty glance, in supplement of the utterances just cited from English writers, at similar utterances by writers of a very different school, the liberalistic school of Protestant scholarship in Germany. The half-dozen names that follow will all be recognized by those who know, as of first rank among the exegetes and Church historians of Protestant Germany.

On St. Peter and the Petrine Texts : B. Weiss, in Meyer's *Kritisch-Exegetisches Commentar :*

Upon this rock : The emphasis lies on *this*, pointing to Peter : upon no other than upon this rock, i.e. upon this rock-nature which, like the rock in the parable (Matt. vii, 24, 25), could ensure the existence of the house, i.e. the continuance and cohesion of the new community. *I will build my church :* the primacy among the apostles is here undoubtedly awarded to Peter. With this accords also his appearing first in the lists of the apostles, and the actual superiority in which we find him throughout the New Testament in the circle of the apostles.

On the same text Hans Holtzmann (*Hand-Commentar*) :

Peter is to be the Rock for the church. The reference of the image is to the person of Peter,—in this the Catholic exegetes are unquestionably right, as against the old Protestants, who saw the Rock only in Peter's faith or his confession of faith.

Again Holtzmann on John xxi, 15-17 : By ' feed my

lambs' is Peter entrusted with the direction of the community. As the apostolic right of authority had already been conferred on him in common with the other disciples (John xx, 21-23), here can be meant only the supreme direction (Oberleitung); and also his restoration to the position conferred on him in Matthew xvi.

Weizsäcker (*The Apostolic Age*, English translation) :

> He sees the pre-eminence and the undisputed predominance of Peter both in the earliest times and subsequently in the further course of events (I, 14); Matthew xvi represents Christ as declaring that the Church would be founded on this Rock (Peter), and as conferring upon Peter supreme legislative power (II, 150); on John xxi : the lofty authority, the dignity and position of the Apostle Peter are throughout assumed (II, 208).

On the early Primacy of the Roman Church.
We shall cite two witnesses as to the question of fact, Harnack and Sohm.

Harnack's Excursus 'Catholic and Roman' is well known. It is found in Vol. II of the English translation of the *History of Dogma*. He recognizes with Lightfoot the tone of authority in Clement's Epistle ; of Ignatius he says :

> Soften as we may all the extravagant expressions in his Epistle to the Romans, it is at least clear that he conceded to them a precedence in the circle of sister churches. Concerning Victor he asks : How could Victor have ventured on issuing such a decree (powerless though he was to enforce it universally), if it were not established and recognized that to fix the conditions of the common unity in decisive questions of faith belonged chiefly to the Roman Church ? How could Victor have made such an unheard-of demand on autonomous communities, if he, as Roman Bishop, were not recognized as in a special sense the guardian of that common unity ?

And in that other work, *The Expansion of Christianity*, speaking of the first three centuries :

The Roman Church was *the* Catholic Church. It was more than the mere symbol and representative of Christian unity, for to it, more than to any other, Christians owed unity itself (I, 470).

Dr. Rudolph Sohm is not so well known in England as is Harnack, but he has no less a name in Germany. His *Kirchenrecht* (1892) has not been translated into English. In it he says such things as this :

It is beyond doubt that the Roman community was in the first three centuries the leading community of all Christendom.

Rome is the ' head ' of the Church without which the Church is not the Church. Without communion with Rome there is no Church. Only in their union with Rome can the individual communities belong to the Church. These persuasions of the old Catholic Church of the second and third centuries show the prodigious power of the Roman community in face of all the others.

On Victor : Rome has the power to cut off from the Church. Communion with Rome is the presupposition for communion with the Church. Rome has thereby power over every other church.

The Roman community possesses the right Christian belief. Her belief *is* the belief of Christendom. She has, according to the earliest Catholic belief, teaching authority (Lehrgewalt) over all the others, but none has teaching authority over the Roman community.

An unbroken progressive development leads on from the exclusive right of the bishop over the Eucharist [Ignatius] to the infallible teaching office of the Pope.

It is thus that these German Protestant historians *see* the *facts* of the earliest history of the Christian Church. Of course Harnack and Sohm, like Sabatier, are ready with a naturalistic account of what they

look upon as progressive corruption of the Gospel
—a corruption that set in with the very death of
Jesus Christ on Calvary. For them the early prestige
of the Roman Church and its Bishop is mainly the
prestige of the City of Rome.

But the Christians of the second and third centuries
had a quite different and quite definite idea. And it
is, at the least, arguable that the living belief of the
early Church is more likely to be right in such a matter
than the speculations of latter-day scholars. In the
second century, witness Irenaeus and Tertullian, the
primacy of the Roman Church was attributed to the
fact that it had been founded and constituted by ' the
two most glorious Apostles, Peter and Paul '; and
in the third, witness Cyprian, this was narrowed to
the fact that it was ' Cathedra Petri '. And so it is
not too much to plead that the Fathers of the Vatican
Council did not act altogether extravagantly, or in
flagrant disregard of history, when they followed
St. Gregory the Great in firmly basing his position
as Pope on the three great Petrine texts :

> To all who know the Gospel, it is manifest that the
> charge of the whole Church was entrusted by the voice
> of the Lord to the holy Apostle Peter, Prince of all the
> Apostles. For to him it is said, ' Peter, lovest thou me ?
> Feed my sheep.' To him is said, ' Behold, Satan hath
> desired to sift you as wheat, but I have prayed for thee,
> Peter, that thy faith fail not ; and do thou, being once
> converted, confirm thy brethren.' To him is said, ' Thou
> art Peter, and upon this rock I will build my Church,'
> etc. Lo, he hath received the keys of the kingdom of
> heaven, the power of binding and loosing is given to him,
> the care and the chiefship of the whole Church is committed
> to him.[1]

[1] Epp. V, 20 (ed. Ben.).

Since the writing of the foregoing pages, a book, *Peter, Prince of the Apostles,* has been produced by yet another of the school of the Cambridge trio, Dr. F. J. Foakes-Jackson, formerly lecturer in Ecclesiastical History at Cambridge, now professor in the General Theological Seminary at New York. The following snippets are from the Introduction :

Peter is the man whom Jesus chose as the leader of the Twelve Apostles, who subsequently appears as their chief in the foundation of the Christian Church at Jerusalem. . . . From the very first Peter is, after Christ, the most prominent person in the history of our religion, and in the Gospels he is always represented as taking the lead among the Apostles. But the history of Peter does not end with his life : he has had a most extraordinary influence on the world to this day. . . . Soon after his martyrdom the Christians connected his name with that of Paul in the foundation of their leading church ; and because of this, the Christian community at Rome was early regarded as the repository of the most reliable apostolic tradition. . . . In his name the Bishops of Rome claimed authority over all churches. . . . For Peter was believed in accordance with the words of Christ to be the Rock on which the Church was built, and as such to be the symbol of Christian unity, and also the Keeper of the Keys of the Kingdom of Heaven, so that none could enter it whom he would exclude. And these tremendous claims were transferred from the humble fisherman to the clergy of his church, and ultimately centred in his representatives, the two hundred and sixty Popes, who claim to be his direct successors. . . . His story is in fact the history of Christianity, not of its theology so much as of its activity, its authority, its influence on the mind of man.

It has seemed worth while to make this somewhat long digression, in order to bring out the fact that some case may be made out from history, as viewed by witnesses with no theological axe to grind, in favour of the theory of the Primacy, and even the Infallibility, defined by the Council; that so all may pass on to the consideration of its proceedings, free from the prejudice that they are going to view an exhibition of singular folly, ignorance, and fanaticism.

CHAPTER IV

THE NEW ULTRAMONTANISM

AT the beginning of the previous chapter we saw
what was the old theological statement of the Ultramontane position as formulated by Bellarmine. We
have now to follow the course of a movement that
set in, primarily in France as a reaction from Gallicanism, but also elsewhere, during the nineteenth
century: this movement Wilfrid Ward has aptly
named 'The New Ultramontanism.' In his book
William George Ward and the Catholic Revival, cc. v-viii,
he gives a masterly presentation of the conflicting
currents of ideas among Catholics during the fifty years
that preceded the Vatican Council, a perusal of which
will greatly repay anyone who wishes rightly to
appraise the forces in play at the Council. Another
book that may profitably be referred to is Rev.
James MacCaffrey's *History of the Catholic Church
in the Nineteenth Century*, I, cc. i, viii; II, c. viii.
Still, good as these reviews are, he who desires to
get into touch with the living movements must
perforce read some at least of the actual sources of
the history, and their volume is immense: the published lives, memoirs, works, letters, pamphlets, of
the leading actors in France would make up a veri-
table library. I have confined myself to two of
these sources, from opposite poles of the controversy: the Lives of Bishop Dupanloup and Abbot

57

Guéranger.[1] Each is frankly partisan, written without attempt or pretence of any impartial judicial presentation of the facts. Still both Lives are richly documented, and each hero was in close personal contact with the leading figures on both sides; so that these two books make the thing alive, and suffice for the purpose of this chapter, which is not to tell the story of the French Catholics in the period before the Council, but to account for the heated atmosphere, both inside and out, in which the Council was held.

The Restoration of the Bourbons in 1815 was an attempt just to set up again the ' ancien régime ' in State and in Church alike; absolute monarchy in the State, and Gallicanism in the Church. The restored ' emigrés ' bishops had been brought up in the Gallican theory, and the Four Articles of 1682 had again to be taught in the theological schools. But the Revolution had shaken to the foundations not only the throne and the old social order, but also the Gallican Church, and there were now strong Ultramontane currents running among the younger clergy and the educated Catholic laity. This movement found eloquent expression in the book *Du Pape* of Count Joseph de Maistre, published 1819. He was not a theologian, but a thoughtful highly educated man of affairs, who had represented the Bourbons at St. Petersburg from 1802 till 1817; his *Soirées de Saint Pétersbourg* was a well-known book in its day.

The *Du Pape* is a strong assertion of the Ultra-

[1] *Life of Mgr. Dupanloup, Bishop of Orleans*, by abbé F. Lagrange (later Bishop of Chartres); translated by Lady Herbert, 2 vols.

Dom Guéranger, Abbé de Solesmes, par un Moine Bénédictin de la Congrégation de France, 2 vols.

montane position of Bellarmine : it vigorously controverts the Gallican as represented chiefly by Bossuet and Fleury. But de Maistre's real interest lay not in questions of theology but in practical problems—the reconstitution of the social order in France after the Revolution : and the positive and constructive side of his argument turns on the necessity of union of papacy and throne for the firm re-establishment of a Christian State. He starts from the idea of ' sovereignty ', asserting that all sovereignty necessarily implies the acceptance in practice of the ultimate decision of authority, in whatever form of government, as being *right*, in the sense that it must be acted on, and so far forth is ' infallible ' in practice : but in the case of the ultimate religious authority such practical infallibility necessarily becomes real infallibility in the full sense of the word. For him religion, Catholic religion, the Catholic Church, is the only stay of society and of an ordered civil and political system— he has his eye on France ;—and so he argues that the Pope must have on the spiritual side, and in a higher degree, the like position of authority, finality, power, jurisdiction, that he conceives the King to have on the side of temporals. The Pope is so necessary for the well-being of society and civil order, that if Christ had not instituted the papacy, it would be necessary to create it. A strong papacy is the great safeguard of Christian society ; Christianity has no stability without the papacy. And so de Maistre took hold of and emphasized and developed the Ultramontane theory as we have seen it in Bellarmine—monarchical position of the Pope, his universal jurisdiction and supreme authority over all, and his infallibility when teaching *ex cathedra*.

W. Ward (op. cit., pp. 89-92) gives a fuller sketch of the argument of *Du Pape ;* also an account of other French writers of the school. But the only one that need concern us is the famous abbé de Lammenais. He took the Ultramontane ideas of de Maistre, and pushed them to such extremes that made them subserve political ideals the very counter of all de Maistre stood for. He called for the alliance of the Church with democracy, and proclaimed an extreme liberalism. With him were a group of earnest able young Catholics, pre-eminent among whom were the abbé Lacordaire and Count de Montalembert. They started a paper, *L'Avenir* ; their platform may be thus described : [1]

On the religious side it was strongly Ultramontane : Lammenais started from a philosophical theory that 'universal consent' is the test of truth, and regarded the Pope as the mouthpiece of this universal consent ; he advocated papal absolutism, and urged that the papal power must be accepted as supreme over the regal. In politics the *Avenir* writers proclaimed themselves at once Ultramontanes and democrats. They demanded complete liberty for the Church, and the only way of securing that liberty was by a complete separation of Church and State. They insisted there should be absolute liberty of conscience and of the press, that universal suffrage was a right that could not be denied. They denounced the concordat as a betrayal of the Church ; they attacked the clergy for consenting to be the paid officials of the State, and the bishops for their attachment to Gallicanism and royalty.

Such teachings naturally stirred up opposition in France and were reprobated at Rome by Gregory XVI as intemperate and in great part erroneous. Lacordaire and Montalembert submitted, but Lammenais apostatized. His influence, which had been immense

---

[1] I have not myself read de Lammenais or the *Avenir* ; the summary is taken from Ward (op. cit., pp. 101-7) and MacCaffrey (op. cit., I, 61-3 ; II, 448).

among the younger clergy, survived in great measure, and was one of the principal forces in the stamping out of Gallicanism.

At this time, the early 'thirties, the state of religion in France was at a low ebb. In most parts the majority of the intelligentzia and of the professional and ruling classes was irreligious and sceptical, without belief in Christianity. But a strong Christian and Catholic revival set in, ever growing in force, associated chiefly with the names of three men : in 1833 began abbé Lacordaire's Conferences in Notre Dame, to which flocked the highest intellect of Paris ; in 1835 Montalembert took his seat in the Chamber of Peers, whence his great speeches in defence of religion and of the liberty of the Church resounded through France ; and at the same time Frederick Ozanam was founding and propagating the Society of St. Vincent of Paul, a widespread association of laymen who brought religion and practical Christian charity into the homes of the poor : in 1840 he was elected to a chair in the faculty of Literature at the Sorbonne, the ancient Paris University, and here he made his lectures a telling apology for Christianity and the Catholic Church, listened to by crowds of young men.[1] Under the influence mainly of these three great outstanding Catholics a return movement towards Christian belief among intellectual circles was set afoot which waxed stronger and stronger throughout the reign of Louis Philippe (1830-48). Thus a compact Catholic party came into being under the leadership of Montalembert, with which, though it was small, the politicians and the Government had to count.

The Catholics concentrated their efforts first on

[1] We may refer to *Le Movement Catholique en France de 1830 à 1850*, by abbé F. Mourret.

winning liberty of education, the right to set up
Catholic schools, both primary and secondary, independent of the State and under the full control
of the Catholic authorities. On the overthrow of
Louis Philippe in 1848, at the election of the President
of the Republic, the Catholic vote on the whole supported the candidature of Louis Napoleon; and in
return for their support a leading Catholic, the Comte
de Falloux, was taken into the new Government and
given the portfolios of public worship and education.
By his great influence and tact a bill was passed in
1850, securing for Catholics the right of setting up
schools, primary and secondary, and the right of
teaching therein for all duly qualified Catholics,
including the members of the teaching orders, even,
after a special battle, the Jesuits. The only limitation
was in regard to secondary education, that university
degrees could be conferred only by the State university.

This proviso occasioned a lamentable division in
the ranks of the Catholics. One party, headed by
Louis Veuillot, the combative editor of the principal
Catholic organ, the *Univers*, asserted it to be an absolute surrender of principle that the Church should
not be able to confer degrees recognized by the State;
and urged that an act containing such a limitation
could not be accepted by Catholics. The others,
Falloux, Montalembert, Dupanloup, maintained that
the act gave the Church a very real and substantive
good, in that it secured for parents a Catholic education
for their children, and that it was the most that could
possibly be obtained; therefore it should be accepted
and worked to the utmost possible. It is worthy
of note that such Ultramontane stalwarts as Abbot
Guéranger and Mgr. Pie, Bishop of Poitiers, took this
view and pressed the *Univers* writers to withhold
their opposition; the Papal Nuncio in Paris urged
the same; finally Pius IX himself said that the law,

while falling short of all that could be desired, still did confer a great boon and should be used by the Catholics, and he made an urgent appeal for healing the divisions among the Catholics of France.[1] For all that, in spite of Nuncio and Pope, the *Univers* continued obdurate, and it pursued with a bitter invective those French Catholics who advocated the acceptance of the law, Montalembert above all.

The irreconcilable and intransigent attitude of the *Univers* writers over the education act and other issues split the French Catholics into two vehemently opposed camps that lasted until the Council, and longer, to the irreparable damage of the cause of Catholicism and religion in France. These feuds were also without doubt a principal cause of the heat, and even animosities, that surrounded, and indeed found entrance into, the Council.

The questions at issue in France were much more politico-social than theological—theories of government and the relations between Church and State. On these issues of the practical order there existed among the French Catholics a liberal party and an intransigent party; and these same parties grew up, with modifications, throughout the whole Catholic world. Naturally, in France the names 'Gallican' and 'Ultramontane' came to be affixed to the respective parties, and were freely bandied about; but they were in reality nicknames. The liberal Catholics were not, as such, Gallicans: Montalembert in a letter to Guéranger declares that he 'detests' Gallicanism, the Four Articles of 1682, the Organic Articles, and the rest; nor, as we shall see, was the foremost leader of the party, Bishop Dupanloup, a Gallican, though freely called such. The idea the liberals stood for was to christianize and catholicize modern

[1] *Guéranger*, I, 426; II, 10; cf. *Dupanloup*, I, c. xxviii.

society and the modern State, without repudiating or combating the democratic idea or the principles of political liberalism. They recognized that the work of the French Revolution could not be undone, and that the modern State with its new ideas of polity, freedom, had come to stay. They believed that the Church could embrace and assimilate the modern State just as well as she had the feudal State, and also in great measure modern social and political ideas. These men held that the principles of 1789—Liberté, Égalité, Fraternité—were capable of a good Christian meaning, and could be applied to the conditions of a sound modern State and society. Their idea was to 'baptize the Revolution', exorcizing the evil elements in it; their endeavour was to control and guide on to right lines the new democratic political and social ideas, rather than to reject them root and branch.

To the other school, the irreconcilables, this was a betrayal in principle, and a delusion in fact. Modern society and all the political and social ideas let loose by the Revolution were so incurably vicious that nothing could be hoped for from them, and there was nothing for good Catholics to do but to stand aloof and protest and reassert uncompromisingly the principles that had held sway in the times when Europe was Catholic. For the present, things could only be left to run their course, and society, after plunging through evil upon evil, might be hoped at long last to find salvation by a return to the polity of olden times.

An article of the *Univers* affords a sample of the politico-religious ideas championed by Veuillot and his school:

Society is on a sewer—it will perish—with the debris of the Vatican God will stone the human race. These stones of the Vatican will roll through the world, crushing thrones and dwellings, even to the tombs. There are no more Catholic Princes in the world. Well, O Church of

God, leave them, and turn to the democracy. The democracy baptized will do what the monarchies have not done. Peter has heard the voice, ' Launch out into the deep ' : the fisher of men will cast his great nets. The multitude of the nations will form one universal confederation under the presidency of the Roman Pontiff, a holy people, as there was a Holy Empire.[1]

This serves to show the sort of thing that Catholic statesmen, such as Falloux, Montalembert, Dupanloup, Darboy, were faced with. The Lateran Treaty is a curious commentary on such dreams.

It will be in place to introduce here the great personality of Bishop Dupanloup, one of the most outstanding figures of the period and of the Council. Born in 1802 in Savoy, he entered St. Sulpice and was ordained priest in 1825. He first came under the public eye as the one who brought about the reconciliation of Talleyrand on his deathbed. As a young priest he used to fill the Madeleine by the wonderful catechism classes that attracted the children and young people of all grades. As Rector of the Episcopal college of Paris he raised it to the very first rank among the colleges and lycées of France, and so became a recognized educational authority, and as such was on the commission that prepared the Falloux law of 1850. After being Vicar General of Paris and Canon of Notre Dame, he became in 1849 Bishop of Orleans. Until the end of his long life, 1878, he proved himself in every aspect of episcopal duty a truly apostolic bishop. And by his eloquent powerful sermons and addresses, his books, and his enormous output of telling pamphlets on all the great religious questions that arose in France, he became a notable public man, able to influence the Government and

---

[1] *Univers*, July 11, 1868; cited by Dupanloup in the *Avertissement*.

the nation at large. He could conciliate such men as Guizot, Thiers, even Victor Cousin, and win them over to support great Catholic causes. His fearlessness enabled him to beard the Government and even the Emperor himself; once he drew upon himself a state prosecution. He soon became the chief Catholic champion in all public controversies, the recognized spokesman of the bishops, the most prominent bishop in France, and one of the most prominent bishops of the whole Catholic world. His attitude to the papal question is of special interest for us. The particular point of the infallibility will be spoken of in a later chapter: but in the matter of the Pope's temporal sovereignty and of the Papal States he was the Pope's great champion in France, asserting in speech and pamphlet in the most uncompromising terms not only the Pope's right to the hereditary States of the Church, and the injustice and revolutionary character of the moves to despoil him of them; but also their theoretical necessity for the Pope's freedom of action in the spiritual government of the Church, and this with a fullness and absoluteness hardly heard nowadays: indeed, put out of date by the Lateran Treaty. He it was who more than any other worked up Catholic opinion in France to such a pitch of protest in 1860, when with the connivance of the French Emperor the Piedmontese had annexed all the Papal States except the Patrimony or territories around Rome, that the Government was forced to yield and to keep the French troops holding Rome and the Patrimony for the Pope from 1860 till 1870. It is hardly too much to say that the prolongation of the reduced temporal sovereignty of the Pope for these ten years longer was the achievement of Dupanloup.

Nor was Pio Nono unmindful of it all. He appreciated and thanked him time after time for his efforts in behalf of the temporal sovereignty, and in behalf of all the great religious issues so often at stake in France, which he ever defended with power and success, in that he, more than any other, could reach the ear and the intelligence of the French public. And the Pope used often to turn to him to use voice and pen in defence of these great causes. A whole volume, near three hundred pages long, has been printed, made up of the rescripts and letters of Pius IX to Dupanloup in recognition of his manifold services to religion.

What must appear strange is that this was the man beyond all others persistently and violently attacked by the intransigent and irreconcilable section of the French Catholics, whose organ was the *Univers*, and whose protagonist was its editor, Louis Veuillot. What is stranger still is that Ozanam was similarly attacked in the *Univers* in 1840 and 1850, for preaching moderation : Veuillot charged him with cowardly desertion, weak compliance, timid silence, false flattery, and so on :[1] Ozanam, who is universally looked on by Catholics as a Christian hero, a great apostle of Christian charity, and as having in him much of the stuff that makes a saint. Again, Lacordaire : he was probably the most liberal of the group of French liberal Catholics—his wish was to die a penitent Catholic and an impenitent liberal. But now that he is well known by his Letters and his Life—who thinks of him as anything else than a real Christian hero, who effected a great work of religious renovation in France ? In fact, whatever was achieved in France in those days for Pope, for Church, for religion, was in far greatest measure achieved by these men, Lacordaire, Montalembert, Ozanam, Dupanloup, Falloux. And this is now recognized. In 1928 the

[1] F. *Ozanam in his Correspondence*, by Mgr. Baunard, trans., pp. 214, 305.

Lenten preacher in Notre Dame of Paris, was Mgr. Baudrillart, Rector of the Institut Catholique, and recently made titular archbishop. Reviewing the religious revival in France he named as the Catholic protagonists of the movement in the middle period of the nineteenth century, Lacordaire, Montalembert, Ozanam, Veuillot, Dupanloup, de Broglie, Falloux, Cochin—' liberals ' all, with the single exception of Veuillot.[1]

It is time to speak of Pius IX. He held a quite over-mastering personal position throughout the Catholic world, such as none of his predecessors for many long centuries had held. In the *Life of Bishop Ullathorne* (II, 297) I have tried to sketch the causes of this influence ; but two chapters (xvi, xxviii) of Wilfrid Ward's *Life of Cardinal Wiseman* afford an admirably clear account of the first twenty years of the pontificate. When he ascended the papal throne in 1846, after the reactionary reign of Gregory XVI, he was acclaimed as the liberal Pope, a sympathizer with Italian national sentiment. He set up a representative government for the Papal States, which was welcomed with enthusiastic acclamation by the people.[2] But the revolutionary element would not have it ; the Pope's Prime Minister, Count de Rossi, was poignarded entering the Chamber ; the revolution broke out ; the Roman Republic was proclaimed ; the Pope was imprisoned in the Quirinal and had to escape from Rome in disguise, aided by the French Ambassador (1848). He found an asylum at Gaeta, in Neapolitan territory, where he stayed for a year, till restored to Rome by a French army, despatched, be it said, through the efforts of the Catholic liberals, Falloux and Montalembert.

---

[1] *Tablet*, 1928, April 14, p. 506.
[2] Ozanam was in Rome and describes the great ovation given to the Pope (F. *Ozanam*, Baunard, p. 245).

Pio Nono's attempt to establish constitutional government in his States, and the amnesty to political prisoners, had won general admiration; one of the London papers acclaimed him as 'the most enlightened sovereign of the age'. But after his well-intentioned efforts at conciliation had been deliberately wrecked by the revolutionary elements in Rome and in Italy, and after he himself had tasted the Revolution and had been forced to flee from his City and See of Rome, it can cause no surprise that he came back cured of all liking for liberal institutions. 1848 was the year of revolutions in most countries of Western Europe, and the revolutionary movements in most places, and especially in Italy, were strongly anti-clerical, anti-Catholic, anti-Christian, anti-religious. In the presence of this spirit of revolt the Pope had again and again to raise his voice; and at frequent intervals throughout his reign were issued protests against the rationalistic and materialistic philosophies then greatly in vogue; against the subversive social and political theories of the revolutionaries; against religious indifference and anti-religious legislation; against the seizure and spoliation of the Pontifical States; against the multitudinous errors of the time concerning society, polity, law.

The issuing in 1864 by the Cardinal Secretary of State to the Catholic bishops, of a Syllabus or list of eighty propositions that had been condemned in some thirty such pontifical utterances of Pius IX, raised a storm of unprecedented fury in all quarters hostile to the Church and the Papacy. When these propositions are now read and pondered in a calmer atmosphere, it will probably be recognized that fully half the condemned errors must appear monstrous to any Catholic, and indeed to anyone who accepts a Christian basis of society. But the secular and anti-Catholic press seized upon the Syllabus as a declaration

69

of war upon modern civilization, society, and thought, as the 'definitive divorce of the Church from the modern world'.[1] Some journalists so far lost their heads as to say the Pope had condemned all the discoveries of modern science and industry, railroads, electric telegraphs, photography, and was about to suppress all such things in the small territory left to him, together with steam engines and gas light.[2]

The eightieth and last censured proposition was the one that above all gave occasion to such notions. It ran : 'The Roman Pontiff can and ought to be reconciled to, and come to terms with, progress, liberalism and modern civilization.' Bishop Ullathorne had to deal with this proposition in his reply to Mr. Gladstone's attack on the Vatican Council in 1874 ; he did so by the simple method of quoting the full context at length from the Allocution of 1861 from which the proposition was taken : the true meaning of the various propositions was to be ascertained from the contexts of the original documents from which they had been culled. I have given the piece in full in the *Life of Bishop Ullathorne* (II, 94-9) ; anyone who reads it will, I venture to think, agree that the Pope could not come to terms with the kind of progress there held up to reprobation : I add, however, that as a piece of indexing, this proposition, thus out of its context, was singularly unfortunate.

The one to stand up in defence of the Pope and in vindication of the Syllabus from the extravagant interpretations placed on it by the world at large, was Dupanloup, who issued a pamphlet exposing the

[1] The best account of the Syllabus in English is Wilfrid Ward's *W. G. Ward and the Catholic Revival*, c. x. But by far the best account is that by the French non-Catholic statesman Émile Ollivier, in *L'Église et l'État au Concile du Vatican* (I, c. iv, §§ iii, iv), to be spoken of below, Chapter VI.

[2] So a Piedmontese paper.

erroneous meanings attached to various of its propositions. This vindication was a work of first importance,
and brought to its author letters from no fewer than 630
bishops in all parts of the Catholic world, congratulat-
ing and thanking him for the pamphlet. The Pope
too wrote thanking him for having 'exploded the
calumnious interpretations' laid upon the Syllabus.
The secular press cried out that Dupanloup had
'denaturalized' it, explaining away its plain import,
and watering down its force : and, what is remarkable,
the extreme section of the French Ultramontanes
joined in the cry, and acclaimed the Syllabus as the
formal and final condemnation of the modern State.
The writer of the Life of Guéranger uses language
that makes it seem as though he held that according
to the Syllabus only an absolute monarchy, like that
of the 'ancien régime', could be fully according to
the mind and teaching of the Catholic Church, all
kinds of representative government being ruled out.
Veuillot definitely endorsed the saying, 'the parliamentary system rests on an heretical principle'.[1]
These men pressed to their extreme limits the terms
of the Syllabus, and urged that not merely revolutionary liberalism, but liberal principles of every grade
and shade, fell under the condemnation of the
Syllabus : there can no more be, they said, any kind of
good liberalism, than any kind of good Protestantism.

[1] It is curious to note how, though religiously poles asunder,
L. Veuillot and M. Maurras of the *Action Française* are in agreement that representative government is against the principles
of the Catholic Church, and that only a non-parliamentary
monarchy is properly according to her mind ; and also to
observe how conservative circles among the French Catholics
rallied, then and now, to this idea. It is needless to say that
any such idea has been strongly repudiated by Leo XIII and
subsequent Popes. There is an instructive article in the *Dublin
Review* of January 1927, by abbé Lugan : 'How Politics has
injured Religion in France.'

And these controversies among the French Catholics were carried on with the lack of restraint, the violence of language, and the bitterness, that too often mark such controversy, religious or political, in France.

The questions thus in agitation in France were of the religious-political order, rather than of the theological ; they were questions of the relations of Church and State, of kinds of government, of theories on the ideal rights of the spiritual power in face of the civil. The slogan, dear to Montalembert, ' Free Church in Free State ', called forth vehement denunciation. It is strange, how remote, after seventy years, the whole thing appears to us. Catholics in the United States, in England, Ireland, Australia, and many other countries, have all this time been living under actual conditions of Free Church in Free State ; they do not concern themselves much with questions of theory, whether this be the ideal ; but they know that under such conditions the Catholic Church functions freely and thrives exceedingly : and recent Popes have more than once expressed their satisfaction with the result.

All this business of the Syllabus was very much alive during the Council, though not coming to the surface. We shall have to revert to it hereafter (Chapter XVII).

If in France the new Ultramontanism had a practical and political character, versed largely in questions of social order and church life, elsewhere the conflict between Ultramontanes and liberals took on other shapes. In England, for instance, it was more theological in character, turning on the question of infallibility, and is therefore more directly concerned with the Vatican Council. W. G. Ward was the protagonist of the English group of extreme Ultramontanes. He was one of the first Oxford converts of 1845, a man of great intellectual power, an original and profound thinker in matters of philosophy and ethics. His interests lay, too, in theological and religious questions, and here he was prone to adopt positions of extreme intransigence. I have tried to depict Ward's mentality in the *Life of Bishop Ullathorne* (II, 305-8). In 1863 he became owner and editor of the *Dublin Review*, and he at once embarked on a vigorous Ultramontane campaign, concentrating above all on the question of infallibility. In this he went far beyond the positions laid down by Bellarmine, which had become the accepted theses of the Ultramontane theological schools as to what were to be accepted as infallible pronouncements of the Pope or infallible teaching of the Church. I had occasion when writing the *Life of Bishop Ullathorne* (II, 41-4) to describe Ward's positions ; so I make no apology for reproducing the sketch here :

> For him, all direct doctrinal instructions of all ency- clicals, of all letters to individual bishops and allocutions, published by the Popes, are *ex cathedra* pronouncements and *ipso facto* infallible. He was not directly concerned with the Gallican controversy—whether the organ of infallibility be the Pope alone, or Pope and episcopate ; his contention was concerned, as he expressed it, not with the ' subject ' of the infallibility, but with the ' object ', the kind of pro- nouncements to which it extends. He held that the in- fallible element of bulls, encyclicals, etc., should not be restricted to their formal definitions, but ran through their entire doctrinal instructions ; the decrees of the Roman Congregations, if adopted by the Pope and published by his authority, thereby were stamped with the mark of infallibility ; in short, ' his every doctrinal pronouncement is infallibly directed by the Holy Ghost '. Pusey in the *Eirenicon* not unjustly objected that such a doctrine of infallibility went far beyond the inerrancy in defining matters of faith or morals guaranteed to the Pope by the special assistance of the Holy Ghost, as laid down by the standard Catholic theologians, and, in fact, practically

amounted to inspiration : indeed Ward held explicitly that infallibility often amounts to ' a new inspiration ', instancing the condemnation of the Five Propositions of Jansenius (*Dublin Review*, October 1869, p. 479). He did not shrink from saying that bulls, as the ' Quanta Cura ' of 1864, were to be accepted ' as the Word of God '.[1] Thus he utterly rejected the idea that infallible pronouncements are few and far between, or need to be marked by the solemnities and conditions laid down by the theologians, or require any theological tribunal to declare them *ex cathedra* or interpret their meaning. On the contrary they bore their *ex cathedra* character on their face, and any man of good will and ordinary intelligence could recognize them and understand their import, and was immediately bound in conscience under pain of mortal sin to accept their teaching with full interior assent. Thus Ward's attitude to encyclicals and allocutions was much like the Protestant attitude to the Bible. For him the eighty propositions of the Syllabus were ' beyond question the Church's infallible utterance ' ; and not only so, but the thirty encyclicals and allocutions from which the propositions were culled were all thereby shown to have been *ex cathedra* in their entirety.

And not only did he urge with merciless logic and great vehemence of language his own view as to the infallible character of this enormous and quite indefinite mass of *ex cathedra* teaching, to be dug out from the Bullarium and Papal Acta of the past ; he insisted with uncompromising assurance that his view was the only Catholic one, and must be accepted as the Catholic Faith necessary for salvation, only invincible ignorance excusing from mortal sin.

The novelty of such ideas was made manifest before the Council. Just at its beginning one of the most prominent of the French Ultramontanes, Abbot Guéranger, published a tract, *La Monarchie Pontificale*, in which, answering the objection that a flood of infallible pronouncements might be expected, he laid down the tests of an *ex cathedra* utterance, which, he

---

[1] It will be seen in Chapter XXVII how far from such ideas stand the theologians since the Council.

said, were unmistakable : The Pope must manifest his decision to the whole Church, declaring his intention of pronouncing on the question of faith or morals, and commanding the submission of faith, qualifying with the note of heresy the opposite opinion, and fulminating an anathema against those who should hold it for the future.[1]

Reviewing this tract in the *Dublin Review*, and one of like tenor by another foremost Ultramontane, Mgr. Dechamps, Archbishop of Malines, Ward declared such limitations on the scope of *ex cathedra* pronouncements to be unduly narrow, and inadmissible—'minimizing '—yet the two tracts, each of them, received a special warm commendation from the Pope ! Fr. Perrone, the great Jesuit theologian in Rome at the middle of the century, had laid down the same tests and limitations : An *ex cathedra* decree is one whereby the Pope lays down something for the Universal Church to be held by faith, or to be rejected as contrary to the faith, under penalty of censure or anathema.[2]

Whatever his intransigence, Ward was a theologian; Louis Veuillot was not—he was a journalist without theological training, and he strained the idea of the Pope's infallibility beyond all theological bounds. He treated it as ' inspiration ' : ' We all know certainly only one thing, that is that no man knows anything except the Man with whom God is for ever, the Man who carries the thought of God. We must unswervingly follow his inspired directions.' Writing from Rome during the Council Veuillot thus posed the question : 'Does the Church believe, or does she not believe, that her Head is inspired directly by God, that is to say, infallible in his decisions regarding

[1] Op. cit., pp. 245-51.
[2] *Praelectiones Theologicae*, ' de Romano Pontifice ', c. iv.

faith and morals?'[1] Consonant with such ideas is what I myself heard a survivor of the Veuillot school say: he did not like the definitions of the Council being spoken of as having been put into shape by the discussions at the Council; 'it is much simpler to think of them as whispered directly by the Holy Ghost into the Pope's ear.' Again, Veuillot said: 'We must affirm squarely the authority and omnipotence of the Pope, as the source of all authority, spiritual and temporal. The proclamation of the dogma of the infallibility of the Pope has no other object.'

As the Council drew near there found place in the *Univers* an almost unbelievable exuberance of quite untheological devotion to the Holy Father, sometimes bordering, it seemed to many, on blasphemy; as when for the Holy Ghost was substituted the Pope in the verse of the sequence 'Veni Sancte Spiritus', thus:

À Pie IX, Pontife-Roi:

Pater pauperum
Dator munerum
Lumen cordium
Emitte caelitus
Lucis tuae radium!

Or when the Nones hymn, 'Rerum Deus tenax vigor', was paraphrased:

Rerum PIUS tenax vigor,
Immotus in te permanens,
Da verba vitae quae regant
Agnos, oves, et saeculum.

Again: À Pie IX qui représente mon Dieu sur la terre: Iste Deus meus et glorificabo eum, Deus patris mei et exaltabo eum!

[1] *Rome pendant le Concile*, II, 50.

Hebrews vii, 26 was applied to him : Pontifex sanctus, innocens, impollutus, segregatus a peccatoribus, et excelsior caelis factus.

'The infallibility of the Pope is the infallibility of Jesus Christ Himself'; 'When the Pope thinks, it is God who is thinking in him'—this last from an Italian Ultramontane source: 'Quando egli medità, è Dio che pensa in lui.'[1]

Of course no trained theologian would accept such aberrations. Still the excesses of the New Ultramontanism, whether Veuillot's entirely untheological extravagances, or Ward's undue straining of infallibility beyond the traditional teaching of the Catholic Ultramontane schools, or the extreme interpretations of the political and social import of the Syllabus, as being a condemnation of modern constitutional forms of government, did exercise a profound influence on the atmosphere in which the Council was held. It is to be understood that they were not the isolated extravagances of a few extremists. The *Univers* wielded a widespread influence in France and had a great backing among the clergy. Ward's views were upheld in England by theologians as Fr. Knox; and Archbishop Manning was more than disposed to accept them.[2] In other countries too, Italy and Germany, the New Ultramontanism was a very living force. This it was principally that caused the bitter hostility of the whole non-Catholic world, and the fears of the Governments of the Catholic States. This too was one real cause of the action of the Minority bishops in opposing the definition —they were afraid of the kind of infallibility that might be defined. As will appear, what was defined

---

[1] The *Civiltà Cattolica*, which ought to have known its theology better !

[2] *Life of Bishop Ullathorne*, II, 44 ; he did not urge such views during the Council.

was the old theological Ultramontane doctrine of Bellarmine.

At the close of this chapter it is again opportune to recommend Ollivier's account of the religious movements in France, op. cit., I, iii, § 3, and first half of c. iv. In justice to Louis Veuillot may be cited Ollivier's summing up. After commenting on his harshness to persons and his tendency to extremes, he says : ' Néanmoins et quoi qu'on en ait dit, l'éclat, l'audace, la puissance, la supériorité, la persévérance de la polémique de M. Louis Veuillot, ont été d'une manière continue plus utiles à l'Église que n'ont pu lui être nuisibles à certains moments, l'exaggeration des thèses et la cruanté des attaques personnelles ' (l.c., p. 304).

PREPARATIONS FOR THE COUNCIL

CHAPTER V

PREPARATIONS AT ROME[1]

ON December 6, 1864, two days before the publication
of the bull ' Quanta Cura ' and the Syllabus, at a
meeting of the Congregation of Rites, Pius IX caused
all officials to withdraw, and spoke to the Cardinals
alone. He manifested to them an idea that had long
been in his mind : that it would be for the good of
the Church to hold an œcumenical Council, so as to
provide in this extraordinary way for the extraordinary
needs of the Christian flock. Let the Cardinals study
the project, each one by himself, and then submit in
writing what seems good in the Lord : all under the
strictest secrecy. This was addressed to the Cardinals
in Curia, those resident in Rome. There were in all
twenty-one responses.[2] Two were definite negatives,
and half a dozen more expressed grave doubts and
hesitations as to the prudence, possibility, opportuneness, of holding a Council at the time. The majority
pronounced in favour. They considered there was
need of a clear statement of Catholic doctrine on
points impugned or controverted, together with
condemnations of current errors ; it should be

---

[1] The documents connected with this chapter are in Mansi,
I (49) ; the more important also in *Collectio Lacensis*, VII (*Lac*),
1013-67.

[2] They are printed in Mansi, l.c., 9-94. Granderath, *History*,
gives a summary that is very full (I, Bk. i, c. 3) ; Manning a
more concise one, *True Story*, c. i.

considered whether the changed conditions of the Church did not call for changes in discipline, and whether certain relaxations of ecclesiastical laws would not secure a better observance; there was need, too, of improvements in the education and instruction of the clergy, and of a general raising of the level of clerical life among seculars and regulars alike. Several thought that the Council might pave the way for the return to Catholic unity of those separated, either in doctrine or in communion, and also for renewed vigour in the Missions to the Heathen. Only two of the Cardinals made any reference to the defining of the Pope's infallibility.

A Commission of five Cardinals was set up to deal with all things relating to the Council. It got to work at once, and passed resolutions, approved by the Pope, to the effect that the convocation of an œcumenical Council was highly desirable and opportune; that the Catholic Sovereigns should not be consulted beforehand, but simultaneously with the announcing of the Council the Holy See should do what was proper in their regard; that a number of representative bishops of different nations should be invited to submit a summary of the matters that they thought ought to be dealt with at the Council.

At the end of April, 1865, a letter was despatched, under strict secrecy, to thirty-four bishops of the Latin Church, chosen by the Pope; and soon after to certain bishops of the Oriental Uniat Churches. It disclosed the fact that the Pope had in mind the convoking of an œcumenical Council and called on these bishops severally to draw up a summary of the matters that they thought should be dealt with at the Council.[1]

The names of these bishops would at present be

---

[1] Mansi, l.c., 105; *Lac* 1017.

mere names, but many of them will be familiar figures as the story of Council goes on. Suffice it to say that among them were Cardinal Pecci of Perugia (Leo XIII), Manning, and Dupanloup. The responses of the bishops are printed in Mansi (l.c., 107-202), followed by a long Report summarizing the views contained in them (202-238) ; this Report is in turn summarized by Granderath (I, Bk. i, c. 4). Some, perhaps six or eight, while recognizing the good that could be done by a Council, still doubted as to the prudence, and even the possibility, of holding one in the existing disturbed state of the world, and advised postponing the project : among these was Dupanloup. But the majority was favourable to the Council.

The general sense of the selected bishops was that the principal errors current should be dealt with and condemned : pantheism, naturalism, rationalism, socialism, communism, spiritism, religious indifference ; also the modern Protestant and rationalistic teachings in regard to the inspiration of the Sacred Books, their authority and interpretation. They thought that the great principles of Theism and of the Christian dogmatic system should be reasserted, including the idea of the Church, the Roman primacy and prerogatives, eight adding the infallibility of the Roman Pontiff teaching *ex cathedra*. They thought that one of the aims of the Council should be the recalling heretics and schismatics to the bosom of the Catholic Church. In matters of discipline : the raising the life of clergy, and the recalling the religious Orders to a better observance and especially to the practice of common life (' vita perfecte communis '). Other things proposed were the drawing up of an official Catechism for universal use ; the promotion of the Christian life by missions, spiritual exercises, sodalities ; the reform of the canon law ; and on the relations of Church and State some urged the necessity of receiving in fact, as tolerated, liberty of worship and of the press, and called for a pronouncement that the exigencies of the Church are not incompatible with the political needs of the present time.

Political events, especially the war between Austria and Prussia, interfered with the progress of the Council for nearly two years, and it was not until a great assembly of the bishops of the entire Catholic world, all invited to Rome for the eighteenth centenary of the martyrdom of the Apostles Peter and Paul, June 29, 1867, that the Pope made the public announcement of the Council.

From the *Life of Dupanloup* (II, c. xvi) it seems that up to the very eve of the celebration the Pope's mind was not definitely made up as to the public announcement, and that Dupanloup now encouraged him to proceed. He went to Rome the middle of May, and at his first audience, on his speaking in this sense, Pius said: 'But you were not of this opinion two years ago.' 'It is true, Holy Father, I did hesitate at first, but now I no longer hesitate'; and he presented a memorandum in favour of holding the Council. It concluded:

My conviction is that the forthcoming Council in Rome will present to the whole world the imposing spectacle of five or six hundred bishops, gathered from all points of the compass, and firmly united in one faith on all the great questions which interest humanity.

The Pope himself was strongly inclined to the Council, but among the Cardinals and others at Rome there were grave hesitations, and in particular Cardinal Antonelli, the Secretary of State, was opposed to it, fearing opposition and difficulties on the part of the Governments. With these, and with many of the French bishops, Dupanloup put forth all his powers of influence to win them over to the idea of the

Council. Soon it became apparent that the Council gained very general support, and the Pope hesitated no longer. Thus on June 18 Dr. Ullathorne wrote to his secretary :

> I have great news, so keep this as a memorandum of history. The Bishop of Orleans [Dupanloup] has just been here and tells us that all is prepared for the General Council. The Pope will announce it in his Allocution on the 26th. The bishops of all nations are strong in its favour. It is contemplated at present to open on the Immaculate Conception of 1868. It is calculated to last six months, and a great congregation will prepare the way for it six months beforehand. The Pope will summon theologians to this preparatory congregation by name from all nations. The great work will be the reform of the canon law, much of which is now in an impracticable shape ; but discipline and doctrine will both be taken in hand.

Accordingly, in Public Consistory on June 26, in his Allocution to the five hundred assembled bishops, Pius IX proclaimed the coming Council, ' in order to bring necessary and salutary remedies to the many evils whereby the Church is oppressed '.[1]

A congratulatory address had to be presented by the bishops thanking the Pope for the Allocution and expressing approval of the project of the œcumenical Council. An account of the drawing up of the Address is given in the *Life of Dupanloup* (II, c. xvi). A general meeting of bishops first was held to lay down the general lines. ' An English prelate ' —without any doubt Manning—advocated a fighting manifesto, ' wounding in order to strike home.' But the presiding Cardinal ruled that the tone should be moderate, so as not to create trouble with their Governments for the French and Italian bishops. It was in reference to this episode that Ullathorne

---

[1] Mansi, l.c., 243 ; *Lac* 1029.

wrote: Grenoble [Bishop Ginoulhiac] said to me, coming to me in a fury against our friend [Manning] in the Consistory of 1867: *Ce n'est pas le temps de casser les vitraux.*[1]

It proving impossible to draft an address at so numerous a gathering, a committee of seven was appointed, the outstanding names being Haynald, Archbishop of Kalocsa, Hungary, Manning and Dupanloup. The drafting was entrusted to Haynald, a consummate Latinist. When his draft was read the word 'infallible' occurred three or four times. No objection was raised by the committee, but Dupanloup proposed that the draft be given to Franchi (later Cardinal) to revise, and when the revision was read the word 'infallible' has disappeared, it was supposed through Dupanloup's influence. Manning now urged that either the word be restored, or else the decree of Florence on the Primacy be inserted. There was general agreement that to use the word 'infallible' was undesirable, as seeming to forestall the Council; Dupanloup opposed the introduction of the decree of Florence; but Manning insisted and got his way.[2] It is certain that on this occasion a hot passage of arms took place between Manning and Dupanloup (see Ullathorne's letter, below, p. 147). The address as finally agreed to by the committee was signed by the five hundred bishops and presented to the Pope on July 1.[3] To the matter-of-fact English mind it sounds flamboyant, effusive, and even adulatory. But Pio Nono was a very old man, and in a wonderful way the object of Catholic affection, sympathy, admiration, enthusiasm.

[1] See below, p. 147.
[2] The details are from a document in App. to ed. 4 of Ollivier's *L'Église et l'État au Concile du Vatican*, II, 601; cf. Manning, *True Story*, p. 52.
[3] Mansi, l.c., 247; *Lac* 1033.

The most significant passage was this :

We profess that our great concern and desire is that we may believe and teach what Thou dost believe and teach, and that the errors Thou dost reject, we also may reject ; that under Thy leadership we may walk with one accord in the ways of the Lord, that we may follow Thee and work with Thee. . . . Thy mouth has never been silent. Thou hast deemed it to belong to Thy supreme office to proclaim the eternal truths, to smite with the sword of apostolic speech the errors of the age, to dissipate the fogs of novel doctrine, and intrepidly to utter, to persuade, to enjoin what is necessary alike for individual men, for the Christian family, and for civil society : so that at length all may know what it is that a Catholic should hold, retain, and profess.

Believing that Peter speaks by the mouth of Pius, what Thou hast said, confirmed, uttered for the safeguarding of the deposit, we also say, confirm, proclaim ; and with one voice and soul we reject all that Thou hast judged to be reprobated and rejected. For we fully accept what the Fathers of the Council of Florence defined in the decree of Union : That the Roman Pontiff is the Vicar of Christ and Head of the whole Church, and Father and Teacher of all Christians, and to him in Blessed Peter has been given by Jesus Christ full power of feeding, ruling, and governing the universal Church.

Though the word ' infallible ' did not occur, the above piece came very near to an implicit recognition of the Pope's infallibility. So it is worthy of note that the two who had the chief hand in drafting the Address, Haynald and Dupanloup, were at the Council foremost opponents of the defining of the doctrine : as also were several of the signatories, as Cardinal Mathieu, Archbishop of Besançon, Darboy, Ginoulhiac, Simor, Melchers, Ketteler, Strossmayer, Kenrick, Clifford, and others whose names will become familiar in the sequel.

The Address was presented July 1, and the Pope in his reply said definitely that the Council would be convoked, but fixed no date.[1] The bull of Indiction was not issued for another year, June 29, 1868, the date fixed being the Feast of the Immaculate Conception of the Blessed Virgin, December 8, 1869.[2]

It ran:

It is at this time evident and manifest to all men in how horrible a tempest the Church is now tossed, and with what vast evils civil society is afflicted. For the Catholic Church, with its saving doctrine and venerable power, and the supreme authority of this Holy See, are by the bitterest enemies of God and man assailed and trampled down; all sacred things are held in contempt, ecclesiastical possessions spoiled, and the ministers of holy things harassed in every way; the religious orders suppressed, impious books and pestilent periodicals and manifold and most pernicious sects diffused on every side. So that not only our holy religion but human society itself is plunged in an unspeakable state of disorder and suffering.

Wherefore we have judged it to be opportune to bring together into a General Council all our venerable brethren of the whole Catholic world, who have been called to share our solicitude. In this œcumenical Council must be examined with the greatest accuracy, and decreed, all things which in these difficult times relate to the greater glory of God, the integrity of the faith, the gravity of divine worship, the eternal salvation of men, the discipline of the secular and regular clergy and its wholesome and solid culture, the observance of ecclesiastical laws, the amendment of manners, and the instruction of Christian youth. And with most intent study, care must be taken that all evils may be averted from the Church and from civil society.

Meantime during the winter of 1867-68 the preparations were going forward at Rome. At the beginning, in 1865, a special ' Directing Congregation ' or ' Central Commission ' of Cardinals had been

---

[1] Mansi, l.c., 261 ; *Lac* 1042.

[2] Mansi, l.c., 1249 (in tome 50) ; *Lac* 1 : see Manning, *True Story*, p. 63 ; Ollivier, *L'Église et l'État*, c. i.

set up for the affairs of the coming Council. This congregation had resolved that five subsidiary commissions should be formed, to prepare the material for the Council : viz.,

on faith and dogma
on ecclesiastical discipline and canon law
on religious Orders and regulars
on Oriental Churches and foreign missions
on politico-ecclesiastical affairs and relations of Church and State.

It had been decided, too, at an early date that select theologians and canonists from the different countries should be brought to Rome as consultors, to be joined to those on the spot in forming these commissions. The Nuncios at the various Courts had been instructed to consult the bishops as to suitable representatives, and report.[1] As the result, Hergenröther and Hettinger, both of Würzburg University, of repute as theologians and church historians, whose works are current to this day, were in the first instance invited from Germany. The selection did not give satisfaction in Germany, and Cardinal Schwarzenberg, Archbishop of Prague, wrote urging that other German and Austrian Universities besides Würzburg ought to be represented, and submitting the names of Hefele, the historian of the Councils, and Döllinger, as suitable representatives of German ecclesiastical scholarship. He received answer from Cardinal Antonelli, the Secretary of State, that Döllinger was to have been invited, but it had been stated to the Pope that he had declared he would not go. Hefele was invited and took a great part in the preparatory work ; he became Bishop

[1] The details of the selection of consultors are given in Granderath, *History*, I, Bk. i, c. 6. He cites an interesting letter of the Nuncio at Munich, with an encomium of Hefele.

of Rottenburg, Württemberg, before the Council. Haneberg, abbot of the Benedictine abbey of St. Bonifaz, Munich, a sound orientalist, who was assigned to the commission for the Oriental Churches, and Alzog, the church historian, were also chosen for Germany. Similarly a number were chosen from the other countries. Ullathorne, as Newman's bishop, had a letter intimating that the Holy Father had it in mind to invite Newman to Rome as a consultor, and desiring him to sound him if he would be willing to come. Though greatly pleased, Newman after deliberation begged off, on score of health, and because he could speak no language but English.[1]

Besides the consultors summoned by the Pope, the bishops of each Province were commissioned to elect a consultor for the preparatory work. The English bishops chose Dr. Weathers, the President of Old Hall. The consultors numbered just a hundred, both those called in from abroad and those belonging to the Roman schools and courts : they were distributed among the five commissions, and got to work early in 1869.[2] Among them all, Hefele was entrusted with what was probably the most important piece of work. He was attached as consultor to the central or directing congregation, and in view of his unique knowledge of the history of Councils, he was called on to draw up a votum or opinion as to the mode of procedure in the transaction of business. His votum, March 1869, a lengthy and weighty document,[3] is of great interest, in that its suggestions were adopted and carried out in almost every particular, so that the machinery of the Council, as we shall find it working, was in effect constructed by Hefele. This is of

---

[1] *Life of Ullathorne*, II, 46.
[2] The minutes of the proceedings of the Commissions are printed in Mansi, l.c., 477-1248.
[3] Mansi, l.c., 531 ; *Lac* 1087.

Mormon and Churchill covers
which I'm laughing at but English — but
How they spoke — !!!

MGR. FESSLER,
Bishop of Sankt Polten, Austria ;
Secretary of the Council

CARDINAL BILIO,
One of the Presidents ;

importance, in view of the dissatisfactions and complaints of the Minority bishops and of those hostile to the Council outside; for Hefele was by no means a neo-Ultramontane; on the contrary, he was soberly liberal, and a leader in the Minority opposed to the definition of infallibility. Yet was he clear that the supreme control of the Council was vested in the Pope alone; and in particular he urged that all contentious preliminary questions of personnel and procedure, that had occasioned such acrimonious debates and such delays at Trent, should be definitively settled beforehand by the authority of the Pope.

Finally, at the end of March 1869, was appointed as General Secretary of the Council Dr. Joseph Fessler, Bishop of Sankt Polten in Austria; he had been professor of ecclesiastical history and canon law in Vienna University, and was author of what was in its day the best manual of Patrology, though long since superseded. He was one of the small group of Austrian bishops of Ultramontane tendency, but on the lines of the strict theological school. Ullathorne's appreciation of him will be read in a subsequent letter (see Chap. XVI, March 25).

Important questions had to be settled regarding the personnel of the Council—who should take part in it; and on this grave uncertainties existed. The early Councils had, in the matter of defining doctrine, been composed of bishops only, although, notably at Chalcedon, the Emperor and his commissaries took part in regulating the debates. In course of time modifications had come in. At the Western Councils of the Middle Ages abbots also sat, and at the Fourth Lateran, 1215, they outnumbered the bishops by two to one. At Constance and at Basle an army of doctors of theology and canon law took part, so that the bishops were an insignificant minority. It seems from the Acts that at Constance the theologians voted even on def itions of faith, as the canons condemning the er rs of Wyclif and Hus.

At Trent a re ersion to the old practice was made, but the Catho Princes were invited and pressed to take part, i person or by ambassadors; and both Emperor d King of France sent ambassadors, who exercise considerable influence on the course of things, but w nout voting on matters of doctrine.

fell to the Central Directing Commission to deal w a these questions. The fundamental principle dopted was, that 'a Council is of bishops', that those entitled to sit at it by divine law (jure divino) are the 'residential' or diocesan bishops. Next, by long-standing custom all cardinals, even if not bishops, are entitled to sit and vote. The case of titular bishops, consecrated but without ordinary jurisdiction over a canonically erected diocese, gave rise to controversy. Finally they were divided into two categories: vicars apostolic or bishops over districts in the missionary field; the right of these to sit and vote, as bishops exercising episcopal jurisdiction, not ordinary but delegated, in their districts, was admitted: merely titular bishops, as coadjutors and auxiliary bishops, higher officials in the Curia and the papal diplomatic service; the admission of these was recommended as a privilege, not as a right, but if present they should be given voice and vote. The Pope endorsed these decisions and the titular bishops were admitted. The case of titulars remains thus in the codex of Canon Law.

In regard to abbots, it was decided that 'abbates nullius', that is abbots who, without being bishops, still are ordinaries of a diocese with episcopal juris-diction, should be admitted: such are the Benedictine abbots of Monte Cassino and of Pannonhalma in Hungary, and half a dozen more, Benedictine and Canon Regular. Of other abbots, not all abbots of individual abbeys, but only the Presidents of monastic congregations were admitted. Similarly the Generals of Religious Orders were admitted : all these on the ground that they exercise over their subjects quasi-episcopal powers.

Vicars capitular, those elected by the Chapter to govern a diocese during a vacancy by death of the bishop, were excluded. The case of procurators sent by bishops lawfully hindered from going to the Council, occasioned much discussion. The precedents were uncertain. At Trent at first the German bishops were allowed to send procurators with full deliberative voice ; but the permission was withdrawn, and again conceded. Hefele advised that, as they were not going to be numerous, they should be admitted ; but the final decision was adverse. They were allowed to be present at the proceedings but not to speak or vote.

These decisions as to the personnel of an œcumenical Council are now the law of the Church, being incorporated in the codex of Canon Law.

One of the good effects of the Council hoped for by many of the bishops was the possible Reunion of Christendom, of the Orthodox Eastern Churches with the Holy See, and even of the return of Protestant Bodies to Catholic Unity. Accordingly in September, 1868, was issued an Apostolic Letter ' to all Bishops of Churches of the Eastern Rite not in Communion with the Apostolic See '.[1] After asserting strongly the Petrine and papal position, the Pope expressed his great desire that the schism of Western and Eastern Churches should be healed. And having just con-voked an œcumenical Council,

we direct our voice to you, and with the greatest possible earnestness of soul we beseech, admonish, and pressingly

---

[1] Mansi, l.c., 1255 ; *Lac* 7.

exhort you to come to the said General Synod, as your ancestors came to the Councils of Lyons and of Florence; in order that the conditions of our former love may be renewed, and the peace of our Fathers may be once more called to vigour, so that the light of desired union may shine brightly upon all. Thus may continual thanksgivings be ever offered up to the Father of Mercies by all His Saints, and especially by those most glorious ancient Fathers and Doctors of the Eastern Churches, when from heaven they look down on the restoration and renewal of that union with the Apostolic See, the centre of Catholic truth and unity, which they whilst living upon earth laboured with every effort and with unwearied toil to cherish, and daily to forward more and more by teaching and example.

Unfortunately the Letter got into the press before it was presented to the Eastern Patriarchs, with the result that when the Vicar Apostolic presented the Pope's Letter to the Patriarch of Constantinople, the Patriarch said that, were it not that he already knew the contents, he would certainly have received and carefully perused the Letter; but as it was, he had read it in a newspaper, and so was able to say at once it contained principles and claims which the Orthodox Eastern Church could not admit; their bishops going to the Council would mean a renewal of the old theological disputes that could only accentuate the disagreements between them, reopening old wounds. The only basis of reunion must be that the Western Church revert in doctrine and practice to the norm existing before the Schism, giving up all that has been added since then. Finally,

if His Holiness the Pope of Rome had respect to apostolic equality and brotherhood, it was fitting that, as an equal among equals in point of dignity, but being first by canonical right and rank of his See, he should have directed a separate letter to each of the Patriarchs and Synods of the East, and not in encyclical and dictatorial form to impose it as lord

94

and master of them all, but as a brother to brethren equal in honour and degree, to ask them how, where, and in what conditions, they would agree to the assembling of a Holy Council.

And the Patriarch handed back to the Vicar Apostolic the Letter unopened. The other Eastern patriarchs and bishops followed the cue given at Constantinople ; none came to the Council and the Pope's gesture was bootless.[1]

The invitation was sent to the Patriarchs of the Armenian Nestorians and of the Monophysites, both Jacobite and Coptic, without result ; but not to the three Jansenist bishops of Holland. The case of the bishops of the Anglican Church was decided negatively, on the ground that the validity of their orders was not recognized. For all that, many members of the A.P.U.C. (Association for Promoting the Unity of Christendom) urged that deputies should be sent to the Council to treat of the conditions of the reconciliation of the English Church with the Holy See. They were, however, a minority so small as to be negligible.

The Pope's Letter of September 1868, ' to all Protestants and other non-Catholics ', attracted more attention and called for a greater response. The Letter exhorted Protestants to reconsider their position in face of the innumerable sects into which Protestantism was broken up, and the consequent dilution of Christian doctrines, and to return to the fulness of Catholic Faith and to Catholic Unity from which their Fathers had broken away.[2]

It is remarkable that the leading French Protestant of the day, Guizot, should have said : ' Pius IX has

---

[1] *Lac* 1110-23. See an English tract, *The Patriarch of Rome and the Patriarchs of the East*, by W. Fraser (London, 1869). Granderath, *History*, I, Bk. ii, c. 12.

[2] Mansi, l.c., 1259 ; *Lac* 8.

given proof of admirable wisdom in convoking this
great assembly, whence will issue perhaps the saving
of the world ; for our societies are gravely sick, and
for great evils great remedies are needed.' But this
was not the common Protestant attitude. Meetings
of representative Protestants held at Berlin, Gröningen,
Geneva, Worms, and also the Protestant Federations
of France and the United States, drew up reasoned
statements of the Protestant position and teaching,
showing why they could not comply with the exhortations of the Pope.[1]

Thus even before the Council were dashed the
hopes of many bishops, such as Dupanloup, that it
might pave the way for the Reunion of Christendom.

[1] The principal documents are given in *Lac* 1123-46 ; see
Granderath, l.c., c. 13.

CHAPTER VI

ATTITUDE OF THE GOVERNMENTS

WHILE the ecclesiastical preparations were thus going on apace, the Governments of the various States, especially the Catholic, were turning their attention to the coming Council. In April 1869, Prince Hohenlohe, Foreign Minister of Bavaria, despatched a letter to the Bavarian ministers at the various Courts. It exhibits in a restrained tone the apprehensions very generally felt among Catholic statesmen : [1]

It is unlikely that the Council will occupy itself solely with doctrines of pure theology. The only dogmatic thesis that Rome would wish to be proclaimed at the Council is the papal infallibility. It is evident that this pretension raised to a dogma would pass beyond the purely spiritual domain, and would become a question eminently political, raising the power of the Pope, even on the temporal side, above all princes and peoples of Christendom. This doctrine is therefore of a nature to arouse the attention of all Governments with Catholic subjects. Moreover, one of the Commissions preparing the matter for the Council is occupied with mixed questions, touching equally matters of public law, of politics, and of canon law. This leads us to suppose that the intention is to promulgate at the Council a series of decrees on questions political more than ecclesiastical.

Again, the *Civiltà Cattolica*, the semi-authoritative organ of the Roman Jesuits, has said that the condemnations of

[1] The principal documents on which this chapter is based are in *Lac* 1199-1253.

the Syllabus of 1864 will be transformed into positive conciliar decrees. But the articles of the Syllabus being directed
against the principles that form the basis of modern public
life as it is developed among all civilized peoples, it follows
that the Governments should ask themselves if it be not
their duty to call the serious attention of their bishops and
of the Council to the disastrous results that would follow
from such a disturbance in the actual relations of Church
and State. It seems a matter of urgency that the Governments should take concerted action by their agents at Rome,
or otherwise, to forestall any decisions the Council might
make, not in concert with representatives of the secular
powers, on matters at once political and religious in their
bearing.

The Bavarian ministers are to lay these ideas before the
Governments of the Courts to which they are accredited,
and to seek to bring about concerted action towards laying
before the Holy See the views of the various Governments
interested.

The attitude taken up by the Governments is noteworthy. Bismarck, the Prussian Foreign Minister,
took up the clear position that ' in spirituals full
liberty would be left to the Church ; but if there
should be any incursion into the civil domain, it
would be resisted. The bishops of the Prussian
territories will be given free and untrammelled facili-
ties for attending the Council.' Similarly Von Beust,
the Austrian Foreign Minister : ' The Government
will not intervene unless it should become clear that
the Council was invading the limits and rights of the
civil power. It trusted, however, to the prudence of
the Holy Father and the Cardinals to avoid solutions
that would embroil the relations between Church and
State. It would not send any special agent to Rome.'
We allow the proceedings in France to stand over
for a moment, merely noting that a like attitude was
finally adopted. The other Governments, including
after hesitations the Italian, fell into line, and no inter-

ference with the Council was contemplated, unless there should be signs of an attempt to issue decrees on political matters touching relations of Church and State. The Russian Government alone prevented its Catholic bishops from going to the Council.

The aforesaid forebodings and apprehensions, though natural enough in view of the kind of things being said by extremists, were in fact without foundation. //There is no evidence among the documents of any idea on the part of responsible persons, of turning the condemned propositions of the Syllabus into positive decrees.// As for the Commission on politico-ecclesiastical affairs that caused such misgiving, its proceedings were conducted with great circumspection.[1] The schedule of subjects laid before the consultors could hardly have led to conflict with the civil authority; and the Cardinal who was chairman laid down that they should confine themselves to matters of doctrinal import, and that the outcome of their work should be communicated to the Commission on doctrine, to be incorporated in its schemata. And so in fact in the dogmatic schema on the Church the last three chapters deal with the relations between Church and civil society and the State, in a way little calculated to cause frictions or practical difficulties. Certainly the five canons proposed on this range of subjects would hardly be disputed by any Christian man.[2] The Council, however, never got so far in its programme.

We must return to France. The attitude of the French Government was of almost decisive importance for the Council. French troops were still holding Rome, as they had been for twenty years, as protection against internal revolution and against annexation by

---

[1] Mansi, I (49), 1171-1210; *Lac* 1103-6.
[2] Mansi, III (51), 545-53; *Lac* 572-8: in Chapter XVII, below, this matter is gone into fully.

the new Italian Kingdom. The withdrawal of the army of occupation would have made the Council impossible. The principal part in determining French policy in the matter of the Council was taken by M. Émile Ollivier ; and as he was author also of one of the most instructive books on the Council, to be used often in these pages, it will be in place here to introduce him and his book.

Ollivier was a lawyer of liberal republican tendencies, who first came to the front at the Revolution of 1848. He entered the Chamber of Deputies as one of the liberal opposition to the autocratic Empire of Louis Napoleon. His opposition in time wore down ; and finally in January 1870 he became the Emperor's principal Minister in the belated attempt to liberalize the Empire and place it on a popular footing. Thus he was Prime Minister during the Council and during the War of 1870, in precipitating which he has to share the responsibility with Bismarck. The disasters of the war ruined his political career. As statesman his great concern was centred on the relations of Church and State in France ; and in 1877 he published a book in two volumes, *L'Église et l'État au Concile du Vatican*, which ran to a fourth edition in 1884. This book being, in certain aspects of the external history, the most important work on the Council, it becomes necessary to appraise it. I have to say that of all books of history I have read, this one comes perhaps the nearest to the ideal of historical objectivity and impartiality. The third chapter gives statements of the Ultramontane and of the Gallican positions : on reading the first I said, ' He surely is an Ultramontane ' ; but on reading the second, ' He is a convinced Gallican ',—so clearly is each case set forth. The general impression made on me by the book was that Ollivier was a sincere Catholic, a moderate Ultramontane in belief, but a liberal statesman keenly desirous to bring about a conciliation between the Catholic Church and the modern liberal State as it existed in France under the Empire. And this indeed was his great object : but he was no Catholic at all, nor Protestant : he was ' incroyant '.[1] But there can be no doubt the author of this book was a Theist, a believer in God and in the social value of religion : a conscientious man, too, who tells us that when, as Prime Minister, it fell to him to suggest to the Emperor names to present to the Holy See for vacant bishoprics, it gave him sleepless nights. Himself he would have preferred Gallican ideas to prevail ; but he recognized that in view of the strong Ultramontane currents running even in France, this was impossible ; and so he faced the inevitable and made the best of it. He held that the question of papal infallibility was of the purely spiritual order, not affecting the State in any way ; he scouted as chimerical the fears entertained on score of the Syllabus : his explanation and defence of the Syllabus is the best— better than Dupanloup's, better than Newman's.[2] In regard to the Council, he defends it from the attacks and criticisms made on it both from without and within. He knew well personally many of the chief actors, not only the leading French bishops and laymen, but Cardinal Antonelli, of whom he makes an eloquent encomium both as statesman and as man, greatly at variance with the usual appreciations.[3] He had a great veneration for Pio Nono, who on his side had a liking for Ollivier : ' Voyez M. Ollivier,' he once said, ' j'ai surtout confiance en lui, il a un fonds très-religieux.' [4]

It is evidently a great advantage to have con-

---

[1] So abbé Mourret, *Concile du Vatican*, p. 252.
[2] Op. cit., I, c. iv, §§ iii, iv.
[3] Op. cit., I, c. v, § xiii.   [4] *Ibid.*, II, 202.

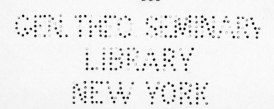

cerning the events and the persons of the Council the judgements of this well-informed, sagacious, quite independent yet sympathetic onlooker, closely associated with all that was going forward : it will be a valuable counterpoise to the violences and exaggerations of those who have hitherto commonly been accepted in the outer world as the best accredited authorities on the Council.

Shortly after the promulgation of the bull of Indiction, June 29, 1868, the question of the attitude of the French Government came on in the Chamber of Deputies. On July 10 a debate took place, opened by Ollivier, still a private deputy, in a remarkable speech.[1]

First he laid down that in virtue of the Concordat the Emperor enjoyed all the rights and privileges enjoyed of old by the Kings of France, and consequently had the right to be present at the Council in person or by ambassadors. But he urged that the claim should not be pressed, as it could not be effectively enforced, nor could it arrest the course of things at the Council : only by threat of the withdrawal of the French troops from Rome could any effective influence be exerted,—a measure he would altogether deprecate. The fact that no invitation to the Council had been given to Catholic Sovereigns was nothing less than the assertion of the severance of Church and State, made on the part of the Church. The State should accept the situation and safeguard its own independence by refraining from any kind of intervention at the Council, so that, while leaving entire freedom to the Council in matters of the spiritual order, it might be uncompromised should there be any attempt to invade the sphere belonging to the civil authority. There should be no semblance of persecution ; no interference with the publication of bulls ; no restraint placed on the bishops in attending the Council ; no attempt to influence the opinions they might express there : above

---

[1] The speech and the whole debate are given in full, *Lac* 1216-29 ; Ollivier, op. cit., I, c. iv, § viii.

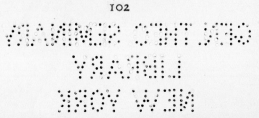

all, no ambassador or representative of the Government should take part in the Council.

The speech made a sensation and was well received; the Government, while expressing agreement, declined as yet to form a decisive determination.

A year later, April 1869, Ollivier again raised the matter in the Chamber, putting to the Minister three formal questions, which were answered thus :

Will the bishops be free to go to the Council ?—Yes, incontestably.

How will they go there ? Will they go with full liberty of conscience, of judgement, and without any understanding with the Government ?—We respect the members of the episcopate too much to seek to influence their decisions ; they will go to Rome with their personal dignity, with their independence, with their conscience, with their patriotism [great applause].

The third question, Will the Government be represented at the Council, the Minister was not in a position to answer.

In fact, some of the Cabinet wanted such a representative ; but the Emperor decided against it. The French Ambassador at Rome reported that the Holy Father expressed himself much pleased : the Ambassador did not anticipate the raising of contentious political issues at the Council.

The question of the Catholic Sovereigns was much exercising minds at Rome. We have seen that at the preliminary meeting of the Central Directing Congregation, March 1865, it had been agreed that they be not consulted beforehand as to the holding of the Council, but when it was proclaimed the Holy See should do what was suitable ; and this had been confirmed by the Pope. But when the actual drafting of the bull of Indiction was under consideration, May 1868, the matter came up again. At first it was decided to adhere to the former decision, and send to the Catholic Courts a printed copy of the bull simultaneously with its promulgation. The question if it should be sent also to non-Catholic Governments having Catholic subjects was deferred, for consultation with Cardinal Antonelli. Then many hesitations began to be felt as to whether the precedents of Trent ought not to be followed, and the Catholic Sovereigns invited to take part, in person or by ambassadors.

The Cardinals of the Directing Congregation veered round to the view that they ought to be invited. Accordingly on June 23, just a week before the date of promulgating the bull, a special meeting of the Congregation was held in the presence of the Pope, at which Antonelli took part, to consider this important matter.[1] A difficulty in the way of inviting the Catholic Sovereigns was that the King of Italy was under excommunication for the invasion and annexation of the Papal States in 1860 ; also some of the Presidents of South American Republics were Freemasons or strong anti-clericals ; moreover, it would be difficult to invite the Sovereigns of Catholic States, and not those of other States with great Catholic districts and populations, as Prussia. The final decision was a compromise : to insert in the bull the sentence : ' and that, as becomes Catholic Princes, they should most earnestly co-operate in all things that may be for the greater glory of God and the good of the Council.'

Antonelli made it plain to the French Ambassador that this, though not an invitation, was intended to give an opening to any Catholic power to take part in the Council, as at Trent ; and that if any did so, their representatives would be admitted and welcomed. In fact, a provisional place was provided for any such,

[1] Mansi, I (49), 503 ; *Lac* 1061.

facing the Cardinals.[1]   But there can be no doubt
that the authorities were relieved that none of the
Governments intervened.

Thus at the opening of the Council the attitude of
the Powers was friendly, or at least neutral.   At a
later stage, as will be seen, there were serious threaten-
ings of hostile intervention.

[1] Ollivier, op. cit., I, 508.

CHAPTER VII

EVE OF THE COUNCIL: CONTROVERSY AMONG CATHOLICS

If there was little trouble or conflict with the secular Governments over the coming Council, a keen and bitter controversy broke out among Catholics, chiefly round the question of defining the Pope's infallibility as a Catholic dogma. What may be called the great central body of Catholic opinion was not moved; it had, at any rate outside France, for a long time accepted as practically true the old theological statement of the Pope's infallibility as laid down by Bellarmine. But between the extremists on either side the battle raged—the neo-Ultramontanes and the ultra-liberals, a school powerful in Germany, especially in Bavaria, but with a strong though small group of adherents in England, and of course elsewhere. Of this school the protagonist was Dr. Döllinger, whom it is necessary now to introduce.[1]

Born in 1799, Ignaz Döllinger was ordained in 1822, and five years later obtained the chair of canon law and ecclesiastical history at Munich University, which he held until his death. In his early days he was regarded as a representative Ultramontane in Germany, standing above all for the freedom of the Church from State control. In the 'thirties he produced a *History of the Church* (English translation, 4 vols., 1840). In this work he laid down what may

---

[1] On Döllinger see Ollivier, op. cit., I, 425-8.

be called the normal Catholic positions in regard to St. Peter and the Papacy : thus the import of the Petrine texts, the position of St. Peter, the pre-eminence of the Roman Church and Bishop in ante-nicene times, the relation of Popes to General Councils, and the papal Supremacy are all set out clearly in a sober Catholic and Ultramontane sense. The sections ' The Pope as supreme Teacher and Guardian of the Faith ' and ' as the Visible Representative of Ecclesiastical Unity ' are especially noteworthy. Hildebrand, Innocent, even Boniface VIII, are dealt with sympathetically, appreciatively ; and in the contest of Papacy and Empire the balance is evenly held. And what is noteworthy, the crucial decrees of Constance are treated as invalid. Thus as to Döllinger's fundamental Ultramontane position in early life there can be no doubt. About 1850 a change began to come over him. He grew more and more out of sympathy with the tendencies and influences prevailing at Rome. For all that, in the book *The First Age of the Church*, published 1860 (English translation, 1866), a remarkable work at that date, he still could write :

St. Peter was the Shepherd appointed by Christ for the whole flock ; the pillar of legitimate unity chosen by Christ as Shepherd of the flock ; the Head of the Church (i, 90-1). Peter held a pre-eminence among the Apostles which none of the rest contested. To him was the charge given to strengthen his brethren and feed the flock of Christ. He is necessarily the Head of the apostolic college and the whole Church. The primacy of Peter displayed itself on all grave occasions (ii, 100-1). So much on St. Peter. On the Papacy : Peter received the keys of the Kingdom and is the Rock on which the Church is built—that is, the continuance, increase, and growth of the Church rests on the office created in his person (*ibid.*).

So Döllinger wrote still in 1860. But during the next decade an ever-increasing estrangement from the

Roman Church and the ecclesiastical and civil policies of Pope and Curia, kept driving him into a state of isolation and opposition to the central authority. He used to attack vehemently the Temporal Power and the administration of the Papal States, the Curia, and the Jesuits. He adopted the most extreme interpretation of the Syllabus, as an attack on modern society and the modern State. He called for the abandonment of the scholastic method in theology in favour of a purely historical treatment : and so on. And so, when the Council was announced, Döllinger settled down into an attitude of determined opposition, and became the storm-centre of the violent agitation stirred up around it. He can be seen behind the letter of Prince Hohenlohe, whose fears were precisely those of Döllinger.

The sign of battle was given by an article in the *Civiltà Cattolica* of February 6, 1869. The *Civiltà* was the organ of the Roman Jesuits, and though not officially representing the Vatican, it was recognized as enjoying the high approval of Pius IX, and as being at any rate semi-authoritative. At the middle of January the Papal Nuncio in Paris, Archbishop Chigi, in response to a requisition, sent to Cardinal Antonelli two Memoirs exhaustively dealing with the state of mind existing in France relative to the Council on the part of Government, press, and the various sections of the general public, Catholic and other.[1] These Memoirs were sent by Antonelli to the *Civiltà*, and were in great part printed, as being from a ' Paris Correspondant '. Among other things the Nuncio had given as the desire of the great body of normal French Catholic opinion, that the teaching of the Syllabus should be defined in such a way as to remove the misinterpretations attached to it ; that the dog-

---

[1] *Lac* 1146-67.

matic infallibility of the Pope should be proclaimed
—and they hoped that 'a unanimous outburst of
the Holy Spirit would define it by acclamation by
the mouth of the Fathers';[1] that they expected the
Council to be of short duration, as that of Chalcedon
(less than a month), believing that there will be such
general accord among the bishops of the whole world
that a minority would not be able to put up any prolonged opposition : so that any protracted conflict of
opinions and discussions at the Council would cause
some astonishment.

This last point reflects the ideas of Veuillot in the
Univers : he laughed at those 'who want the Fathers
to discuss, and wish the Holy Ghost to take time in
forming an opinion; and have a hundred arguments
to prove how much time for reflection is indispensable
to the Holy Ghost.' Again : 'It is worthy of note
that in the Upper Room no discussion preceded the
outpouring of the Holy Ghost.'

Such prognostications of what was expected to
happen at the Council were so wholly out of keeping
with the elaborate preparations on foot, that it springs
to the mind to ask if their publication by the Pope's
Prime Minister, the Cardinal Secretary of State, was
not a 'ballon d' essai', to test how such ideas would
be received. Be that as it may, their publication in
an organ so closely associated with the Curia and the
Pope himself, and above all, the idea of defining the
infallibility by acclamation, was surely a regrettable
adventure. For immediately they called forth during
March and April a series of articles in the Augsburg *Allgemeine Zeitung,* of which, whatever collabora-
tion there may have been, the author-in-chief was
Döllinger.[2] These articles, expanded and re-enforced

[1] On espère que l'explosion unanime de l'Esprit-Saint par la
bouche des Pères définira par acclamation.
[2] *Lac* 1167.

with a wealth of curious learning, were reissued in July in book form, *The Pope and the Council*, by ' Janus ', promptly translated into the principal languages, the English translation being published in the autumn, just before the bishops started for Rome. The thesis of the book is laid down in the Preface :

Every faithful Catholic is convinced—and to that conviction the authors of this book profess their adherence—that the Primacy rests on divine appointment. The Church from the first was founded upon it, and the Lord of the Church ordained its type in the person of Peter. It has therefore, from the necessity of the case, developed itself up to a certain point ; but on this has followed, since the ninth century, a further development—artificial and sickly rather than sound and natural—of the Primacy into the Papacy, a transformation more than a development. [And on the Primacy :] During the first Christian centuries we meet with abundant facts which prove unmistakably that the Roman Bishops not only believed themselves to be in possession of a divine right, and acted accordingly, but that this right was actually recognized by others. And if it was often affirmed, as by the Council of Chalcedon, that the Roman Church had received its privileges from the Fathers, we shall have to consider that the Primacy itself, the first rank among churches, was not given to it by any Synod at any fixed time, but had always existed since the time of the Apostles ; and that to any heathen who asked which among their churches was the first and principal one, whose voice and testimony had the greatest weight and influence, every Christian would have answered at once that it was the Roman Church, where the two chief Apostles, Peter and Paul, sealed their testimony with their blood, just as Irenaeus has expressed it (pp. xxi, xxiii).

Thus it was not the Primacy that was attacked—it was accepted as of divine institution : it was the ' Papacy ' and its works and pomps, as manifested in the Middle Ages, in the Renaissance, in the Counter-Reformation, and in modern times, that was attacked.

It was indeed a vehement frontal attack on the political papacy, the papal monarchy as conceived by Hildebrand and Innocent, the centralizing tendencies at Rome, the Roman Curia, the Inquisition, the Temporal Power and the administration of the Papal States, the Syllabus taken as the condemnation of modern political ideas, Ultramontanism both new and old, with the Jesuits as the principal devils of the piece. False Decretals, exactions, arbitrary acts, scandals in papal history, political mistakes, are all raked together out of a perhaps unique knowledge of medieval and modern church history, and piled up into an imposing onslaught on the Popes, probably the most damaging ever compiled. ' It is the gravest and severest attack on the Holy See and the Jesuits, and especially on the policy of Rome for a thousand years, and will be a great storehouse for the adversaries of the Church,'—so wrote Ullathorne (October 22).

' Janus ' was greatly moved at the idea of ' making the Syllabus dogmatic '. Here he could point to the fact that this had already been done by the Viennese Jesuit Schrader, of the neo-Ultramontane school, and he was able to quote with effect samples of the propositions Catholics might expect to have imposed on them by the Council as articles of faith. Such anticipations have already been shown to have had no foundation in any responsible quarter. But his chief fear was the papal infallibility. His idea was that, once defined, it would be in constant use, and all attempts to set limits to its exercise would be futile. Herein he took for granted that the theories of Ward and Veuillot were going to prevail. Looked at in the atmosphere then prevailing such fears do not appear altogether fantastic ; but looked at in the light of what has happened during the past sixty years they are seen to have been exaggerated and vain.

An answer, ' Anti-Janus ', was promptly produced

III

by Hergenröther, a learned church historian; but to answer effectively such a book in one of the same size is wellnigh impossible. 'Janus' caused a great conflagration in Germany. A meeting of Catholic laymen held at Coblenz drew up a memorial to the Bishop of Treves, expressing the fears caused in them by the *Civiltà* article, and their objection to its programme, and setting out the burning questions of the day, social, industrial, political, on which they hoped the Council would lay down the great lines of Catholic teaching. They asked for the removal of the Index of prohibited books. At the end, they declare it is their determination to live and die true sons of the Church, in unity with her and her centre, the Roman See, and under the obedience of their bishop.[1] This was in May; the manifesto was circulated widely, and led to much correspondence in Catholic Germany. A meeting of Catholics in Berlin prepared another manifesto to be sent to the German bishops.[2] They pledged themselves to obey whatever decrees might be made at the Council; begged that there should be no interference with it on the part of the secular Governments; accepted the Catholic teaching, as laid down by the Pope, on the ideal relations between Church and State, but thought that in applying this teaching consideration must be had of the actual condition of civil society; rejected the idea of a national church; finally, they thought the definition of the infallibility unnecessary.

During August was circulated, in all the languages, among the bishops of Germany, England and Ireland, United States, Spain, France, Italy, an anonymous tract, 'Observations on the question, Whether it be opportune to define the infallibility of the Sovereign Pontiff?' its argument being that the definition would

[1] *Lac* 1175.   [2] *Lac* 1185.

be most inopportune. The German was the original, and Döllinger acknowledged the authorship.

In view of these movements and the general excitement prevailing in Germany, the bishops felt they had to take the matter in hand; and so during the first six days of September the twenty bishops of Germany (not Austria) met in synod at Fulda.[1] They discussed the situation, especially the definition of papal infallibility. They agreed that theological questions as to the truth and the definability of the doctrine were matters for the Council; they confined themselves to the question whether the definition would be opportune, and precisely from the point of view of religious interests in Germany. As the outcome of their deliberations they issued a joint pastoral letter,[2] a fine loyal manifesto, reminding their flocks that

the Council would be an œcumenical Council, and therefore, according to Catholic teaching, under the special guidance of the Holy Ghost, so that its decrees would come to Catholics with the like authority as those of earlier General Councils. They sought to calm the fears and misgivings sown in the minds of Catholics by the suggestions of ' Janus ', that there would not be free discussion at the Council, that the bishops would be intimidated and afraid to speak their minds, so that the freedom of the Council and the validity of its decrees would be questionable. Such suggestions they repudiated as unworthy of the Catholic bishops, and they regretted that the insinuations hitherto made by the enemies of the Church should now be made by Catholics. Finally they called on all Catholics to rally round the Church, the Council, and the Holy Father, and to hold aloof from all party movements and conflicts that were being stirred up around the Council.

Fourteen of them sent also a letter to the Holy Father:[3]

[1] *Lac* 1188.
[2] *Lac* 1191 : it is given in full by Granderath, I, Bk. ii, c. 6.
[3] *Lac* 1196 : Granderath, l.c.

They say they deem it their duty to make known to him the excitement of mind and the unrest existing throughout Germany, among Catholics and Protestants alike, at the idea of the definition of papal infallibility. They have received numerous representations from clergy and laymen, devoted to the Church and the Holy See, begging that the definition be not made. And they express their own conviction that, in view of the actual state of things in Germany, the definition would be inopportune.

This letter was signed by fourteen of the twenty bishops; among them the Archbishops of Cologne and Munich, the Prince Bishop of Breslau, the Bishops of Treves and Augsburg, Ketteler of Mayence, and Hefele, the elect of Rottenburg. Naturally, all these bishops will figure among the Minority at the Council.

The turmoil of feeling in Germany can hardly be imagined unless such account of the newspaper and pamphlet warfare as is supplied by Granderath (I, Bk. ii, cc. 3, 4, 5) be read. So great was the popular excitement that the Nuncio at Munich reported to Antonelli that on their way to Fulda the Archbishop of Cologne and other bishops had been publicly insulted and almost mobbed by the populace.[1]

In other countries also controversies among Catholics broke out, but nowhere did they assume the same character as in Germany. It was inevitable that in France controversy should arise between the two schools that divided French Catholics, the liberal and the neo-Ultramontane, the protagonists being Dupanloup and Louis Veuillot, the editor of the *Univers*. On his return from Rome, July 1867, straightway after the announcement of the coming Council, Dupanloup issued a pastoral letter uttering in words of glowing enthusiasm all his hopes of what the Council might achieve—the reunion of the Eastern Churches, the return of the Protestant Bodies :

[1] *Lac* 1197.

To dissipate current errors, to throw the bright light of Christian tradition and Catholic science upon great questions overshadowed by present clouds ; to revive in the bosom of the Church the ardent flames of charity and devotion ; to disperse by explaining misconstructions ; to make plain the way for a great movement of return to the true fold : in a word, to accomplish a vast work of illumination and pacification—who would not applaud such an effort on the part of the Catholic Church ?

The bull of Indiction not appearing, he sent early in 1868 a letter to the Pope urging the importance of speeding up the Council. On March 4 the Pope replied :

It is with deep gratitude that we have received the observations you have addressed to us. They have given us a fresh proof of the ardent zeal with which you are filled for the honour of the Church and the Holy See. And, in consequence, we have determined to issue sooner than we had intended our Apostolic Letter for the convocation of the Council.

It was promulgated June 29, 1868. Dupanloup issued another pastoral, November, said to be the finest thing he ever wrote :

There will be at the Council two great objects : the good of the Church and the good of human society. Great misunderstandings have arisen over all questions concerning the Church. Let humanity rejoice at the magnanimous resolution of Pius IX, for it ought to be for those who believe, and for those who have not the happiness of believing, a solemn hope. From the simply human point of view what can be more worthy of sympathy and respect than this great endeavour of the Catholic Church to work, in what concerns her, for the illumination and the peace of the world ?

This letter made a great impression ; it ran to many French editions and was translated into all the languages.[1] Pius IX wrote an affectionate brief of thanks :

> It is with thankfulness that we have received your writing. It will dissipate, such is our hope and our desire, the shadows which ignorance and malignity have shed over men's minds, and it will incline all hearts to desire this most efficacious remedy of the Council.

As Bishop Dupanloup is going to figure as one of the leaders, perhaps in a way the chief leader and chief driving force, of the opposition to the defining of the papal infallibility, it will be well at the outset to make clear his position, which was the position also of nearly all the members of the opposition or minority at the Council. It is of the utmost importance for any right understanding of the Council that the mind of those who opposed the definition should be rightly understood. Fortunately in the case of Dupanloup materials are at hand sufficient to make quite clear his whole attitude without possibility of misconception.

Dupanloup spent four months in Rome during the winter of 1841-42. While there he took the degree of doctor of divinity at the Sapienza, and the doctorate thesis he defended was ' The Infallibility of the Roman Pontiff'. The substance of the thesis was :

> The sense of the Church is implied in a definition *ex cathedra*, which is always in conformity with it. The Pope recognizes it and defines it. He is *caput ecclesiae*, the head. The whole strength, light, and speech are in the head. . . . In the Church there is a perpetual circulation of doctrine and truth, as in the human body there is a perpetual circulation of blood—only if life be in the heart, the eye that sees everything, the ear that hears all things, the strength which wills everything, and the mouth which speaks when necessary, are all in the head.[2]

---

[1] English translation, 1869.   [2] *Life*, I, 211.

And his biographer, Bishop Lagrange, who knew him well, adds :

He never held any other theological opinion on this point, from first to last, having a horror of what is called Gallicanism. He wrote in 1843 : ' Gallicanism is inevitably dying out in France . . . there are not more than eight moderate Gallican bishops left.' [1]

In a pamphlet of 1861, *La Souveraineté pontificale*, he said :

For us Catholics the Pope is the universal doctor, the judge in the last resort of questions of faith and of Christian morals, the supreme interpreter of Holy Scripture and of the divine teaching ; he judges, interprets, defines, approves, condemns. . . . It is his function to watch over the sacred deposit of truth and of morals, to maintain discipline, to define doctrine, to condemn errors, to extirpate abuses.

And though he went to the Council fully determined to oppose as inopportune the defining of the papal infallibility, he made beforehand perfectly clear his frame of mind in regard to whatever might finally be defined at the Council. Thus in a pastoral letter to his flock :

I declare beforehand that obedient unto death, I adhere to whatever may be the decision of the Head of the Church and the Council : and I adhere to it from the very bottom of my heart and soul, whatever may be these decisions, whether conformable or contrary to my particular ideas, and whether they confirm or contradict them. We are all human, and in this Council as in all others, human imperfections may have their share. But our belief is precisely this—that the Holy Ghost directs, fashions, and consumes these imperfections, and turns them to the service of the truth. No one is a real Catholic who has not this faith, which is mine ; and therefore I declare beforehand that whatever happens, I adhere, I submit ; that I am happy thus to adhere — joyous thus to submit. After having

[1] *Life*, I, 212.

fought frankly and openly, acted courageously, and laboured valiantly, submission will be our victory; and Thou wilt give to us all the grace, O my God! to find peace in the Faith and joy in obedience. *Haec est victoria quae vincit mundum, fides nostra.*[1]

He spoke in like manner at a meeting of his clergy, assembled to wish him farewell and godspeed on his departure for Rome. The Dean of the Chapter spoke of the ' sentiments of absolute submission with which the Orleans clergy was prepared to receive the decrees of the Council'. The Bishop said :

We must have confidence in the word of Him who has said to His Church, ' Teach all nations. I am with you till the end of the world ; ' and who is going to teach us again by the mouth of the successor of Peter and of the bishops assembled around him. And after the Council, when Peter and the Apostles, when Pope and Bishops, have spoken, entire docility, absolute submission to all that the Spirit of God shall have dictated to the holy assembly. As for myself, I go to the Council summoned by the supreme Head of the Church. I go there as judge and witness of the faith. I shall be there, I hope, by the help of Our Lord, a free judge, attentive and firm, without human respect ; a watchful and faithful witness.

And when the Council is over, whatever its decisions have been, whether conformable or contrary to my desires and votes, I shall return submissive to all without the slightest effort, submissive in mouth, in spirit, and in heart, docile as the humblest sheep of the flock.

Such is my faith, and such is yours. It is by it that we live, and for it, if need be, we would die.[2]

[1] *Life*, II, 367.
[2] Et le Concile achevé, quelles qu'aient été ses décisions, conformes ou contraires à mes vœux et à mes votes, je reviendrai soumis à tout, sans le moindre effort, soumis de bouche, d'esprit, et de cœur, docile comme la plus humble brebis du troupeau. Telle est ma foi, Messieurs, telle est la vôtre. C'est par elle que nous vivons, et pour elle, au besoin, nous saurions mourir (*Lac* 1281).

And he was good as his word. After having at
the Council used his influence to the very utmost to
avert the definition, in February 1871, as soon as the
armistice with Germany ended the war and com-
munications were once more opened up with foreign
countries, he wrote to Pius IX :

It has been made known to me that your Holiness
wishes for something from me relative to the constitution
of July 18. I have no difficulty in this matter ; I have
written and spoken only against the opportuneness of the
definition. As to the doctrine I have always professed it,
not only in my heart, but in public writings, for which the
Holy Father has been pleased to felicitate me by most
affectionate briefs. And I adhere to it again, too happy if
I can by this adhesion bring to your Holiness some consolation in the midst of your bitter distresses.

I am preparing an ordinance in which I propose to promulgate the constitutions of April 24 and July 18.[1]

Soon after this the pastoral was issued promulgating
the decrees of the Council, to which he gave his
formal adhesion.

We have here, even in an extreme case, the attitude of nearly all the bishops of the Minority that
opposed the definition. Manning[2] and Ullathorne[3]
both bear witness that there were not more than a
half-dozen bishops who upheld the historical Gallican
position and questioned the doctrine.

The beginning of controversy over the Council
in France was in the summer of 1868, when the news
went round that Mgr. Maret was writing a book on
the Council and the topics to be dealt with at it. He
was Dean of the Catholic theological faculty that still
existed in the Sorbonne, and had been *honoris causa*
made titular Bishop of Sura *in partibus infidelium*. He

---

[1] *Lac* 999.   [2] *True Story*, p. 99.
[3] *Life of Bishop Ullathorne*, II, 72.

was a learned and able man of high character, and a known upholder of the old Gallican school; and now the secular press, notably the *Figaro*, gave it out that his book was going to demolish the Ultramontane position. Veuillot retaliated in the *Univers*, and a controversy ensued between him and Maret.

The book was published a year later, September 1869: *Du Concile général et de la paix religieuse*, two volumes. The main propositions are extracted in a document, *Lac* 952-7.

The general thesis is that the government of the Church is a constitutional monarchy, the spiritual sovereignty being composed of two essential elements, the one principal, the papacy, the other subordinate, the episcopate. Though subordinate, the body of bishops have their place in every act of authority in the Church, and each bishop has the right of examining, judging, contradicting even *ex cathedra* dogmatic decrees, unless they be accepted by the general body of bishops; the supreme authority of a General Council over the Pope even in matters of Faith is strongly asserted; the doctrine of the personal infallibility of the Pope is strongly denied: finally, the holding of General Councils every ten years is advocated as the best remedy for the ills of the Church and of the world.[1]

Maret by the French Ambassador presented a copy to the Holy Father along with a personal letter (*Lac* 912); also a copy was sent to every bishop of the Catholic world, and of course the book was put on the public market. These proceedings let loose a great wave of controversy among the French bishops, which over-flowed into the newspapers.[2] Mgr. Pie of Poitiers, the leader, though by no means the most extreme, of the Ultramontanes in the French hierarchy, criticized the book in an address to his clergy; Maret responded

[1] On Maret's book see Ollivier, I, 407-10; Granderath, I, Bk. ii, c. 7.
[2] Ollivier, l.c. 410-14.

in the *Univers ;* and Pie again at the end of October, in bidding adieu to his clergy on departing for Rome, renewed his criticisms in vigorous language (*Lac* 1263-83). In a letter in reply to one of his episcopal antagonists Maret declared that when the matters in debate had been fully discussed at the Council, new light would shine forth : ' I hope God will give me the grace never to shut my eyes to this light. In every case, submission will be sweet to me.' After the Council he wrote to Pius declaring his full adherence, of heart and mind, to the decrees of the Council (*Lac* 1001) ; and he withdrew his book from circulation.

On October 10 of the same year, 1869, was published what was regarded as a manifesto of the French Catholic liberals, the group of laymen represented by de Falloux, de Broglie, de Montalembert (now on his deathbed), with whom was closely associated Dupanloup. It was an article, ' Le Concile ', of near fifty pages in the *Correspondant,* the organ of the party, and it was recognized as the joint utterance of the leaders. For anyone who wishes to understand the real attitude of the great French Catholics of that school, it would probably be the most enlightening source of information he could find.[1]

It deals with the two great subjects absorbing the interest of all : The relations of Church to Pope, and of Church to State. It begins by setting out the twofold fear widely entertained on these subjects: the fear that the outcome of the Council will be to concentrate all the authority of the Church on the head of the Sovereign Pontiff, so that the Church will appear transformed from a mitigated (temperée) monarchy into an absolute monarchy governed without control by a single head ; and the fear that condemnations may be passed on politico-religious principles

---

[1] It is printed in full among the ' Pièces justificatives ' in L. Veuillot's *Rome pendant le Concile.*

which are part of all modern constitutions, so that the Church would be put in open hostility with civil society, and Catholics be placed in the sad alternative of having to choose between obedience to the Church and the attachment they owe to the laws of their country.

The authors declare that they do not themselves share these fears. In regard to the most burning question in the first category, the definition of papal infallibility, their hope and expectation is that it will not be defined. But whatever the Council may do in the matter of defining the infallibility, we have but to remember our catechism to know that, if the marks of infallibility may be doubtful when Pope and bishops are separated, when they are united all shadow of legitimate doubt disappears and the infallibility is certain. A conciliar decision clothed with the pontifical assent, or a pontifical utterance corroborated by the consent of the episcopate—infallibility is there, or it is nowhere.

Although the treatment of the question of Church and State was at the time subjected to severe strictures, especially by the legitimist royalist section of the French Ultramontanes, I cannot think it would cause much, if any, stir now. It was urged that in no country, not even in the Catholic countries of Europe, in Austria, Spain, France, does the Church now hold the privileged position of former times, and the idea that it should or could be restored to its old position was a mere dream, and a mischievous dream. The Church had to take its place amid the conditions of liberty that obtain in all modern states, except Russia. The bishops assembled from all parts of the world would deal wisely with all such questions of Church and State, and with the great social and industrial problems of the day. It concludes :

It matters little that these questions are badly judged by the press ; they will be well judged by the Council, by the Sovereign Pontiff in union with the bishops ; and for every Catholic conscience the voice of the Church is the voice of God. The Council can by its voice restore the great truths attacked by the rebirth of an atheistic materialism, and protect reason, no less menaced than faith. It can recall the eternal principles of justice, and condemn usurpation, the abuse of war, slavery. It can restore the great law of the Sunday rest, the only means of breaking the servitude of manual toilers. . . . What a sublime mission with the help of God. The Vatican Council we believe will mark in the history of this century, and of all centuries, an important date ; and it will win for itself the admiration of unbelievers, as it has already, beforehand, secured for itself the adhesion, entire, respectful, joyful, unanimous, of Catholic believers of all schools, of all tongues, of all countries.

It cannot but seem to us, now, extraordinary that Granderath should argue that, in spite of difference of language and of tone, the spirit of the article is the same as that of ' Janus ', and that the sincerity of the words may be doubted. It is less surprising that at the time in France it was vehemently denounced by Ultramontane bishops, as Pie of Poitiers, and of course by Veuillot in the *Univers*. Time, however, has its revenges. In April 1929 took place in Paris a religious celebration in memory of the centenary of the *Correspondant*. Pope Pius XI was specially represented ; the Nuncio took part and Cardinal Dubois, Archbishop of Paris. One of the bishops preached a panegyric on the *Correspondant* for the great work it had done for religion, and on the principal contributors by name, the great Catholic liberals of the 'sixties.

As was to be expected, Dupanloup took a great part in these preliminary skirmishings, though he did not go down into the arena until the last moment. In the November he issued a farewell pastoral letter conformable to those of 1867 and 1868, breathing no word of controversy, but encouraging his flock to look for great things from the Council, and to help it with their best prayers ; it concluded with the declaration, already cited p. 117, of his full acceptance beforehand of whatever should be defined at the Council.

The pastoral was followed by a letter to the clergy, November 11, which being the most public and the clearest popular formulation of the case of the ' Inopportunists ', will be summarized here.

The title was : *Observations sur la controverse soulevée relativement à la définition de l'infaillibilité au prochain Concile* (56 pages).

He laid down at the start that he did not intend to speak of the doctrine itself, but only of the opportuneness of defining it as an article of Catholic Faith. Against the opportuneness he urged the following reasons :

(1) there is no necessity for defining it : that the Church is infallible has sufficed for eighteen centuries.

(2) though raised at Trent, it was shelved by the prudence of the Pope, to avoid division among the bishops.

(3) it will create a fresh barrier against the return of the Oriental Churches and the Protestant Bodies to Catholic Unity.

(4) it will antagonize the Governments, by whom it will be taken as confirming the ' Unam Sanctam ' of Boniface VIII.

(5) theological difficulties, as the difficulty of determining the conditions of an *ex cathedra* act, and of distinguishing between the Pope as private doctor and as Pope. On these points the differences among theologians are very great ; he instanced the extreme ideas of Ward. Some Ultramontane theologians have discarded the received term *ex cathedra* and any conditional infallibility, maintaining an infallibility of the Pope absolute, unconditional and universal, so that he cannot err even if he wished to fall into any error privately or publicly ; and a French theologian has held it to be an open opinion that the Pope, even as private doctor, is infallible.

(6) historical difficulties, questions of fact.

(7) in the eyes of the faithful the position of bishops will be depressed ; they will no longer be looked on as

witnesses and judges of the Faith : for their witness will no longer be needed and may be dispensed with ; and as judges they will be obliged simply to endorse the judgement of the supreme judge.

The following picture of the rightful position of Pope and Episcopate is after the manner of Bossuet at his best :

See the Pope, successor of St. Peter, Vicar of Jesus Christ, in whom resides the plenitude of apostolic power ; the Head of all the bishops, Pontiff of the principal See, in which all the others preserve their unity ; universal Pastor, not only of the sheep, but of the pastors ; mouth of the Church, keystone and arch of Catholicity, the head of the teaching Church.

And see the Bishops, successors of the Apostles, judges and doctors, with whom is Jesus Christ every day to the end of the world, placed by the Holy Ghost to shepherd the Church of God.

As was inevitable, Dupanloup's *Observations*, issued at the middle of November, being the first and weightiest pronouncement by a bishop against the opportuneness of the definition, attracted much attention and called forth protests and replies. A summary of the argument has been given ; but he also inveighed against the imprudent and provocative way in which the subject had been treated by some of the Ultramontane papers, naming particularly the *Civiltà* and the *Univers*, accusing the last-named of introducing the methods of journalism into the affairs of Faith : it had engineered a campaign in favour of the definition by a kind of plebiscite, slips of paper for signatures being scattered broadcast by the thousand, and long lists of adherents being printed day by day in the *Univers :* this was said to be the modern way of ascertaining the ' sensus fidelium '. Naturally the *Univers* retaliated vigorously, as was its wont. The article is printed in the Introduction to Veuillot's book *Rome pendant le Concile*, p. cxxvi. It filled to overflowing the vials of Dupanloup's indignation, and called forth on November 21 a personal *Avertissement* to M. Veuillot, as editor-in-chief of the *Univers*. It is a lengthy diatribe, thirty pages long.[1] The actual *Avertissement* is only a couple of pages :

> The moment has come to defend ourselves against you. I raise then, in my turn, my voice. I charge you with usurpations on the Episcopate, with perpetual intrusion in the most delicate matters ; I charge you above all with your excesses in doctrine, your deplorable taste for irritating questions, and for violent and dangerous solutions. I charge you with accusing, insulting and calumniating your brethren in the Faith. None have merited more than you that severe word of the Sacred Books ' Accusator fratrum '. Above all I reproach you with making the Church participate in your violences, by giving as its doctrines, with rare audacity, your most personal ideas.[2]

The rest is a recital of words and acts of the *Univers* writers in justification of so strong a condemnation. They have been used in setting forth the ideas of the most extreme school of the New Ultramontanism (Chap. IV). It is necessary to remember that French

---

[1] It is certainly courageous and candid of Veuillot to print it in full, almost without comment, among the ' Pièces justificatives ' of *Rome pendant le Concile*, pp. 551-83.

[2] The Nuncio at Paris in the Report spoken of at the beginning of this chapter, referring to the Ultramontane press, and especially the *Univers*, said there were many complaints that it overstepped the bounds proper for lay writers, that it was bitter, intolerant of opinions that are free, violent against the persons who do not share its opinions, and often extravagant in its theses and its attacks (*Lac* 1151). In 1872 Pius IX spoke out : ' There are in France two parties, one of which lacks humility, the other charity '—' qui oublie totalement les lois de la charité '. Veuillot recognized that the *Univers* was meant, and suspended the paper for a period, ' nous disparaîtrons' (*Life of Guéranger*, II, 403).

journalism often conducts its political and religious controversies with a vivacity, a violence, a bitterness, and an insulting language, that are rare with us ; and there seems to be no doubt that the *Univers* was an offender in these respects. Veuillot's reply was short and restrained : If the Bishop's accusations were true, the ecclesiastical authorities would not have tolerated the *Univers* for ten days. It is the fact that it had the support of a number of the bishops, and a large and enthusiastic following among the clergy.

Ollivier speaks in terms of severe condemnation of both these tractates, in themselves and in their effects. Maret's two learned volumes, of 500 pages each, had been read only by theologians and discussed only in the religious periodicals : but Dupanloup's pamphlets stirred the crowd and set loose a prodigious uproar :

Discussions began in the market-place, and every one took part, even society ladies between the acts at the Opera. Every discussion of the market-place is of its nature intemperate. A shoal of pamphleteers rushed in with injurious language and extravagant ideas : for them the official theological *ex cathedra* infallibility in faith and morals was not enough ; they wanted an infallibility absolute, unconditional, unlimited ; an inspired infallibility in matters of science, of politics, of government : the Pope, even if he wished, could not fall into any error public or private. Extravagance of language accompanied extravagance of ideas ; invectives, recriminations, outrageous proposals, denunciations, were bandied about.[1]

Maret was an heresiarch ; he and Dupanloup and the great Catholic liberals were branded as schismatics, heretics, more dangerous than infidels. The excitement caused by Dupanloup's pamphlets spread to Rome, to the entourage of the Pope. It is pleasing

[1] Ollivier, op. cit., I, 448.

to know that Pio Nono kept his head: 'Oh, the Bishop of Orleans has given proof in defence of the Pope, of the Holy See, and of religion, of a zeal, a devotion, and a courage that I can never forget.'[1]

It is perhaps necessary to say a word on England. There the controversy never reached the pitch of excitement and bitterness that we have seen in France. Still the *Tablet* did carry on a strong Ultramontane, perhaps even neo-Ultramontane campaign. The owner and editor was Fr. Herbert Vaughan, the future Cardinal, at that time wholly under the influence of Manning and Ward. On the appearance of Dupanloup's *Observations* a leading article accused him of 'servility and tyranny'—afterwards, on a remonstrance from Dupanloup, withdrawn partially;—the 'servility' lying in the desire to avoid creating difficulties for Protestants and Easterns! A respectful tone was maintained towards the Bishop; but on December 4 was printed the following 'Letter from Rome':

The Bishop of Orleans' late unhappy letter is generally attributed in well-informed quarters to an interview Mgr. Dupanloup had with the Emperor Napoleon at Compiègne a few days before, in which his Majesty offered to present Mgr. Dupanloup to the See of Lyons in consideration of his taking the lead of the Gallican party—[Lyons being the primatial see of France, and the Archbishop nearing his end].

Dupanloup took the trouble to give a categorical denial to this story. The *Tablet* did give great offence and incur strong disapprobation in many quarters: witness the utterances of two of the English bishops:

The *Dublin Review* and the *Tablet* have taken upon themselves not merely to advocate the infallibility, but to denounce everybody else as little less than heretics and infidels. Another: In regard to the *Tablet* I have not

[1] Ollivier, op. cit., I, 448.

hesitated to express loudly my disapproval, also my apprehension of the serious evil likely to ensue from the course pursued by Herbert Vaughan and his party in England.

Unpleasant reading all this : but necessary for an understanding of the atmosphere in which the Council was held and of the course of events during it.

NOTE.—Though they made a great stir at the time, the cases are passed over here, as not belonging to the actual Council, of Père Hyacinth Loyson, Carmelite, who apostatized; and abbé Gratry, who after vehemently opposing the definition and the Council, accepted the decrees when enacted.

CHAPTER VIII

THE FORGATHERING OF THE BISHOPS

*Portraits of the bishops here named will be found
throughout these volumes.*

TOWARDS the end of November 1869, the bishops
from all quarters of the world began to forgather in
Rome.   This will be the place to introduce those who
are going to take foremost parts in the Council.

And first Mgr. Dechamps, Archbishop of Malines,
later Cardinal.   To my mind he must be looked on
as the leader of the Ultramontane Majority.   The title
Mr. Leslie gives to Manning is happily chosen : he
was the ' chief whip ' of the party ; but Dechamps was
the leader.   He was a great figure in Belgium, brother
of the Catholic leader and statesman.   Shortly after
ordination he entered the Order of Redemptorists, and
for thirty years worked as preacher, missioner, controversialist, writer on apologetics on all the great
questions of the day.   His writings fill fourteen
volumes.   He was a highly trained theologian, and
his speeches and pamphlets during the Council were
among the very best.   He was a convinced Ultramontane, but of the Bellarmine type, untouched by
neo-Ultramontanism.   It is probably true to say that
no other bishop had so great a hand in the actual
formulation of the two great dogmatic constitutions
of the Council.   He was a man of great charm and
attractive personality ; and while uncompromising in

CARDINAL SCHWARZENBERG,
Archbishop of Prague

CARDINAL RAUSCHER,
Archbishop of Vienna

urging his views, he was always friendly and conciliatory to opponents.[1]

In an English book there can be no need to portray
Archbishop Manning, for his personality is well
known.[2] Suffice it to repeat that his will inflexibly
pursued its objects, and his mentality was such that
whatever view he held, he held it with whole-hearted
conviction of its truth, so that to differ from him was
simply to be wrong. His great powers of organization
and diplomacy found an open field at the Council, so
that he was the great driving force on the side of the
Ultramontane Majority, and his influence and activities
will stand out again and again in these pages.

Another protagonist on the same side was Cardinal Cullen, Archbishop of Dublin. He had grown
up in the traditions of the Roman schools, and had
been Rector of the Irish College in Rome. He was a
good hebraist and classicist. On becoming Archbishop
of Dublin he was the great propagator of Ultramontane teaching in Ireland. At the Council, though
not one of those most in evidence, he made powerful
speeches, being a sound theologian; and it was he
who put forward the actual formula in which the
Pope's infallibility was defined.[3]

The leaders of the Minority throughout the
Council were the two Austrian Cardinals, Schwarzenberg, Archbishop of Prague, and Rauscher, Archbishop
of Vienna. Anyone wishing to form a just estimate
of these two men, may read the articles contributed

[1] See Saintrain, *Vie de Cardinal Dechamps;* also Mourret,
Concile du Vatican, p. 169.

[2] See the Lives of him by Purcell and Shane Leslie; also
the *Life of Bishop Ullathorne.* For French appreciations of
Manning, see Mourret, op. cit., p. 165; and Ollivier, *L'Église et
l'État au Concile du Vatican,* II, 8.

[3] See art. in *Catholic Encyclopædia,* by his nephew Cardinal
Moran. Also Ollivier, op. cit., II, 9.

to the *Catholic Encyclopædia* by Dr. Wolfsgruber, a Benedictine of the Schotten, Vienna.[1] They had proved themselves pillars of the Church and of religion in Austria during the troublous times after the revolutionary movements of 1848. They, especially Rauscher, had been the chief negotiators of the Concordat of 1855 between the Holy See and the Austrian Government. They had promoted a great reorganization of church life in all its aspects, and a great revival of religion throughout the Austrian Empire, and they stand out as great and devoted Catholic bishops. Rauscher was a man of wide erudition, especially in patrology. On arrival in Rome for the Council ' he was greeted with universal respect, and hailed as one of the glories of the Council ' (Ollivier).[2]

Among the German bishops the outstanding figure was Melchers, Archbishop of Cologne. As professor of theology he held and taught as the true theological opinion the infallibility of the Pope ; but at the Council he was one of the chief opponents of defining the doctrine. After the Council he was the first of the Opposition bishops to accept publicly and promulgate the Vatican decrees, hardly a week after their enactment. He was a great bishop and Catholic leader in Germany ; and in the struggle with Bismarck over the Falk Laws he proved his fidelity to the Catholic Church and the Pope by enduring six months' imprisonment, and then ten years of exile. He resigned his see for sake of peace and retired to Rome, where he was made Cardinal ; but after a short time he entered the Society of Jesus and died a Jesuit.

The other most outstanding German bishop of the Minority was Hefele of Rottenburg, Württemberg,

---

[1] A more personal portraiture is given by Ollivier, op. cit., II, 10, 11.

[2] Wolfsgruber has written a massive life of each of them, bringing out their great rôle in the religious life of Austria.

perhaps the most learned bishop of the Council in the domain of church history and patrology. His *History of the Councils* is the classical work on the subject. It is probable he was one of the few who before and during the Council questioned the doctrine itself of the papal infallibility ; but after the Council he declared his submission to the decrees. He had been one of the consultors called to Rome to prepare for the Council, and we have seen that what was in one way the most important piece of preparatory work was entrusted to him. When there was question of his being invited to Rome as consultor, the Nuncio at Munich, while pointing out certain tendencies of his writings, strongly recommended him, bearing witness to ' the merit of his works, his priestly virtues, his great love of the Church and of the Apostolic See, and what he had done for the Church, the papacy, and for Christian life '.[1] He was made Bishop of Rottenburg on the eve of the Council.

Although most of the Austrian and German bishops were of the Minority, there were conspicuous exceptions. Not to speak of Fessler, the General Secretary, two of the best theologians of the Council were Gasser of Brixen and Martin of Paderborn,[2] both strong Ultramontanes, who took prominent parts in the proceedings. There were some half-dozen more, among them Senestréy of Ratisbon (Regensburg), Manning's companion in arms in the effort to secure a definition of the infallibility as stringent as could be got through the Council.

Two prominent Hungarian bishops of the Minority were Simor, Archbishop of Esztergom (Gran), Primate of Hungary, and Haynald, Archbishop of Kalocsa. Both of them learned theologians and apostolic

---

[1] Cited Granderath, I, Bk. i, c. 6.
[2] For Martin see *Catholic Encyclopædia*.

bishops, they were conspicuous as two of the best Latin orators at the Council. Haynald as bishop had got into trouble with the Vienna Government for his strongly national Hungarian proclivities and had to withdraw to Rome for some years. He returned to Hungary as Archbishop of Kalocsa. He will appear as one of the most combative of the Minority; yet of him also Manning was able to say: 'Mgr. Haynald never opposed the doctrine or the word. It was he who wrote the word in the Address of 1867, and, as he has told me, had always taught the doctrine.'[1] Haynald was made Cardinal by Leo XIII; Simor by Pius IX.

Mgr. Strossmayer, Bishop of Bosnia and Sirmium (Slavonia), was the chief fighting member of the Minority, and the storm-centre of most of the ' scenes ' of the Vatican Council—there was only one proper scene, be it remarked, to be described in Chapter XV. Of German race, but of a family long domiciled in Croatia, he was by birth and sympathy a Croat and a pan-Slavist, one of the chief pioneers of the South Slavonic national movement that has finally issued in the formation of Yugo-Slavia. The late Dr. Adrian Fortescue has given a discriminating but sympathetic account of Strossmayer in the *Dublin Review* (October 1918) well worth reading. His diocese, including Bosnia, Dalmatia, with Servia as a vicariate, was in 1870 partly in the Austrian Empire and partly in the Turkish. Thus, though of the Latin Church and the Latin rite, he lived in close contact with churches of Oriental rites, both Orthodox and Uniat; and one of the dominating ideas of his life was to conciliate the Slav Orthodox communions, especially Russia, and reunite them with the Catholic Church. This explains

[1] Leslie, *Life of Manning*, p. 214. Ollivier gives an interesting and pleasing picture of Haynald, op. cit., II, 11; see also *Catholic Encyclopædia*.

the vehemence of his opposition to the infallibility, in which he saw a fresh barrier to such hopes. He was by universal consent the outstanding Latin orator of the Council. On February 4, 1870, Ullathorne wrote of him :

Strossmayer sits just under me : he is a warm-hearted affectionate Croat, as eloquent as he is warm, but apt to get over vehement. We have taken quite an affection for each other.

He was a friend of Leo XIII, who wanted to make him Archbishop of Zagreb (Agram) and Cardinal ; but the Austrian Government objected, on account of his Slav propaganda.

The bishops of Eastern Europe, as of Hungary, Transylvania, and the Slavonic countries of the then Austrian Empire, living in the presence of strong communities of the Eastern Orthodox Churches, and some of them bishops of Uniat Churches of various Eastern rites, were nearly all strong ' inopportunists ' at the Council ; they opposed the defining of papal infallibility on the ground that it would bar the door against any hope of the Reunion of the Eastern Orthodox Churches with the Catholic Church of the West. And this was too a principal motive with all those who opposed the definition. The case of the Protestant Bodies weighed similarly with the inopportunist bishops of Protestant lands.

This fear, of putting a difficulty in the way of return to Catholic Unity of those out of communion with the Holy See, was real and valid. In a lecture at Cambridge in 1927, on ' The Russian Church and Prospects of Reunion ', Count George Benningsen, a recent convert from Orthodoxy, while setting out certain political obstacles to Reunion, said that the only real outstanding difficulty in the theological order is the doctrine of the papal infallibility as defined at the Council. And anyone who has had direct personal dealings with Protestants,—I mean, of the real old brand,—will know that with them also it is a principal rock of offence. This is not to say that the definition was not, on the whole, opportune—that the ending of controversy in the Catholic Church itself, and the making unmistakably clear what is involved in Union, was not a good so great as to outweigh the incidental difficulties created for those without. But this objection of the Minority had reality in it, and was not fictitious or factious opposition.

When we turn to the English-speaking countries we meet four archbishops of the United States who were prominent figures at the Council. Spalding of Baltimore was of the Majority that favoured the definition ; but he took up a middle position, desiring the definition, but wishing it to be framed implicitly without use of the word ' infallible '. With him stood half a dozen of the United States bishops. But the greater number followed Kenrick of St. Louis and Purcell of Cincinnati in strenuous opposition to the definition. McCloskey of New York also at first opposed. These four were all of them great builders up of the Catholic Church in the middle years of the last century, powerful organizers, zealous pastors, fine bishops.[1] Mgr. Connolly, Archbishop of Halifax, Canada, was another outspoken member of the Minority.

By common consent Verot, Bishop of Savannah, and then of St. Augustine, Florida, was the ' enfant terrible ' of the Council. He was born in France, was a Sulpitian, and went to the States in 1830. He was probably one of the few real Gallicans at the Council, having made his studies in France at the

---

[1] See the articles in *Catholic Encyclopædia*.

time that the Gallican articles were publicly taught in the schools. He was a frequent and lengthy speaker at the Council, and the one who succeeded in raising frequent laughs. He was often in conflict with the Presidents because of these sallies ; but he received their rebukes with irrepressible good humour. Those who know him only at the Council would be apt to judge him by these encounters ; but that would be unjust ; anyone who wishes to judge him justly should read the article on him in *Catholic Encyclopædia.* He was a great bishop of ' boundless zeal and resource-fulness ', who played a giant's part in the work of reconstruction in the South after the catastrophe of the Civil War.

Clifford of Clifton and Moriarty of Kerry were the only members of the English and Irish hier-archies to take a strong inopportunist line. Clifford stands out in the *Life of Bishop Ullathorne* (Index). Moriarty was Newman's great friend among the Irish bishops, and his supporter over the business of the Catholic University. His position at the Council and his character will be seen very clearly in the series of letters to Newman, to be cited in due course. The estimation in which he was held is shown by the fact that in the preface to a volume of his sermons pub-lished in 1901, Bishop Coffey of Ardfert and Aghadoe calls him ' the most illustrious of the successors of Brendan '.

Of the Irish Majority bishops Mgr. Leahy, Arch-bishop of Cashel, should be named ; he took a promi-nent part, and made more than one important speech. If the Italian and Spanish bishops are passed over here, it is because, being almost solidly of the Majority, they are not going to take so conspicuous a part in the public action of the Council. They of course contributed their share of the speeches ; and one of them, d'Avanzo of Calvi, showed himself to be among the best theologians and best speakers of the Council.

We have allowed the French bishops to stand over till the last, because, inevitably, the controversy among them was the sharpest and keenest, Gallicanism and neo-Ultramontanism alike being French products. And here special reference should be made to M. Ollivier's characterizations of the leading French bishops, whom he knew well personally.[1] They were divided into three groups, each having at its head a Cardinal. Cardinal Donnet of Bordeaux headed the Ultramontanes, but the outstanding leader was Mgr. Pie, Bishop of Poitiers, made Cardinal by Leo XIII. Son of a village shoemaker, he was a big man with red hair, of a dignified and majestic presence. He had by deep study developed a remarkable intelligence ; his pastoral and apostolic writings are of a writer at once nervous and elegant, and of a theology of robust calibre (Ollivier). An uncompromising Ultramontane of the school of Bellarmine, we shall see him maintaining a studiously quiet position in the extra-conciliar agitations that went on during the Council, like Ullathorne holding aloof from all party movements outside the Council : his name does not figure even among the 450 bishops who petitioned for the introduction of the question of the Pope's infallibility. But in political issues and questions of Church and State Pie was intransigent. He was a strong royalist and legitimist, looking for the restoration of the elder branch of the Bourbons, and of the ' ancien régime ' ; thus he was an opponent of the Empire, and of modern ideas of parliamentary government, which he included under the condemnation of ' naturalism '. Certainly he was one of the most striking figures of the Council.

---

[1] *L'Église de l'État au Concile du Vatican*, I, 410-24, 442-4 ; II, 13-16 : also Mourret, *Concile du Vatican*, 161 ff.

Mgr. Darboy,
Archbishop of Paris

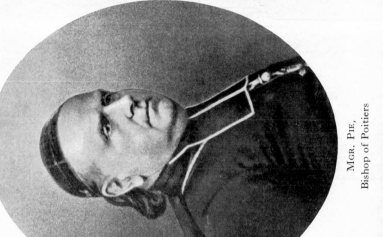

Mgr. Pie,
Bishop of Poitiers

Cardinal Bonnechose of Rouen headed a middle party among the French bishops, those who desired the infallibility to be defined, but in the mildest and most conciliatory terms compatible with fixing the doctrine, so as to secure general agreement. Of this group the leaders were Guibert, Archbishop of Tours and later of Paris, and Lavigerie, Archbishop of Algiers, the great missioner, both of them afterwards Cardinals.

The French Inopportunist group was presided over by Cardinal Mathieu, Archbishop of Besançon. If Manning was the chief whip of the infallibilist Majority, Dupanloup was incontestably the chief whip of the Minority, not merely of the French section, but of the whole party. His personality and position have been sufficiently set forth, and his activities at the Council will stand out no less clearly than Manning's.

Distinguished French bishops of the Inopportunist group might be named : Meignan of Chalons, afterwards Archbishop of Tours and Cardinal ; he was a sound Scripture scholar and apologist, the chief Catholic combatant against Renan : Ginoulhiac of Grenoble, translated to the primatial see of Lyons during the Council, pronounced by Ollivier to be the first theologian among the French bishops, and by Mourret to be a prelate ' of great science and profound piety '.[1]

But without question, not Dupanloup but Darboy, Archbishop of Paris, was the most influential leader of the French Inopportunists. He must have been a man of singular personal charm, as witness Manning's tribute :

The Archbishop of Paris was a man of great culture and intellectual gifts. The playfulness of manner with

[1] Op. cit., p. 39.

which he bore himself towards those who were most opposed to him took off all sharpness from the conflict in which they were mutually engaged. We then little thought of the vision of horror in which he was soon to be enveloped, and of the death which should so soon be inflicted on him *in odium Christi*. His heroic refusal, for the sake of others, to save his life has raised him to the fellowship of those who have won a martyr's crown.[1]

But Ollivier's ten pages, with their touching account of his death, are the classical tribute to Darboy:[2]

Penetration and serenity, reflective resolution and concentrated vigour, a sweet dignity with a winning air that captivated, this is what appeared in his countenance. His powerful spirit, more diplomatist than ecclesiastic, animated a fragile body. Although pious, regular, of exemplary character, and very devoted to his episcopal duties, he was in the line of Richelieu rather than of Vincent de Paul. Gracious, with much urbanity, ready with delicate and amiable sallies, he brought into his intercourse an ease, a grace, a charm, that were irresistible.

He got into trouble with Rome by resisting papal action in his diocese: a curé suspended by his predecessor had appealed to Rome and the suspension had been removed by the Pope; Darboy would not recognize the act, and persisted in treating him as suspended; and he declared in the Senate that the receiving of such appeals by Rome made the government of his diocese impossible. Also he insisted on making canonical visitations of exempt religious houses. And so for some time he was under a cloud at Rome and with the Ultramontanes of France. In March 1869, on the occasion of Pio Nono's golden jubilee of priesthood, celebrated throughout the Catholic world, Darboy made a declaration of affec-

---

[1] *True Story*, p. 156.   [2] Op. cit., I, 416 ff.

tionate loyalty and prayer that quite placated the Holy Father. He said to the French Ambassador : ' See this good Archbishop who has been writing to his clergy about me. Oh ! (he added smiling) he committed an indiscretion : eh bien, nous voilà bons amis.'

During the Council Darboy was one of the most determined opponents of the definition. Yet on March 2, 1870, as soon as the siege of Paris was raised, he wrote to the Pope to declare that he ' adhered purely and simply ' to the decree of July 18.[1] In a letter to *The Times* after Darboy's death at the hand of the Commune, Manning declared :

I am able to attest that the resistance of the Archbishop of Paris to the definition did not touch the truth of the doctrine, but the expediency of defining that truth. I make this statement not on hearsay, but on personal conference with him in Rome.[2]

Ollivier tells with great beauty and pathos the story of Darboy's tragic death. He was arrested by the Communists, April 4, 1870, and held as a hostage. When urged to fly before arrest, he said : ' I will abide, for I ought to give example to my priests ; and my flight would be the signal for a general massacre of priests.' Efforts were made to save him : it has to be said with sorrow that the English Ambassador refused to intervene, and it was left to the American Minister to act. He visited the Archbishop in prison and found him bent down under maladies, suffering, pale and haggard, his beard long and unkempt ; yet resigned, benevolent, without a word against his gaolers : ' I have never seen such resignation, nor

[1] *Lac* 997.
[2] Purcell, *Life of Manning*, II, 468. At the same place is told Manning's endeavour to save him from the Paris Communards.

such Christian spirit in any man, nor anyone so raised above the things of the earth.' The Communists offered to exchange him for one of their leaders in the hands of the Government. Thiers refused, ' avec une dureté de cœur inqualifiable ' (Ollivier), and Darboy was shot in cold blood, May 24, and died blessing his executioners. When Pius IX heard of it he exclaimed : ' He has washed away his defects in his own blood, and has put on the martyr's robe.'

Ollivier prints ' les superbes paroles ' addressed by Darboy to Pio Nono, not to be spoilt by translation :

Votre blâme est puissant, ô vicaire de Jésus-Christ ! Mais votre bénédiction est plus forte encore. Dieu vous a fait asseoir sur la chaire apostolique, entre les deux moitiés de ce siècle, pour absoudre l'une et pour inaugurer l'autre. C'est à vous qu'il appartient de réconcilier la raison avec la foi, la liberté avec l'autorité, la politique avec l'Église. Du haut de la triple majesté dont vous revêtent la religion, l'âge, et le malheur, vous ne sauriez rien dire ni rien faire qui n'ait une portée considérable, qui ne déconcerte ou n'encourage les peuples. Tirez de votre grande âme de pontife une de ces paroles qui amnistient le passé, rassurent le présent, et ouvrent les horizons de l'avenir. L'Europe moderne ressemble au navigateur ballotté par les flots et ne pouvant doubler le cap des tempêtes : institutions et lois, mœurs et croyances, œuvres et doctrine, monarchie illustrée par quatorze siècles de services rendus, empire fait à force de gloire et de génie, trônes s'appuyant sur l'intérêt et l'opinion, depuis soixante ans, l'ouragan de la libre pensée chasse devant lui toutes ces puissantes choses, comme les flots mobiles d'une mer en tourmente. Au milieu de ces agitations et de ces minaces, vous seul, ô pilote inspiré, successeur du batelier de Galilée, vous seul pouvez aider efficacement l'humanité à doubler le cap orageux de l'avenir et à reprendre, avec moins d'incertitudes et de perils, la route de ses destinées éternelles. Benissez donc la noble voyageuse, Saint-Père ; benissez surtout la France, afin qu'elle reste à jamais chrétienne et prospère, et que ses entreprises, fondées sur la justice, soient toujours couronnées par le succès !

So one of the ' enemies ' of the Papacy !

These are the bishops whom we shall see principally figuring, on this side and on that, during the Council. And, in spite of the attempts of extremists on either side, pre-eminently the journalists, to vilify their leading opponents, it may with truth be affirmed of these men that they were one and all fine bishops, worthy pastors, and devoted sons of the Catholic Church, loyal to the Holy See and the Holy Father. Their personalities will stand out as the story is unfolded, and we shall get to know most of them familiarly.[1]

As Bishop Ullathorne is, in a way, the central figure in this Story of the Vatican Council, it will be proper to bring out his position in regard to the great controversy : and all the more so, in that he was representative of the great central body of opinion among the bishops that carried the definition as it is. His position is explained in the *Life* (ii, 47). As a theological student he had been brought up on the Four Gallican Articles ; but he had got hold of de Maistre's *du Pape*, and had assimilated it, and had read himself at an early age out of his Gallicanism into a sober Ultramontanism of the theological Bellarmine type. A letter written to an intimate friend, Bishop Brown of Newport, on the very eve of departure for the Council, defines his position quite clearly :

The Pope, I believe, is bent on the definition, if he can, as the crowning of his reign, and I think it will in some shape probably pass. What I am anxious most about is to

[1] Ollivier's character sketches should be read, op. cit., I, 405-25 ; II, 6-17.

get a balance on the side of the episcopate, by defining its divine origin as a counter-balance, and by putting landmarks about the *ex cathedra*. If this is not done we shall have a wild enthusiasm, especially on the part of converts ; and a disposition on the part of the clergy and even laity to lower the power of the episcopate ; and a stronger centralization, leading ultimately to reaction ; and a narrower door presented to those who are seeking the Church ; and a fanatical extending of the papal prerogatives beyond the fact, after the style of Ward.

In a pastoral letter to his flock just before starting for Rome Ullathorne explained the functions of Pope and Bishops at a General Council :

In a General Council the office of the bishops is twofold : they are witnesses and judges. As a witness, each bishop bears testimony to the traditions, teachings, and customs of the church over which he presides ; and so, when all the bishops have given their testimony, the doctrine and practice of the Universal Church becomes manifest. The bishops are also the judges and definers of the questions that come before the Council ; hence every bishop signs the decrees of the Council like the Pontiff himself, adding the word *definiens*, which indicates the exercise of the judicial office. It does not, however, follow that the judicial authority of the bishops is equal in its force and result with that of the Supreme Pontiff. This may be illustrated from our own Parliament. For after both Houses of the Legislature have agreed to a Bill, it has no force or effect until it has received the consent and approbation of the Sovereign. Yet we must not forget the difference between the cases. For the authority of the Head of the State is professedly of human institution, even although loyalty to constituted authority rests upon the divine law ; but the authority of the Head of the Church rests directly upon the authority of God, and was instituted by God Himself, with the promise that the Church should be built upon that authority, that faith with that authority should never fail, and that its possessor should ' confirm the brethren ' in the things of faith. For to Peter himself

and his successors, Christ gave the power of supreme
and final judgement, when He established the Church on
him as on a rock, when He gave him as head pastor the
feeding of the entire flock, when to him, first of all, and
singularly, He gave the Keys of the Kingdom of Heaven,
and the power to bind and loose. It is for the bishops,
then, in Council to bear witness, to deliberate, and to deliver
their judgements by their votes on the matter in hand ; and
it is for the Pope to confirm or withhold consent from their
decisions. The Church does not consist of body alone, or
of head alone, but of head and body moving in joint action ;
but the head is the crowning authority alike in the Church's
capacity of teacher, of lawgiver, and of ruler.

Not all the bishops, however, kept so carefully
off contentious ground, and a keen controversy arose,
the first brewings of the storm that was to break out
at the Council. The first prominent bishop to raise
the question was Mgr. Dechamps, Archbishop of
Malines, who in May 1869, published a pastoral
letter to instruct his flock on the coming Council and
the questions likely to be dealt with at it. The title
was : *L'Infaillibilité et le Concile Général*. Its tenor was
(1) that the doctrine of the Pope's infallibility *ex
cathedra* was definable—i.e. it could be declared to be
of the deposit of Faith, as revealed by our Lord implicitly in the Petrine texts ; (2) that it would be rash
to wish to anticipate the judgement of the Council ;
(3) that his own expectation was that it would be
defined, exposing his reasons in favour of it ; (4) that
if defined it would not be a new dogma, but a dogmatic definition of a doctrine as old as the Church
herself ; (5) as against current extravagant ideas, he
laid down the theological limitations of the doctrine :
the Church's infallibility reaches only to things *per
se* and proximately relating to faith and morals,
not merely *per accidens* and remotely ; it does not require any new ' inspiration ' ; no pontifical act is

ex cathedra which does not expressly declare an obligation of interior assent.

Dechamps received from Pius IX, June 26, a letter of thanks, giving unqualified approval to his clear statement of principles, his doctrine, and his sagacity.[1]

As might be expected, Archbishop Manning took the field with a long letter to his clergy, early in October.[2] He made a statement of the arguments in support of the doctrine of the Pope's infallibility, and strongly urged the reasons in favour of its definition at the Council. He made an appeal to the bishops of France,

that they should, in this first Council of the Vatican, stand forth to lead the voices of the episcopate in asking that the infallibility of the Vicar of Jesus Christ may be declared by a decree of the Universal Church (p. 122).

At the last moment he added a Postscript dealing with Maret's book, just published.

The following letter of October 26 to his intimate friend, Bishop Brown, discloses Ullathorne's mind on the whole situation :

Since I have read Janus, I can scarcely think it to be Döllinger's, it is so outrageous and extreme. Dr. Newman, who thinks it will do immense mischief, thinks also that it cannot be Döllinger. It is evident however that the Acton party, now in possession of the *North British Review*, have adopted it, if they have not had a good deal to do with its concoction.[3]

The Unionist party [the A.P.U.C.] had got their book on their Orders ready for the Council, and a petition was going round for signature, submitting on certain terms, if the Council condemned the Orders, when the paragraph in the *Register* caused alarm, and stopped the whole proceeding.

[1] *Lac* 1261.

[2] Reproduced in the volume *Petri Privilegium*.

[3] In the October number was an article of Acton's in support of ' Janus '.

I am sorry for this, as it was desirable they should appeal to the Council.

I have it on second-hand authority that the Archbishop was to have put the proposition about infallibility to the Council, and the priest is named to whom he told it. I do not doubt myself but that there was an understanding between him and Rome about it. Only the Continent gave signs which were obliged to be attended to. The result you will see in the last *Tablet* and in the new Pastoral Letter. It is now denied.[1]

It is a certain fact that at our last meeting in Rome [1867] he got a hint from the Pope to check Orleans in the commission for drawing up the Address, and you know what a fight there was between them, and what a different edition Orleans subsequently gave to the story from that we received on the spot.

I think, however much more moderate the Archbishop's new pastoral is, until it reaches the Appendix on Maret's injudicious book, he has committed a blunder by inviting the French bishops to bring the infallibility forward, angry as many of them are against him, and divided as they are into three parties.

You should have seen the former production before it was revised, and several pages cut out of it; it would have put France in a fury. It was by my advice it was sent to Murray [the principal theologian at Maynooth] after I had given my objections, and others had done the same.

I do believe that moderation will prevail, and that the bulk of the bishops will feel the pressure of the times, and control the enthusiasts. As Grenoble said to me, coming to me in a fury against our friend in the Consistory [1867] : *Ce n'est pas le temps de casser les vitraux.*

---

[1] On November 6, 1869, the *Tablet* had the following editorial paragraph : We have twice contradicted upon authority the statement that the Archbishop of Westminster intends to take the initiative in proposing to the Council a definition of the Church's doctrine on the infallibility of the Holy See. We repeat for the third time that we have authority for stating that the Archbishop has not, and never has had, any such intention.

[Here comes the piece on the Infallibility, cited above, p. 143.]

I want to see a good chapter drawn up in the Council on the status, sanctity, and obligations of the pastoral clergy, and some such word as 'pastoral' consecrated to their designation, that we may not always be tied to that detestable word 'secular' to mark them off. Everyone to whom I have spoken, the Archbishop and Reisach included, all think this of the utmost importance for the future well-being of them who have the real responsibility of souls on them.

I think also that we ought to have by common law a title for ordaining, especially now that benefices are everywhere gone. 'Ascriptus Diocesi' was proposed as a general title at Trent, but in those days its need was not felt.

I have other views I deem of importance, and have long meditated on ; especially the expedience of active orders of women being cast into diocesan congregations, with diocesan novitiates and administration. For teaching brothers the same.

But I will not tire you with my notions.

Other bishops, as Simor of Esztergom, Primate of Hungary, and Darboy of Paris, issued pastorals of a pacificatory character, striving to allay the excitements stirred up in the minds of all men, whether Catholics or not.

In such an atmosphere it was that the bishops came together in Rome towards the end of November 1869. It is not surprising that Ullathorne wrote :

Things are daily growing hotter and hotter, thanks, in great measure, to the constant straining after extremes on the orthodox side. A great deal of controversy is raging round the question of proposing the infallibility, and there will be warm work at Rome. Prayer will have to carry the Council through.

Dr. Ullathorne arrived in Rome towards the end of November, and was lodged, along with half a dozen other English bishops, at the English College. He found himself in the thick of controversies that had already blazed out between Dupanloup and Manning and Dechamps, arising out of the letters to their clergy.

In the Postscript to his letter, which Manning had added on receipt of Maret's book, as against Maret's thesis, that the Pope is infallible only in conjunction with the body of bishops, by concourse or consultation, he had laid down the counter-thesis, that ' judgements *ex cathedra* are in their essence judgements of the Pontiff, apart from the episcopal body, whether congregated or dispersed,'—' even apart from convocation or consultation with the episcopate as a body, whether congregated or dispersed '.

Dupanloup in his *Observations* had seized on these words, repeating them half a dozen times, in the following terms :

quand il prononce seul EN DEHORS DU CORPS ÉPISCOPAL RÉUNI OU DISPERSÉ ; et qu'il peut définir les dogmes seul, SÉPARÉMENT, INDÉPENDAMMENT DE L'ÉPISCOPAT, sans aucun concours exprès ou tacite, antécédent ou conséquent, des évêques.

Manning in a French letter to Dupanloup, written at Rome, November 25,[1] protested against this translation, saying that it ' denatured ' his words, making them seem, by over-emphasis, to suggest opposition and scission between Pope and episcopate, and not merely that the Pope speaking *ex cathedra* is infallible without any concourse of the bishops : and he called on him to retract this publicly.

Dupanloup replied in a printed letter of December 15 : He had not intended to suggest that Manning had meant any scission of Pope from episcopate : the translation of Manning's words was not his, but that

[1] The letter is incorporated in Dupanloup's reply.

of the *Univers*, which had printed Manning's letter : English friends assured him that the French did fairly represent the English. He concluded : ' And now that the Council is open, let us think of nothing else than to contribute to the great work of pacification and of light, that the Holy Father wishes for the salvation of souls, and that the world is looking for.'

The controversy with Dechamps was on a higher level and of greater importance. Dupanloup in the *Observations* had animadverted on Dechamps' letter as well as Manning's. Dechamps now published in Rome, November 30, a lengthy dignified letter to Dupanloup, that in tone of remonstrance and in clear calm counter-statement of the Ultramontane position leaves nothing to be desired.[1] In so far as serious theological discussion of the Infallibility is concerned, these two, Dechamps and Dupanloup, may be taken as the protagonists of the two sides ; long letters, really theological treatises, continued to pass between them.

The question of ' separate infallibility ' continued to be a chief bone of contention throughout the Council. Dechamps treats of it in this first reply to Dupanloup :

When the sovereign Pontiff declares or defines the Faith, he declares the truth divinely revealed and he declares it by Scripture and tradition. And how does he declare tradition ? Sometimes by consulting the bishops ; sometimes by convoking Councils ; sometimes doing neither, when tradition is indubitable and springs to the eyes of all, as in the condemnations of Jansenism and Febronianism. Why then do people speak of ' separate infallibility ', as if the faith of the successor of Peter could ever be exclusively personal, or separate itself from the faith of all the centuries ? If by the term ' separate infallibility ' people mean to say that in order to declare the tradition the Pope has not always the need of convoking Councils, or even of consulting the

[1] *Lac* 1286-95.

bishops, they mean to say what is true, but they say it very badly. The Church is a living body, and in order that the infallibility of the head could be separate, it would be necessary that the head itself could be separated from the body.

All these obscurities arise from the fact that people lose sight of the object and nature of the infallibility. It has for object only the preservation of the deposit of faith and to declare when necessary its content; and it is not by new revelations or by inspirations that the supreme doctrinal authority preserves the faith and declares it, but by the fidelity divinely promised to the employment of the means necessary to preserve and declare it.

It is not to the private person, but to the public person that infallibility is promised, and only for the exercise of his supreme charge, the conservation and definition of the Faith. There is no infallibility in acts which are not definitions of faith, or which do not lay upon the whole Church the obligation of believing.

Ex cathedra means the teaching given by the head of the Church when he speaks, not as a private person, but as the supreme authority, and when he proposes to the Church as a dogma of faith a truth contained in the deposit of revelation. All *ex cathedra* definitions have this threefold character : they come from the Pope as Pope ; they are addressed to the universal Church; and they are proposed to it to be believed as a dogma of faith, a truth contained in the deposit of revelation. Pontifical documents which have not this threefold character are not definitions *ex cathedra*. The thing has always been clear, and whenever a Pope has defined dogmatically the Church has never been in doubt as to the fact. When he promulgates a dogmatic decree he promulgates a law, and he gives it the clearness of a law. If then certain theologians wish to see dogmatic definitions everywhere, in every rescript, in every Latin letter, in every brief, in every one of the acts or words of the Holy Father, we must just let them abound and not trouble ourselves over it.

So like are many turns of expression in this piece to those of the dogmatic preamble to the definition, that Dechamps' hand in the formulation of the decree may clearly be discerned.

After arrival in Rome and before the beginning of the Council Ullathorne sent two letters home, picturing the atmosphere that he found there :

Nov. 26, 1869. It is expected the Council will last until end of June at least. The Congregation Aula is ready and very handsome, in one transept of St. Peter's.

There is much excitement about the Bishop of Orleans' attack on Archbishop Manning. Every one thinks he has gone much too far. One paragraph is insulting to the Holy Father. It will require great prudence to avoid a severe conflict in the Council. But Rome has a large store of prudence for emergencies, and I think they will scarcely let the question [i.e. Infallibility] come on early at all events. For my part I think it better that extreme parties should show what is in them before entering the Council, as it will show beforehand the great prudence and management required. I hear much and say but little for the present. As soon as we assemble, we shall have the printed materials of the committees of the last two years in our hands.

The Pope has just sent the English bishops a present of twenty-four woodcocks. He is very well. He receives the bishops by nations. Our audience will be on Monday or Tuesday.

Nov. 29. The Archbishop asked me to ride with him yesterday, and assured me with every solemnity that there never was an understanding that he was to bring on *the question*. I told him what I had heard had been said by Lockhart and de Lisle. He still denied, but would write to Lockhart. I then told him I should have congratulated him on his pastoral, if he had not called on the French Church to act, and had not written the hasty Postscript. He said the French bishops thought otherwise. I replied, ' Some of them no doubt.' Now Grant [the Bishop of Southwark] had revised it, and advised him not to touch the French Church, etc. ; but he changed nothing, and still sees all things in rose colour. He admitted the Postscript was a rapid addition.

If *the question* comes on early by being forced it will put the Council in a strife. If it is delayed, as I think it will be, for I believe it is not amongst the prepared *proposita*, all will go well. I think it will not, and that we shall set to the prepared business. The Pope says to a special friend that he has said nothing about it.

THE COUNCIL

CHAPTER IX

GETTING UNDER WAY

THE Vatican Council began with a Presynodal Congregation held on December 2 in the Sistine Chapel.[1] The Pope made an Allocution, and then nominated the five Cardinals who, in his name and with his authority, were to preside over the General Congregations : they were Cardinals Reisach, de Luca, Bizzarri, Bilio, Capalti : on Reisach's death, December 29, Cardinal de Angelis was put in his place. Bishop Fessler of Sankt Polten, Austria, was appointed Secretary of the Council ; also were appointed a number of other officials, including a body of twenty-four stenographers. A brief, ' Multiplices inter ', was issued, laying down the order of procedure at the Council. Ullathorne wrote :

Dec. 2. A solemn Novena is going on all over Rome prior to the Council, and Exposition in nearly all the churches that one enters. This morning the bishops were all packed in the Sistine, the whole body of which was filled with seats, and the prelates also filling the space behind the screen. 405 had arrived last night, and they now come in very fast. The snows on the Alps have sent a number back to come by sea, including Bishops Clifford and Amherst not yet arrived. The Pope gave the most beautiful Allocution, I think, he ever gave. No doubt you will have it in the newspapers. The officials of the Synod were then appointed and sworn to secrecy, and the

[1] Mansi, II (50), 1 ; *Lac* 13.

157

regulations of the Synod were distributed in print. This was the work this morning of the presynodal assembly.

The Rules of Procedure of the ' Multiplices inter ', promulgated at the Presynodal Congregation on December 2 had best be set forth here.[1] It was laid down that the right of proposing questions for the consideration of the Council was vested in the Pope ; but the bishops were invited to suggest subjects in writing to a special Congregation set up for the purpose of considering such proposals and reporting to the Pope, with whom rested the final decision whether they should be brought before the Council.

The business of the Council was to be transacted in General Congregations and Public Sessions, the latter being the solemn and final functions marking each stage of the Council. The procedure was that the schemata on the different topics, prepared beforehand by the commissions of theologians and canonists, should be distributed in print to all the Fathers some days before being brought forward at a General Congregation : anyone desirous to speak should give notice beforehand to the Cardinal Presidents, and they should all speak in order of precedence. When all on the official list had spoken, others might speak with permission. If no serious difficulty or discussion arose, the schema might be passed forthwith by the Congregation ; but to meet the case of difficulties appearing, four Deputations, each of twenty-four Fathers, should be elected by secret ballot, for Faith, for Discipline, for Regulars, and for the Eastern Churches and Missions. Matters in controversy should be referred to the proper deputation or committee, whose deliberations and report should be printed and circulated to all the Fathers, to be voted at another General Congregation after further discussion, the

[1] Mansi, I (49), 1271 (in vol. 50) ; *Lac* 17.

Fathers being allowed to read their vote and the reasons impelling them to it.

When a schema had been finally passed at a General Congregation, a Public Session would be held, presided over by the Pope. The decrees and canons would be solemnly proclaimed and the Fathers would give their votes ' placet ' or ' non placet '. The result of the voting would be told to the Pope, and if favourable, he would order them to be promulgated by the formula : The decrees just read have pleased all the Fathers, so many excepted ; and We, with the approval of the Sacred Council, decree enact and sanction them as read. The letter of December 2 goes on :

Rome is tranquil, and all is peaceful, except that the Bishop of Orleans' pastoral [*Observations*] has raised much excitement amongst the prelates ; nor is it the only one that has done so ! Replies are coming out, and so we have a combat outside and before the Synod begins. But I apprehend we shall begin our steady work next week, and Rome is too prudent to put before the Synod, at its commencement, any topic that would divide the prelacy.

Of course we shall be all bound to secrecy as to what passes in the Council, and you will have endless unreliable reports. But depend upon it the bishops will be intent upon their grave responsibility, and will be immersed in what concerns the real wants of the Church.

From all I see of the bishops, I believe that never did a Council begin in better or holier dispositions. And the Holy Father is certainly most solicitous that prayer shall not be wanting.

The Council apartment was only prepared for 500 bishops, and they have had to increase the accommodation considerably since. I think we shall surpass Chalcedon in numbers.

I hear the Archbishop [Manning] is preparing a reply to the Bishop of Orleans, aided by one or two other bishops ; so the war will go on.

Dec. 6.   Our two missing bishops, Clifford and Amherst, are come at last, so we shall now get our audience.   Propaganda is working day and night to clear off its affairs.   After three calls, I found Cardinal Barnabò, as usual, amongst the clerks.   As soon as he saw me, up he came—' Why, Ullathorne ! ' grasping me round, and pressing one cheek after the other, ' What has made your hair so grey ? '   I could only return the compliment ; but he was warm and affectionate as an old friend could be.   He then whispered the thing of all others I wanted to bring about.   He said : ' Get your bishops to meet and agree what you want, and join with the Americans and others, where you agree, and I will meet you whenever you like, after you have got your wants on paper.'   The American bishops are strong on many points.   Halifax (Connolly) wants a special Congregation formed in place of Propaganda, and that we pay for our work in fees.   I don't see this as he does.

The zelantes are determined to press on *the question*, our Archbishop, Plantier, Pie, and Mermillod, etc.[1]   All I ask is that it does not come on early.   As to my own line on the point, if it comes on, I have satisfied myself.

A reply to Orleans is expected daily from Dechamps. It is said another is preparing by our Archbishop, aided by others.   I think perhaps not, but he is immensely active.

The Pope did not come down to the Capella, he is reserving himself for the Session, which will last six or seven hours.   After it begins I shall be tied to secrecy as to what passes.   But the Pope has given the bishops the election to each of the four special deputations of twenty-four bishops to each, retaining none to himself.   I am making all inquiries I can about the qualities of different men of the various nations for the voting.

The Spaniards have proposed to vote for our men, if we will vote for theirs for the special deputations.   Some contrivance is necessary to get at unanimity.   If each nation thus agreed as to its own men, it must turn them up at last.

600 bishops had arrived last night, preparations are now

[1] Plantier of Nîmes, Pie of Poitiers, Mermillod Auxiliary of Geneva.

made for 800 in the aula [hall] ; with the cardinals, officials, theologians, etc., 1400 persons are calculated. I hear the division of the aula from the nave is made to roll back, so the people will see something. The whole Session will be in the aula.

The day after to-morrow comes the opening Session, when we shall get the matters that are prepared, and start in earnest. The first Congregation will be on Friday, the second day after the Session. I left a letter with Cardinal Caterini explaining more fully why Dr. Newman did not come.

We expect our audience to-morrow.

Writing on the same day Bishop Amherst of Northampton described the aula :

The hall of the Council is admirably managed. You see nothing of it on entering the church, so that strangers obtain the full effect as usual. It is in the right transept as you go up, and is walled off by what looks like a massive partition of solid marble of various colours, with an immense pair of bronze doors. But the whole thing folds up like a screen ; and on the opening day and other public functions there will be no obstruction to the view from the dome and the opposite transept. There are reading-rooms, withdrawing-rooms, etc., managed in an extraordinarily clever way.[1]

The Council was formally opened at the First Public Session by Pius IX in person, on December 8, the Feast of the Immaculate Conception of the Blessed Virgin Mary. The official Acts, along with the Pope's Allocution are given, Mansi, II (50), 7-36, and *Lac* 27-44. The Pope put to the bishops the question :

[1] The extracts from Bishop Amherst's letters, etc., are taken from the printed Memoir, *Francis Kerril Amherst*, 1903. My endeavours to trace these papers have been unavailing. Besides letters there was a Diary he kept during the Council that would have been of great interest. He was inclined to the inopportunist attitude.

Right Reverend Fathers, does it please you, for the praise and glory of the Holy and Undivided Trinity, for the increase and exaltation of the Faith and the Catholic religion, for the extirpation of current errors, for the reformation of the clergy and the Christian people, for the common peace and concord of all, that the beginning of the sacred œcumenical Vatican Council be made, and be declared now to have taken place ?

The bishops answered ' placet ' by acclamation, and the Pope said : ' The Decree just read has pleased the Fathers without dissentient, and We, the Sacred Council approving, decree, ordain, and ratify it as read.'

Ullathorne described the scene in a letter the following day :

Dec. 9. The opening Session was held yesterday. Such an assemblage of prelates, whether you consider numbers, or the character of their training and breadth of experience, was never witnessed in this world before. About 7 a.m. began the move towards the Vatican. By 9 all were assembled in the great hall above the Portico of St. Peter's, formed into a chapel. Four rows on each side from one end to the other of prelates, waited the Pope's coming. The rain poured all day. But we were unconscious of what was passing in the outer world. At 9 the procession moved, turning from the Scala Regia into the porch of St. Peter's, up the nave, the Blessed Sacrament being exposed on the high altar, and so it turned into the aula conciliaris, the screen separating it from the body of the church being drawn back during all the function.

When all, after the protracted winding in of procession of prelates, were seated the scene was marvellous. You will have it all in the newspaper descriptions, but you cannot easily realize the effect of those two long ranges of prelates rising in eight tiers on each side, in silver copes, and pure linen mitres. There were some 600 bishops besides the cardinals ranged from the two sides of the apse, ten patriarchs in advance of them, and the abbots and generals of Orders down in front of the bishops, the officials occupying the mid-space between.

The royal persons, including the King of Naples, ex-Dukes of Tuscany and Parma, Empress of Austria, etc., and the ambassadors, had tribunes on the sides above the Fathers of the Council. Above them was another tribune on each side for the theologians of the Council, amongst whom I saw several Dominican fathers. Outside was the dense mass of the faithful, and the sound of their voices and feet was as the sound of many murmuring waters on a seashore.

The 'Veni Creator' was the processional hymn. The Pope chanted the prayers before the Blessed Sacrament at the high altar before entering the aula. The Mass of the feast was sung by the Cardinal Dean at an altar at the entrance end of the Council, the Pope being in the opposite apse. Before the last gospel the sermon was preached by a Capuchin bishop.[1] The Pope then vested in pontificals. The prayers were recited by him with short intervals of silent meditation. The Litanies of the Saints were chanted and responded to by all the bishops. The Gospels were enthroned on the altar of the Synod. The Gospel of the Synod was chanted—the one in Luke where Our Lord instructs the Seventy-two before sending them forth. The 'Veni Creator' was again intoned by the Pope and sung in alternate verses by the choir and the bishops, the people beyond joining like a distant echo. And after the Pope had sung the prayer, the aula ought to have been closed for the voting the decrees, and all but the Council commanded to withdraw; but as the decrees were matters of course, and as there would have been an unnecessary delicacy in ordering the Royal personages to withdraw, they were proposed in public. First the decree for the opening of the Synod was put to the 'placet', and then the decree fixing the Session to be next held for the feast of the Epiphany. They were read by a bishop from the pulpit in the centre of the floor, and in response to each, the bishops rang out in a loud volume of sound their 'Placet', and the decrees were registered. The Pope read an Allocution,

[1] Mansi II (50), 12 ; *Lac* 764.

the ' Te Deum ' was grandly chanted, and at 3 o'clock the Pope had retired, and the bishops were winding their slow way out to the unvesting chapels, recognitions of old friends taking place in all directions amongst them. You saw continental prelates meeting their old school companions come from remote and strange countries, and all sorts of joys, tendernesses, and congratulations.

As you may wish to know where I sit in the Synod, know that I am in the third row from the top, having the primates and archbishops at my back, being amongst the few nominations of Gregory XVI ; my number on the seat is 275, the numbers going from 1 to about 900, including primates, archbishops and bishops ; and I have one of the snuggest places, as it is in the division nearest the Pope, and just the outside corner seat, from which I can slip out without having to tread on anyone's toes.

To-morrow we have the first Congregation to vote the judges of excuses, and the judges of complaints, and the members of the four special deputations. Then we shall receive the printed matter from the preparatory commissions that have been working the last two years, and shall set to real work.

What I have alone been anxious about has been that the question so much debated before the Synod should not be allowed to come on at the beginning. I had a talk with the large-headed Secretary of the Synod [Bishop Fessler] in the Pope's antechamber the day before, and he assured me that this would be the case ; and in the audience the Pope gave us English bishops on that day, he also said that what has already been prepared will come on first. This is like Rome's prudence. When the Synod has once got under its normal influences, I do not fear for any question that may come on before it.

In a letter of Dec. 8 Bishop Amherst writes :

We have returned from the great ceremony of opening the Council, which lasted from 8.30 a.m. to 3.30 p.m. ; but it was magnificent beyond description, and well worth a little fatigue. As far as I can make out there were 659 bishops present ; and the effect of all that number, with

the Pope on his throne at their head, all in white copes and
mitres, is quite indescribable. We all walked into St.
Peter's behind the Pope, who was carried on men's shoulders
in his chair of state. The Zouaves kept a narrow passage
open for us, the enormous church being literally crammed.

The Blessed Sacrament was exposed on the high altar,
and we only genuflected and passed on into the hall of the
Council, at one end of which is the altar for Mass, at the
other the throne.

The cardinals sit in a large semi-circle on each side of
the Pope, and the patriarchs in a smaller and inner one;
then there are eight or ten steps down to the floor, and the
bishops are placed at each side of the hall in five rows of
seats rising one above the other. The seats are very com-
fortable, and each has a small table which hangs by hinges
on the back of the bench in front, and can be used either
sloping as a desk or flat like an ordinary table.

All the people in the church joined in the 'Veni
Creator', the Litanies, and the 'Te Deum'; and those
who were outside say the effect was wonderful. They tell
me that there were 50,000 people in the church.

The first General Congregation was on December
10.[1] There were present 43 cardinals, 605 bishops,
31 abbots and generals of religious orders: 679 in
all. The General Congregations always opened with
a Low Mass 'de Spiritu Sancto' celebrated by an
archbishop. The names were announced of the special
Congregation of twenty-six, 'Congregatio de postulatis', appointed by the Pope to consider proposals
made by bishops of matters to be brought before the
Council to be reported on to the Pope, with whom
the final decision lay. There were twelve cardinals—
among them Rauscher, Archbishop of Vienna, Bonnechose of Rouen, Cullen of Dublin; and fourteen archbishops and bishops—among them the Patriarchs
of Antioch (Melchite), and Jerusalem (Latin); the

[1] Mansi, II (50), 35; *Lac* 710.

Archbishops of Tours, Turin, Baltimore, Westminster, Malines, and the Bishop of Paderborn (Martin).

The schema prepared by the theologians for the dogmatic constitution ' On Catholic doctrine, against the manifold errors flowing from rationalism', was distributed among the bishops. The election also took place of a board of five Judges of Excuses, to consider applications for permission to depart from the Council, which became numerous as time wore on ; and another board of five Judges of Complaints and Controversies that might arise on personal matters, as of precedence, etc. An attempt was made to count the votes, but it at once appeared that this was going to be a lengthy process, ' defecerunt scrutantes in scrutinio' (Psalm lxiii, 7), said the Secretary ; accordingly it was proposed by the Presidents and carried unanimously that a board of scrutators be set up, to count the votes after the Congregation and announce the result at the following one. This method was pursued at all elections.

Of the Congregation Ullathorne wrote the same day :

Dec. 10. We had the first General Congregation this morning, lasting from 9 to 1. The four Cardinal Delegates presided. The next will be on Tuesday the 14th.

In our audience with the Pope on the 7th, we found him looking very well. He stood, and gave us, the English bishops, a little address on the spirit of the Synod, and then solemnly blessed all our clergy, nuns, and people, and specially our special friends. After which he saw our priests.

From the English-speaking countries there are about 146 bishops, Italians 100, Spaniards including their Colonies 100, French 70, Germans 40, etc. ; so you see England has most subjects of any nation in the Council, only you must put 40 out for the United States.[1] My next neighbour in

[1] The number of Italians is much under the mark ; there were over two hundred.

the Council is a Frenchman from the Burmese Empire, speaking English well and interesting about the Buddhists; next to him is the Bishop of Charleston; behind me are two North American archbishops; before me is Bishop Persico, a Capuchin once on the English mission. This may illustrate the force of the English language in the Council.

Battle over the definition of the Pope's infallibility was, after the skirmishing already described, first definitely engaged over the election of the deputation on Faith, which took place at the second General Congregation, December 14. It will perhaps be best to hear first Ullathorne's growls, and then the full story of the transaction will be recorded.

Dec. 16. We are now in the agony of electing the special deputation *de Fide*. Everybody feels that on the twenty-four much will depend when *the question* comes on. We are waiting for the result of the scrutiny, the lists having been given in at Tuesday's Congregation. After a failure, we English got a meeting at the last day before the Congregation, and, to the Archbishop's surprise, evinced by sundry snortings [1] and extra politeness, we turned up Dr. Grant by our secret votes. The Irish and Americans took up our vote, and we theirs. But the Spaniards had put out a lithograph list, taken up by all the sheep tribe, who follow at a gap. The French are divided into two camps, thirty-five in one, under Cardinal Bonnechose [the infallibilists], thirty-four under Cardinal Mathieu [the inopportunists], one solitary bishop hanging between the two and attending both meetings. The Germans are also divided into two parties. Everybody believes the Spanish list was concocted by and with Manning, Dechamps, Pie, Plantier and Mermillod. Mermillod wrote to propose St. Austin's example of retractation to Dupanloup.

The Americans want all the English speakers to act as a body, and through Dr. Moriarty [Kerry] they proposed

---

[1] Manning had a way of sniffing when annoyed.

it to me.   But I recommended them to consult de Luca as President of the Council before making any reunion beyond that of individual nations.   And on sounding the higher Irish prelates, they evidently were a little shy of the go-ahead Americans, although the Australians want it.   This is only for making certain *proposita*.   All the cautious people, as opposed to the zelantes, feel that our Archbishop's rooms are the centre of a determined intrigue, and that if they get their committee it is because they are organized, restlessly active, and have the strongest backing.   It will only transfer the conflict to the General Congregation.[1]

We are calling out for a smaller place for the debates, and I suppose we shall get one.   The present aula is utterly impracticable for deliberation, though well suited for Sessions.   There is talk of the Sistine, but it is long and narrow and high ; some cry out for a small church.

You may rely on it this Council will do great service to religion.   The matter we have already in hand is admirable. The Pope has also issued a constitution annihilating a quantity of effete censures, and reducing all that remain into one schedule, abolishing all else that are incurred *de jure*.[2] This shows that we shall have clean work.   On the Constitution *de Fide* now waiting debate, I can say nothing, as it is under pontifical secrecy.   There were 678 valid votes for the appointing the Judices querelarum and excusationum, not including votes that failed from some defect. All the members of the Council are not yet however arrived. I don't think we shall have much matter ready for the Session on Epiphany.   There seems no likelihood of another Congregation this week.

I have just heard that the French on Orleans' side are not more than twenty-one, and that Cardinal Mathieu finds himself in so awkward a position that he has asked for leave of absence.   This comes of connexion with Orleans.   The

---

[1] It is perhaps worth noting that we shall later on find Manning also using this ugly word ' intrigue ' of the proceedings of his opponents (Purcell, *Life of Manning*, II, 455).   After all, ' intrigue ' is the recognized word by which we all designate diplomatic action displeasing to us.

[2] The bull ' Apostolicae Sedis '.

dogma is certain to be brought in by the zelantes, and my impression is that it will pass ; all depends on the terms of it. Every engine that can is being brought to bear upon it.

I think it not unlikely that I may come on either the Discipline or Regulars deputation, more probably the latter. But I shall not be sorry to be free from them, though I do not much mind. I quite expect the Archbishop will be on the one *de Fide*, though many votes will be for Grant.

Dec. 18. What I told you before I left is even more true than I had anticipated about the need of open ears and a guarded mouth. There has been much excitement and diplomacy amongst the Fathers about the election of the twenty-four for the special deputation on definitions of faith, and we English are not the only ones, though the chief ones, whose united wish, *one excepted*, has been out-witted by what everybody considers an intrigue. How-ever, our character, conscience, and self-respect is saved. All the world knows that most of the nations have got the man on it they wished, except ourselves. We chose and put forward Bishop Grant as our ablest theologian, and several nations and half-nations voted with us ; but there is an intense passion in certain men, committed beforehand to a certain definition, in whose zeal we had more confidence than in their discretion, and of course you will know which Englishman was manœuvred upon it. Still, the General Congregation has first to entertain each subject, and it will only go to the special deputation if any great difficulty arises, after which it returns to the General Congregation. It is supposed that what has been done will only result in throwing the point into sharp controversy in the General Congregation. All we have done yet is to elect that one deputation, and the scrutiny of some 20,000 votes, each one voting for 24 names, has taken three days to get through. We elect the deputation on affairs of Ecclesiastical Discipline and on Diplomacy on Monday the 20th. I am recommended for this deputation and have just received a list put forth by several nations with my name on the list. You need not tell everybody this. I should have preferred the deputation for Regulars, but it can't be helped. I suppose Bishop Grant will have that. I shall not be sorry if I escape the election.

The aula of the Council is to be arranged afresh, the prelates brought closer together, and I hear an awning stretched over it is 150 feet high and opens into the great dome. It is impossible to carry on a discussion in it as arranged, and it is only a new experiment to meet a difficulty. If it fails, we shall have to take another place for the Congregations, reserving the aula for Sessions. We have still two more deputations to vote, and shall get to no real work until after the Christmas holidays. Depend on it, it will be a long affair, and happy shall we be if we finish with June. The French and Germans are so divided that each of these nations meets in two separate bodies, all however on one point of policy. There is no difference as to doctrine. From what has come into our hands already, under pontifical secrecy, I can say that the work will be wide-reaching and of a thorough character.

I have just got five documents from the Papal messenger, two regulating the Christmas functions. The Pope is to preside at the Vespers, and sing the last Mass, but not to have a midnight function. One announcing Monday's Congregation, a form of schedule for the next voting, and with the list elected in the last Congregation as turned up in the scrutiny. We have already a folio vol. of papers. The Pope says, if the Council lasts six months, he will be bankrupt.[1] It is an actual fact that one of the well-off cardinals wrote to claim the Pope's hospitality which was only intended for poor bishops, such as the struggling remote missioners.

When the discussions begin they will be daily printed, and ready for next morning. Each reporter is to write for five minutes, then another takes up the word, and he retires to write in full for the printer. We expect some severe debates on certain points. It is thus that the human element gets cleaned off, and the pure truth is finally left standing. This, you know, is the literal sense of the Latin

[1] A *bon mot* of Pio Nono is recorded : ' Non so se il Papa uscirà di questo Concilio fallibile od infallibile ; ma questo è *certo* che sarà fallito ' (bankrupt).

word 'disputatio', the pruning away of superfluity and incumbrance from the vine.

The facts of what Ullathorne qualifies as an 'intrigue' are known, and were not disavowed but gloried in by Manning. The important rôle going to be played by the deputation on Faith, particularly in regard to the issue uppermost in all minds, the definition of the Pope's infallibility, was evident to all ; also the need of some kind of organization to bring order into elections made by a crowd of 700 bishops from all quarters of the globe, for the most part quite unknown to each other. In such circumstances it was inevitable that the extremists on both sides should meet to take concerted action in furtherance of their views ; and so in fact from the outset private international committees, on the one side and on the other, were formed. Naturally, each side said it was the others that began ; we shall hear Ullathorne's judgement that it was the 'zelantes' for the definition that began : but in any case it was in the nature of things that each side should try to organize its forces and propagate its ideas. Manning relates the beginning of the international committee of infallibilists :

Ratisbon, Carcassonne, Malines, Paderborn, and I began meeting in order to watch and counteract the French and German bishops who were united in an international committee. We met at my rooms and Ratisbon's and Paderborn's rooms, and finally at the Villa Caserta [the Redemptorist's Roman house].[1]

Ullathorne has given the same names of the 'zelantes', adding Plantier and Mermillod ; he adds also Pie of Poitiers, but in this he was wrong : Pie was a strong Ultramontane, but he kept aloof from all extra-conciliar movements, and took no part in

[1] Purcell, *Manning*, II, 453.

the activities of the committee. Thus the inner circle of infallibilists who were acting together to push forward the definition of the infallibility were : Manning, Senestréy of Ratisbon, Dechamps of Malines, Martin of Paderborn, Roullet de la Bouillerie of Carcassonne, Plantier of Nîmes, Mermillod coadjutor of Geneva. Others co-operated, but these were the moving spirits.

Their first objective was the election of the deputation *de Fide*. A preamble to the Acts of the deputation relates how the election was brought off.[1] A meeting of the committee was attended by some forty infallibilist bishops, and it was agreed (1) that no one should be elected to the deputation who was opposed to the definition ; (2) that those to be elected should be taken from the various nations ; (3) that the names chosen should be transmitted to the Archbishop of Westminster. In this way a list of twenty-four names, all favourable to the definition, was formed ; it was submitted to the influential Cardinal de Angelis, later, but not at the time, one of the Presidents, in place of Reisach ; the list was then lithographed and distributed among the bishops, as being approved by Cardinal de Angelis, and ' in honorem Beatae Mariae immaculate conceptae '. The result was that the whole list of twenty-four was elected, the Minority not securing the return of a single representative to voice its views at the deputation *de Fide*, the most important committee of the Council.

After going through the proceedings of the entire Council, I have to say that this appears to me as the one serious blot on its doings. It was surely an error of judgement not to accord to a considerable and influential minority, counting among its members a number of the foremost and most justly respected

---

[1] Mansi, V (53), 157 ; *Lac* 1646.

MGR. SENESTRÉY,
Bishop of Ratisbon (Regensburg)

MGR. MANNING,
Archbishop of Westminster

on the Majority list and actually elected.[1]   As things
turned out the Minority had one to represent it.   By
a mistake Archbishop Simor, the Primate of Hungary,
was included in the committee's list ; before leaving
home he had issued a pastoral letter of strong Ultramontane tenor ;[2] but on arrival at Rome he went
over to the Minority.

Ullathorne's letters have shown how displeased
the English bishops were at their candidate, Dr. Grant,
not being elected, and all the more in that he was
known to be an infallibilist, though of a less ardent
kind than Manning.   But seeing that Manning was
the heart and soul of the zelantist self-appointed committee of selection, and was the chief driving force on
that side, it was inevitable he should be on the list
adopted by the committee.   As a matter of fact, the
lithographed list was in circulation before the meeting
of the English bishops that elected Grant.   Manning's
account of how he came to be on the deputation is
not correct :[3] it was not that the Italian bishops put
him on their list, but that he was on the list circulated
by his own committee.

This election of the deputation *de Fide* was the
first trial of strength between the parties, and it
brought out into clear light the indisputable fact that
the advocates of the infallibility and its definition were
in a decisively preponderating majority.

At the third Congregation, Dec. 20, the names of
the deputation on Faith were officially promulgated,
and the votes taken for the deputation on Discipline.
It will be well to consider the composition of the deputation on Faith, which played so important a rôle
at the Council.   A Spaniard was at the top of the
poll, the Dominican Archbishop of Saragossa ; second

---

[1] Granderath gives the Minority list, II, Bk. i, c. 5, p. 69,
note.

[2] *Lac* 1296.   [3] Purcell, *Manning*, 454.

was Pie of Poitiers, the leading French Ultramontane bishop; third Leahy, Archbishop of Cashel, Ireland; fourth Régnier of Cambrai; fifth Simor, Primate of Hungary : of the rest may be named Ledochowski of Gnesen and Posen, Senestréy of Ratisbon (Regensburg), Dechamps, Spalding, Gasser of Brixen, Manning (the nineteenth), Martin of Paderborn. They were well distributed among the nations : Italy had three; the following countries two each, Spain, France, Germany, United States, South America, and there were two Orientals; the following had one each, Austria, Hungary, Poland (Prussian), Holland, Ireland, Belgium, Switzerland, England, and a Vicar Apostolic from India. They were all intended to be of the one theological colour in regard to the defining of the infallibility; and in fact they all were, except Simor of Esztergom.

After the sweeping victory on the deputation *de Fide*, the one that really mattered, the Majority allowed the Minority to have an adequate representation on the other three deputations. The votes for the deputation on ecclesiastical discipline were cast on 20th. Ullathorne wrote :

Dec. 20. This morning we had a General Congregation for election of the second deputation of discipline and diplomacy. It will be two days before we know the result, but from all I hear I shall be upon it, as I have been put in all the canvassing lists of the different nations, and was told by a number of bishops that they had voted me one of the twenty-four. This means anxious work should a division arise in the General Congregation on any point that comes under this important head. We don't expect another Congregation before Christmas, and we shall require two more for elections, before we come to discussions. 750 votes were given in the previous Congregation, which shows the present number of the Council having deciding voices. A cardinal, Pantini, has died, a bishop also from Gallicia, and another from Panama is dying. All hopes are given up of the life of Cardinal Reisach, one of the five Presidents. He worked himself out in the preparations.

A new list of the Council has been published, showing about 800 votes, including cardinals, and sixteen generals of divers nationality, present. The aula has been changed. The altar put by the Pope's throne, the eight rows on each side made into nine, and the far end seats turned round, and put across to be nearer. But it still won't do for discussions. Amongst the changes I am two nearer the Pope, on the same bench, first below the two rows of archbishops, third from top, on right hand of Pope, the side of the uneven numbers, the even numbers being on the opposite, and the first of the four blocks into which each side is divided by stairs. You can scarcely imagine what a large mass the bishops look, ranged . . . [page lost].

Dec. 23. It is now proposed to hold our Congregations for discussion in a great hall of the Quirinal, reserving the aula in St. Peter's for Sessions. I had appointed to-day to go with an American bishop to see it and give our opinion as to its fitness, but special business connected with the Council prevented me. At all events the cry of the bishops for a better auditory has made itself heard.

I had a long talk with two American archbishops deputed by their body, this morning, about a scheme for all the English-speaking bishops preparing what they have to propose to the Council for their special requirements, and have been moving in other directions for the same end. Our plan, likely to be realized, is this. The bishops of Ireland, England, Scotland, America, Australia, India, etc., will each meet separately and draw up their proposals, then two delegates of each country will meet together and settle what we shall bring together jointly. It is only by contrivances of this kind that in so large a multitude things can be brought to bear in action.

The special correspondents of the great newspapers naturally chafed before the thick veil of secrecy that concealed all that was going on in the Council. They were for the most part altogether hostile, and their reports sought to damage the Council in every possible way. Prominent among them was the special correspondent sent out by *The Times*, Rev. Thomas Mozley, who sent home much strange news. In excuse for him must be allowed his own statement that 'he was known to have no acquaintance with the Italian language and people', and was compelled to rely on the English gossip he could pick up.[1]

On December 23 Ullathorne writes :

The *Times* correspondent has entertained the world with the most astounding decisions, dissensions, and confusion in the Council. President stopped bishops by his bell, 130 bishops walked out of the Council in disgust, and all sorts of protests have been made against oppression of our liberty of speech and action : the fact being that not a bishop has yet opened his mouth, except in prayer and singing and uttering certain formularies. The *Times* has much to say about a certain bull that has angered the bishops until the Pope durst not publish it in the Session : the fact being that this so-called bull is the method of proceeding distributed at the Presynodal Assembly in the Sistine, containing the ordinary rules of a General Council. The correspondent has even got a glimpse of it, and quoted from it, as an astute obtaining of secret information,—the document being posted all the while on the walls of the city. He tells a conversation between the Pope and Cardinal Bonnechose, how the cardinal told a piece of his mind to the Pope, and the words are given : that cardinal being the actual leader of what may be called the Roman and papal party amongst the French. The lies with which people have deluded the poor correspondent are so huge, so ludicrous, so utterly antagonistic to the facts, that we read them at our table as they arrive from London with roars of laughter. He says the bishops were kept two and a half hours at devotions, Mass, etc., before beginning discussions, thus wearing us down first : the fact being that we have simply the Low Mass of the Holy Ghost, then give in our votes, prepared

[1] *Letters from Rome*, I, 7.

beforehand, and that is hitherto all we have done, except to receive printed documents to take home with us. Discussion begins next Tuesday for the first time. He even tells who spoke Latin, who French, and who got into a passion. Well! I suppose England will believe all this, and it will become part of the Protestant tradition. Let us turn to something less revolting to truth and common sense. But almost all English papers are going in the same vein. Even the *Tablet* has made some very egregious statements, having no truth in them. Well did I advise the Faithful in the pastoral to trust nothing but authentic documents.

A few days later Bishop Amherst wrote in the same sense :

You must not believe one word that the Protestant papers say about dissensions amongst the bishops, etc., etc. The *Times* says that the General Congregation last week broke up in great agitation ; the fact being that we walked out as quietly as if we were going from the dining- to the drawing-room at Fieldgate, and with just as much dissension as usually occurs under that roof. And so it has been throughout. Even the *Tablet* is misinformed and tells stories, particularly about the poor Bishop of Orleans, which have not the slightest foundation.

On Christmas Eve Ullathorne wrote :

The list turned up in the scrutiny for the special deputation on Discipline and Diplomacy has just come in. The Archbishop of New York [McCloskey] is first, your humble servant second, and Archbishop MacHale third on the list of twenty-four, showing that these have as they stand in their order got the most votes ; of the other twenty-one members, the Archbishop of Mexico is the only one I yet know personally. There will be a cardinal appointed by the Pope as president, and difficult matters on discipline, canon law, and diplomatic questions that the General Congregation cannot easily decide upon, will go to this deputation. The deputation for things of Faith was previously elected, and on the 28th we meet in the Quirinal to elect the deputation for Regulars, and also to begin discussion and to ascertain if the room chosen will do for the discussions.

It was looked on as remarkable that the three English-speaking bishops should head the poll. McCloskey and MacHale were Inopportunists.

Bishop Amherst gives a description of the Christmas functions:

Christmas Day was rather a tiring time for us. We went to hear the Pope sing vespers on the Eve, came home, dined, and at 8 lay down till 10.30. At 11.30 I went to the Bodenhams, having leave to say three Masses at midnight in their private chapel and to give Communion to any who came. At 2.30 to St. Peter's for Matins and High Mass in the canons' chapel. This office, called Pastorale, is supposed to be in special commemoration of the song of the angels and joy of the shepherds. Anything more exquisitely beautiful I never heard. We had places in the stalls, and I had to give out one of the antiphons. The hymn at Matins was just such a song as one could imagine the shepherds singing after hearing the angels; joyful beyond expression, yet quite in character with good church music. There was a bass voice which sounded like the great bell at Bruges booming away, while the little trebles seemed to dance among the stars. Then there were stops in the organ to imitate the song of birds as an accompaniment, and the air kept coming in in unexpected places in the responses to the lessons and throughout the Mass. I thought I could listen for ever. It lasted till 6.30, when we came home to breakfast, then off to St. Peter's again for the Pope's High Mass.

Imagine a great church with a high throne at the altar end of cloth of silver, backed by a canopy and hangings of crimson damask and gold extending quite across the church. Imagine the Pope on this throne and the altar for his Mass about two hundred feet down the church, and on either side, in five rows of stalls, seven hundred cardinals, patriarchs and bishops, all in white copes and mitres, except some of the Orientals, who wore gorgeous dresses of all colours and crowns of gold and silver. Then the various members of the court in robes of the middle ages, some in cloth of gold, others in black velvet and point lace; the noble guard in full armour; gentlemen of all nations in the uniform of their countries, some in the red of England, as Mr. Monteith, Lord Denbigh, etc. In a balcony or gallery of red and gold are the Empress of Austria, the Queen of Württemberg, the Grand Duke and Duchess of Tuscany, the King of Naples and other royal people; in another lower down the ambassadors in brilliant uniforms, stars and garters; a dense crowd in the church, the country people being in bright costumes. And then imagine, at the Elevation, the sound of the silver trumpets pouring down from the dome and filling the whole of the immense church, seeming as if it came from heaven,—and you have some idea of the Pope's High Mass.

To resume Dr. Ullathorne's letters:

St. Stephen's, Dec. 26. Whatever the *Times* correspondent may say, there has not yet been a word of dispute or even of discussion in the Council, and nothing can be kinder or more courteous than the bearing of the prelates towards each other. Of course there was sharp work out of doors about electing the special deputation *de Fide*, one side having been long organized and very active, whilst the other was scattered. And this was mainly owing to the great probability of *one* question being brought in by the organized party. We met, like most of the nations, and proposed our candidate, and with the Archbishop in the chair voted in Dr. Grant. The Archbishop however was returned, though low in the list, showing he had not a large majority. We simply put forward our best theologian, but we were late in the field, and the Spaniards and Italians stuck to their English candidate. I also find that a good many votes were split between Dr. Grant and myself, or I think Dr. Grant would have been in. He would have been no doubt for the question, but he would have been moderate.

For the deputation of Discipline and Diplomacy, I was

put forward, and was voted second on the list, after the Archbishop of New York, and before the Archbishop of Tuam, who comes third on the list of twenty-four. Thus we three English speakers got the three first places, showing that we had most votes. I should have thought Grant much best for this deputation and myself for the third on Regulars, for which we vote next Tuesday. We are then to have also the first discussion in the largest room in the Quirinal, to see if it will answer better for the Congregations than the aula Concilii, reserving it for the Sessions.

To-morrow we English meet to agree on our own *proposita*, and after each English-speaking nation has done the same, we have agreed that two deputies from each are to meet, to see what we can settle to be proposed in common. I have drawn up a few subjects which seem to be considered desirable, and I am talked of as one of the English deputies. Thus you see I am getting my hands full. Moreover, I have let myself be drawn in for one of the Epiphany sermons at Sant' Andrea.

We have still two deputations to elect; to that for Orientals will be attached all questions also relating to missionary countries. But Tuesday will begin the discussions *de Fide*. We have had a great deal of wind, hail, rain, thunder and lightning ever since St. Bibiana, who is supposed if it rains on her feast [Dec. 2] to carry it on for a month and a week.

There has been a sharp passage of arms between Dr. Manning and the Bishop of Orleans, which I read yesterday in the *Univers*. It is fair however to remember that Dr. Manning gave the challenge, calling on the Bishop publicly to retract, and no doubt Orleans knew that the Bishop of Nîmes, or Poitiers, or Mermillod, *all* or some, were in Dr. Manning's council in the matter. There is a pasquinade that is not bad. Orleans lives in a villa outside the walls, the name of which you will hear directly. 'Why are all these purples in Rome? They are the bishops come to the Council. Has the Pope got them all lodged at the Vatican? No, they are scattered all over Rome. Which of them is the farthest from the Pope? The Bishop of Orleans. He is at Macao.'

He put me on his rival list for Discipline and he called yesterday, or rather sent his card, but I have only seen him at a distance. He works six secretaries here.

Dec. 28. After putting in our votes this morning for the third special deputation, that of Regulars, the first discussion began in the aula conciliaris, and seven prelates spoke. The matter in debate has been long before us in that green book which the correspondent of the *Times* is so anxious to get a look at. Tied by the pontifical secret, I yet may say that clear signs were given that there will be no absence of freedom in discussion. We are to try the Hall of the Switzers in the Quirinal so soon as it is ready, but the Pope and Antonelli think it will be a failure. One prelate spoke from his place this morning, and was heard all over the hall, and applauded at the end, but he had a fine voice. I have one of the best positions in the Council and hear every word, but many bishops could not hear those who spoke from the pulpit. When we change, the shifting of numbers might bring me into a bad position for hearing. Bishops Grant, Turner and Clifford were so placed this morning that they could hear scarcely anything from four of the speakers.

It has been arranged at last for each English-speaking territory to draw up its scheme of *proposita*, and that deputations of two from each should meet at the American College, to see on what we can agree in common, and to exchange our lights generally. In a congress of us English, the Archbishop and myself were deputed on this task. We have pretty well agreed on our own, all of them having originated from myself, except one good point suggested by the Archbishop, and valuable hints from Dr. Grant. The Archbishop put forward Cornthwaite and myself, but Cornthwaite could not trust his memory, and when we met, I proposed the Archbishop and induced him to accept.

You have perhaps seen the short correspondence between the Archbishop and the Bishop of Orleans. The Archbishop tells me he has sent another note to Orleans, still holding that Orleans does not fairly translate him. I told Dr. Manning I had read his pastoral nearly in the same sense, and that others had done so. People certainly imagined that by *apart from* the Episcopate, he meant isolated, and *not* merely acting apart although in union with them. However it is a pretty quarrel which has damaged both combatants.

I see by the *Times* of 24th that its correspondent is backing out of some of those many absurdities that have made him the laughing stock of Rome.

Now that the deputation *de Fide* is settled, the Archbishop no longer affects to be ignorant of what goes on in preparing lists of candidates, so to call them, for the other deputations. He is altogether more open with us, after the lesson given him, and it is much noticed his being the fifth from the end of the list, whilst I am turned up second on the second list, half of which consists of archbishops. I suppose Bishop Clifford will get on the third. Except on the one point, the second is considered to be the most important.

Many poor Spanish and Italian bishops have to walk, even through heavy rain, to the Council, a sign of their impoverishment. It must be serious for their health to thus have to sit long hours in damp things.

You may wish to know how we live here [at the English College]. We English bishops breakfast at 8, lunch at 1, when the Council is not later, and dine after the Ave Maria (nightfall). If a morning is free, it sometimes is spent in calls, otherwise in study. After lunch Dr. Vaughan [Plymouth] and I drive out, and when it is fair above and clean below, get out somewhere for a walk. After dinner study again. I do not go out to evening conversaziones, but occasionally dine out, as at the Denbighs, Scott Murrays, Monteiths, etc. But I avoid this as much as possible. One meets a great many people after dinner on these occasions. But I expect we shall soon be too busy for this kind of thing, which you know is no diversion for me.

The election of the other two deputations need not delay us, for no work of theirs came before the Council. The English-speaking representatives on the

deputation for the affairs of the Religious Orders were
Derry of Clonfert, Ryan of Buffalo, Clifford of Clifton ;
on that for the Oriental rites and the apostolic missions,
Grant of Southwark, MacGettigan of Raphoe, Lynch
of Toronto, Quinn of Brisbane.

CHAPTER X

THE FIRST DEBATES

The Council may be said to have really settled into its work with the New Year, December having been taken up with preliminary formalities and setting up the machinery. True, the discussions did begin at the fourth and fifth General Congregations, held December 28 and 30. Henceforward there usually were two or three of these Congregations each week, eighty-six in all being held up to the prorogation in July. They were regularly attended by upwards of six hundred Fathers, and lasted from 9 a.m. to 1 p.m., a low mass of the Holy Ghost being said each time by an archbishop. The actual business procedure, which was, if thorough, somewhat elaborate and even cumbersome, will be seen in the narrative.

At the first Congregation, December 10, had been distributed to the Fathers the schema of a dogmatic constitution on ' Catholic doctrine against the manifold errors flowing from rationalism '. As has been explained, the schema had been prepared by a commission of theologians in session for some months before the Council. It is a lengthy document, covering fifteen of the folio columns of Mansi and twelve of the closely printed 4° columns of the *Collectio Lacensis* volume, and it was accompanied by Annotations running to three times the length of the document itself.[1] There were eighteen chapters : they opened

[1] Mansi, II (50), 59-74 ; 74-119 : *Lac* 507-18 ; 518-53.

186

with condemnations of materialism, pantheism, and rationalism ; then came chapters on divine revelation, on mysteries of faith, on the nature of faith and motives of credibility, on the supernatural virtue of faith and its firm assent, on the relation between human science and divine faith, and on the unchangeable truth of that sense of dogmas which the Church has held and holds. These were chapters I to XI ; chapters XII to XVIII had to do with particular doctrines : the Unity of God, the Holy Trinity, Creation, the Incarnation and Redemption ; then the origin of the human race from Adam, the original state of justice, original sin and eternal punishment, the supernatural order of grace. It will be seen that the entire schema was a piece of highly technical dogmatic theology ; and it may be surmised that the average elderly bishop, whose recollection of theological niceties had grown dim in the work of the pastorate, must have perused this very stiff bit of theology for the subject matter of debate with feelings akin to consternation. It was four months before the first half of the schema was enacted as the Dogmatic Constitution *de Fide Catholica* at the Third Public Session, Low Sunday, April 24. It may safely be averred that perhaps never in the history of the world has any legislative act been subjected to a discussion more free, or a sifting more thorough, or a criticism more searching, or a weighing of objections more painstaking, or a transformation more complete, than found place in this Vatican dogmatic Constitution on the Catholic Faith.

The bishops had the schema in their hands for eighteen days before the discussions began on December 28, and so had had ample time to study and digest it. The public debate on 'the schema as a whole' was inaugurated by Cardinal Rauscher, Archbishop of Vienna, to whom thus fell the honour of the first speech of the Council. The contents of the various schemata, and the subjects discussed, and what was said by the speakers, was all under strict pontifical secrecy, though the names of those who spoke were published day by day. But all has now been made public, so that Mansi prints the speeches in full from the stenographic reports. Granderath's *History* gives summaries of the principal speeches.[1]

The burden of Rauscher's speech was that the schema was too long and vague and academic, and did not really come to grips with the prevailing errors of the day; the articles on pantheism, rationalism, and materialism were inadequate; it is not now, as it was for Trent, a question of heresies, but of the very foundations of belief and religion: what is needed is a decree of a General Council condemning current errors, not a resumé of dogma for the use of professors of theology.

The second to speak was Archbishop Kenrick of St. Louis, U.S.A., very briefly, but on the same lines: The schema departs from the traditional method of General Councils, which is to assert Catholic truth against errors, but not to enter on their refutation; Catholic doctrines should be simply and shortly stated, and the errors opposed to them anathematized, but without any argumentation or bringing forward of reasons; the schema invites the Council to go over the whole series of revealed truths. It should be remitted to the deputation *de Fide*.

There followed four Italians, three of them critical, only one approving of the schema. The debate that first day was concluded by Archbishop Connolly of Halifax. His was a most trenchant attack on the whole substance and manner of the schema: unlike all previous Councils, and notably Trent, it discourses ' de omni scibili in re dogmatica ', and raises theo-

---

[1] This first debate is in Mansi, II (50), 122-276.

logical speculations into articles of faith; questions recognized as open in the theological schools are decided in a particular sense; the theologians of Trent will rise from their graves and say, 'Look how we did the thing!' The schema should not be patched up or emended, but decently buried (cum honore sepeliendum): it should be wholly recast by the deputation *de Fide*.

It was after this first day's debate that Ullathorne wrote: 'Tied by the pontifical secret, I yet may say that clear signs were given that there will be no absence of freedom in discussion.' The seven speeches fill twelve folio columns of Mansi.

The general debate on 'the schema as a whole' ran its course through six Congregations, till January 10, thirty-five Fathers speaking, and their speeches taking up 130 columns of Mansi, an average of nearly four columns each. It is no wonder that one bishop mounting the ambo after some lengthy speeches, and saying he would not be more than a quarter of an hour, was greeted with cries of 'Bene! Optime!' The speakers came from all parts of the world, and the speeches were in great part concerned with points of high theology and philosophy: some showed themselves jealous in safeguarding the tenets of particular theological schools; one, an Augustinian, discoursed at length on 'a state of pure nature' and on 'original justice'. Only concerning two or three of those going to take leading parts in the proceedings of the Council will it be necessary to make any comment.

Strossmayer, Bishop of Bosnia and Vicar Apostolic of Servia, both at that date still parts of the Turkish Empire, has already been introduced. His first speech, on the second day of the debate, called forth the first intervention of the Presidents. On this occasion he voiced the feelings of many of the bishops by taking objection to the title of the Constitution: 'Pius episcopus, servus servorum Dei, sacro approbante Concilio ', and urging that, as at Trent, all decrees should be promulgated not as the Pope's, but as the Council's, ' Sacrosancta Œcumenica Synodus '. After he had spoken on this point for four columns, the President's bell sounded, and Cardinal Capalti, who on such occasions usually acted as spokesman for the five Presidents, called him to order, as wandering from the subject proposed for discussion : the introductory clause could not be changed, but was the traditional formula always used at General Councils when the Pope presided in person, the Tridentine formula being used only if the Pope was not present personally, but by delegates. The Fathers were invited to express their mind with full freedom on the contents of the Constitution, but they must not wander from it : ' Now the Right Reverend Father may go on with his speech.' There was nothing of the nature of a scene ; it was a perfectly proper calling to order, and it was the one intervention of the Presidents during this six days' debate. Strossmayer who had been sitting in the ambo while Capalti was speaking, went on for another four columns, criticizing most severely the schema, as dealing rather with questions of the schools than with the errors current in the wide world ; he also strongly protested against the needlessly offensive language employed, which was not of a kind likely to impress or conciliate those outside of the Church : the schema should be sent out to the deputation *de Fide* to be wholly recast.

At the next Congregation Verot, Bishop of Savannah, Georgia, U.S.A., as coming from one of the old slave States, where just after the Civil War the negro problem was acute, said that instead of condemning obscure errors of German idealists, it would be more to the purpose to condemn the theory that negroes have not souls ; and he proposed a canon anathematizing any who dare to assert that blacks are not of the human family.

Among the most remarkable members of the Minority, and indeed of the Council, was Meignan, Bishop of Chalons, later Archbishop of Tours and Cardinal. He was a distinguished Scripture scholar, a competent orientalist, a sound theologian and effective apologist, who had made his studies at Munich, Berlin, and Rome. He fixed on the biblical question as enunciated in the schema : while agreeing that every Catholic would take the Bible in its entirety as the Word of God 'simpliciter', he questioned the prudence and the correctness of declaring it to be, in all its parts, the Word of God 'vere et proprie', and argued at length against such a definition. As a fact, the expression does not find place in the actual Constitution.

The debate on 'the schema in general ended on January 10. During it Ullathorne wrote the following letters :

Jan. 1, 1870. I believe we shall succeed in keeping to the aula conciliaris for our discussions, without trying the Quirinal. At the last Congregation, one-third of the length of the aula was separated off, an awning stretched over about a quarter of the length, where the speaking pulpit is, and during the four hours' discussion most of the Assembly, nearly all, indeed, heard very well. With a little more alteration I hope, that is now making, we will hear well. Hitherto there has been no difficulty on account of diversity of pronouncing Latin, though we have had English, French and Spanish as well as Italian speakers, some of them very able and eloquent, most of them speaking with real episcopal freedom. Our next Congregation is on Monday. We begin at 9 a.m. with Mass of the Holy Ghost ; the last was in the Armenian rite, a prelate being selected from a different nation for each day ; and then the discussion goes on until about one, when we disperse.

The special deputations are not yet set to work, but one

will most likely have plenty of work soon. The fourth is not yet elected, as we are waiting for the publication of the result of the scrutiny of the third. Meanwhile, the English-speaking nations, like most of the others, are having their meetings, first by themselves, then together by deputies, the Archbishop and myself being the deputation for England. We had our first meeting yesterday for two hours at the American College and resume on Tuesday morning next. Some nations, or parts of nations, have already printed what they want to bring in, by way of propositions, into the Council. These will first undergo the judgement of the Congregation *de postulatis* appointed by the Pope, and be referred to his Holiness, before leave is got to introduce them into the Council. Some such provision is needful to prevent the time and patience of the Fathers being consumed by all sorts of things, fit or unfit, being introduced.

The reference to the diversities in pronunciation of Latin is of interest, as it has been asserted (e.g. by Salmon [1]) that the bishops could hardly understand one another's Latin. I have come across only one indication of such difficulty. While Pie was making a great speech some Italian bishops called out that they could not understand. He repeated a sentence slowly in his best Italian style, and then said 'Gallus sum, et Gallice loquor!'
Ullathorne's letter to Newman of January 20 (below, p. 210) repeats the same quite explicitly.

Jan. 2. We have had some very good Latin discourses in our Council; one a Hungarian, took the admiration of the Council by his grace and eloquence, and the fluent ease and pliancy with which he used the Latin language, which to the Hungarians is as their native tongue. Another, a blind Italian prelate, first apologizing for not ascending the tribune, owing to his infirmity, spoke from the floor with a splendid voice that filled the hall, a distinctness and closeness to the point, which was followed by Latin exclamations

[1] In the account of the Council in his book *Infallibility*.

of applause from all the benches. A French bishop too, one of my old friends [Ginoulhiac], made a very clever and forcible speech, with much learning and aptitude. Sometimes we get a long prose read from a paper, perhaps, without a point in it, pure muff, its providential use being to tame the prelates, practise their patience, and prove the liberty of the Council. Such a one we had from a venerable old Spanish friend of mine. There is no want of sifting or plain speaking.

I have not inscribed my name to speak on the contents of the green book we are now handling, for it is being handled enough, and it is pretty sure to be sent to its proper deputation for revision, although a most splendid piece of theology. It is not the first time that I have seen the work of the ablest theologians, when the episcopate bring their deeper instinct and keener experience upon it, go to pieces like chaff and consigned to reconstruction. It was so with the Constitution on the Immaculate Conception.[1] It does not however follow that the preliminary work is not of great value, or that it is not thoroughly orthodox.

It has been arranged that infirm or weak-voiced bishops, who could not be heard in the Council, should put their sentiments on paper and lay them on the President's table. Two of our bishops have availed themselves already of this privilege. I see I am running on the verge of confidences, but am still, I trust, within the prescribed limits. Our oath ties us as to the subjects debated, and to say nothing as to who speaks on this side or that; but the names of the speakers themselves are put in the official Roman Journal.

Dr. Amherst also wrote:

Jan. 3. We are at last getting into full work at the Council; but the debates go on slowly, owing to the number of people who want to speak and great length of

---

[1] On that occasion he said: 'I am delighted to see the bishops capsizing the theologians; the bishops are all authority, and the theologians all reason' (*Letters of Archbishop Ullathorne*, p. 59).

the speeches. However, the Italians, who are not accustomed to hard work, are at length seeing the necessity of it. We were in Council from 9 a.m. till 1.30 p.m. to-day, and only had four speeches !

Again :

Jan. 4. We have got home from a meeting of the Council where we were almost stunned by a Swiss bishop, who spoke for an hour, and roared as if he were talking from one mountain to another against wind and thunder !

This was Greith of St. Gall, the only Swiss of the Minority.

The course of the debate was interrupted on January 6 by the Second Public Session. Let Ullathorne describe it :

Jan. 6. This is the Epiphany and the second Public Session of the Council. The general character of the function was the same as the first. The High Mass sung by the Cardinal Vicar, the Pope presiding. After Mass the ' Veni Creator', Litanies, well and unitedly responded to by the whole episcopate. The Gospel of the Council sung, the Book of the Gospels enthroned on the Altar, and then the profession of Faith, which lasted two hours. The Pope first read the Creed of Pius IV, then a bishop ascended the ambo and read the same Creed aloud, then the prelates beginning with the cardinals and patriarchs went up one by one to the Pope, and laying a hand on the Gospel each after the other said : ' Ego N.N. Episcopus N. spondeo, voveo, atque juro juxta formam praelectam, sic me Deus adjuvet, et haec Sancta Dei Evangelia ', then kissing the Book. The archbishops and bishops went up two and two, the abbots and generals four and four, secretaries taking down each name as it was uttered. Just imagine the line of prelates going on unbroken for two hours, those in their seats carrying on a quiet conversation all the while. Nor is this conversation out of place, as it chiefly regards the Council, and communicates information. For instance, I got some very valuable information during the time, which fixed me on a line of policy I had been reflecting on for six months at least before, on perhaps the most important point that may come before the Council. The profession of Faith over, came the ' Te Deum ', alternated between the choir and the bishops. Then the Pope's blessing and an indulgence of thirty years. As no decrees were far enough advanced for the final voting none were brought forward.

It was given out by those hostile to the Council—Friedrich, ' Quirinus ', Mozley—that the solemn profession of Faith was an afterthought, to save the face of the authorities by covering up the fact that there were no decrees ready for promulgation at the Session. Likely enough it had been supposed that there would be decrees ready ; but the public profession of Faith was one of the functions of the Council, and had been fixed for the Second Public Session of January 6 before the Council had assembled.

Jan. 6. He went on :

We meet again in General Congregation on Saturday, when we may hope, as only six speakers are inscribed, that we shall have finished the first stage of discussion of the first dogmatic constitution. What it is all about and what has been said about it, is our one secret, at present, everything else is made public.

The English bishop elected on the deputation concerning Regulars, you will know by this time is Bishop Clifford. I do not see much of him, or of Bishop Amherst, as they live in the neighbourhood of the Piazza di Spagna. Another bishop has died, the Bishop of Panama, making three bishops and two cardinals. The Bishop of Meaux fainted in his place this morning, he however contrived to make his profession of Faith half an hour afterwards. There are some very old bishops in the Council, who have to be helped down the steps and up them. One old gentleman moves by inches on his stick, but some bishop is sure to step forward and help him on. What a little world of its own a Council is, yet it is a world full of courtesy and kindness, evinced perhaps the most strikingly between those who are the most strongly opposed in ecclesiastical policy.

I hear the Pope talks of allowing the bishops in the summer to go into the country for air and rest, but not of returning to their sees. I suppose he apprehends it would be difficult to get them back again. Everything looks like a long sojourn here.

Jan. 8. Just returned from the Council. Discussion as usual from 9, including the Mass, up to a quarter to one. We had hoped this morning would have completed the first stage of discussion on the first constitution, and have handed it over to the special deputation on Faith; but more speakers had inscribed their names, and so we begin again on Monday, which will surely bring us to the first stage.

To-day two more constitutions were put into our hands, which belong to discipline. These will then be the next points for discussion. It is far more amusing than *Punch* to read the Roman correspondent of the *Times*. He is sure to get hold of the direct opposite of the truth in almost everything he states, and even the *Vatican* commits the greatest blunders.[1] There was however one article in the *Tablet*, a letter from Dr. Grant on the modes of procedure, which was quite correct and very able. It did not appear under his name, but was written in reply to the *Times*

Sundry *proposita*, that is to say schemes of questions to be proposed to the Council, have been drawn up by different groups of bishops, and these are seeking for support. I read one this morning, whilst a drowsy speech was going on, 40 pages octavo ; and I am indeed myself on a deputation, as you know, for drawing up certain others.

The aula conciliaris has now taken its final shape ; there Congregations are held, the bishops being brought into half the length which they occupy at a Session. The steps of the apse are covered with seats and all the space in front of the cardinals, and the sixteen rows of bishops are made twenty, so as to be within hearing distance, and an awning is stretched over half the space. I shall keep my

---

[1] The *Vatican* was a Council supplement to the *Tablet*.

old place, and our Archbishop is just opposite me in the second row from the top.

The Council costs the Pope £200 a day of itself. His income is, and long has been, but 30 million frs. a year, whilst his expenditure is 60 millions. The Peter's pence goes but a small way to meet his expenses.

Jan. 10. We had a Congregation to-day up to 1½ p.m., and finished the discussion on the first scheme on Doctrine, and it is sent to the special deputation.

You must remember this, that everything is discussed first in the General Congregation, and only when grave difficulties arise is it afterwards sent to a special deputation; and when they have reformed the constitution, then it returns to be reconsidered in the General Congregation, so that everyone has the opportunity of expressing their sentiments, and that at any length.

Dr. Amherst: Jan. 13. The Bodenhams have a reception for bishops every Wednesday evening, and have fitted up an Oriental divan for the Easterns, where they sit cross-legged and smoke and drink coffee. The hour for the reception is 8.30; but the Orientals seem to like it so much that, yesterday, they arrived at six, before their hosts had dined!

About what goes on in Council we are not allowed to speak. I envy the Hungarian bishops their facility in speaking Latin, which they are so accustomed to that they talk as easily as if they were chattering the language of the country. Two of them, Strossmayer and Haynald, together with the Archbishop of Malines, formerly Père Dechamps, C.SS.R., have made the most eloquent speeches I have ever heard.

The Council-hall has been re-arranged, and we hope it will do and so save the expense, trouble, and disappointment of removing to the Quirinal. The Pope continues wonderfully well.

I am sorry to see a lecture in the *Tablet* by Father Christie, in which he speaks of the Bishop of Orleans as being in an 'intrigue' against the definition of infallibility. I wish they would let the poor man alone. There is no such thing as an intrigue. He merely has expressed in the most open way his own opinions ; and no one has been received with greater kindness by the Holy Father.

This last remark was true; on December 14 Dupanloup wrote in his diary : ' Hier, audience du Pape. Très bienveillant, comme toujours.'[1]

The general sense of the assembly was against the schema as it stood : it was too long and elaborate, too abstract and obscure, and it did not meet the needs of the time. And so it was sent out to the deputation *de Fide* to be remade : ' mangled and pulled to pieces', and ' bleeding in every limb', as Ullathorne put it. The fate of the schema came as a surprise to the theologians and the Curia and the Presidents and the Pope himself ; it had been taken for granted that the prepared schemata would go through easily and quickly with little amendment ; it was not anticipated that the bishops were going to take things so seriously. It should be made clear that, though the most outspoken, the Minority bishops were by no means the only critics of the schema. Mourret, relying on M. Icard's Diary, says it was received with almost general disapprobation. Though the work of two German Jesuit theologians, Franzelin and Schrader, it was disavowed at a meeting of the Jesuit bishops and theologians taking part in the Council, convened by the General. The famous Jesuit moral theologian, Padre Ballerini, characterized it to Icard as ' Moles indigesta, opus de novo conficiendum '—' an undigested mass, a work to be remade'. The strongly Ultramontane theologian, abbé Gay, also expressed to Icard his dissatisfaction : ' it is concerned too much with errors hardly known outside the schools,

[1] Mourret, *Concile du Vatican*, p. 139.

too little with those that trouble men's minds and are a peril to society '.[1]

Two months elapsed during which the deputation worked at the remodelling of the schema, before, on March 18, the revised constitution was brought before a General Congregation for renewed discussion. During this period the Council gave itself up to matters of ecclesiastical discipline and the reform of the canon law, as will be narrated in Chapter XII.

The deputation lost no time in getting to work; indeed, already on January 7, the trend of general criticism being apparent, a preliminary session was held. The Pope had made Cardinal Bilio, one of the Presidents of the Council, Chairman of the deputation *de Fide*, and henceforward he exercised a preponderating influence in the preparation of the dogmatic material for the Council.

At the session of January 7 Bilio put to the deputation the two questions : Should the schema be put aside and an entirely new one framed ; or should it be retained in substance ? And, if so : Should its form be changed ?[2] The deputation resolved with unanimity that it should be retained in substance, but emended : it should be shortened and made more clear ; its tone should be tranquil, as befits the decree of a General Council ; the language of the schools should be eschewed, and all harshness of expression eliminated ; also anything restricting the allowed liberty of the theological schools should be avoided.

At the second session, January 11, the theologians assisting the deputation were instructed to make a full analytic synopsis of all that had been said in

---

[1] Mourret, op. cit., p. 191 : on this work, and M. Icard and his Diary, see below, Chap. XIV.

[2] The full Acta of the Deputatio de Fide are given in Mansi, V (53), 157-332 ; somewhat abridged, *Lac* 1646-95.

criticism of the schema;[1] and the great Jesuit Austrian theologian Franzelin, whose handiwork the schema principally was, was invited to defend it before the deputation. This he did in a spoken theological disquisition taking up twenty-two columns of Mansi, some 12,000 words.[2] He did not, however, satisfy the deputation, and it was determined that the schema must be drastically remodelled. The work was entrusted to a sub-committee of three, Archbishop Dechamps of Malines, and Bishops Pie of Poitiers and Martin of Paderborn; and they in turn entrusted it to the last-named, Conrad Martin, of Paderborn, one of the foremost bishops of Germany, a learned theologian, a sympathetic controversialist, and a strong apostolic bishop.[3] He took two theologians to help him, Fr. Kleutgen, a German Jesuit, and, as appears from the second volume of his *Correspondence*, the abbé Charles Gay of Poitiers, one of the theologians called to Rome by the Pope, and during the Council theologian to Bishop Pie, to whom later he became assistant bishop on his elevation to the purple. Gay's notes in letters on the work of revision are very interesting: he speaks of his emotion in recognizing much of his own wording in the dogmatic definition of the Council. It was not for six weeks that Martin, on March 1, was able to lay before the deputation the result of his labours. Leaving him at work on his task we may return to the public affairs of the Council.

[1] Mansi, II (50), 277-310.
[2] Mansi, II (50), 317-40; *Lac* 1611-27.
[3] See *Catholic Encyclopædia*.

CHAPTER XI

INFALLIBILITY MOVEMENTS: OUTSIDE THE COUNCIL

WHILE the debates on the schema of Catholic Faith
were going on inside the Council-hall, the movements and counter-movements around the Infallibility went on outside. It should be understood that
the commission of theologians for preparing beforehand draft schemata to be laid before the Council as
a basis of discussion, had drawn up a comprehensive
schema *de Ecclesia*, holy Mother Church having never
yet formally defined herself. In regard to the Pope's
infallibility the query had been submitted to the theologians whether the doctrine was theologically definable, and whether it was advisable to include it in the
schema. They answered that the doctrine was definable; but that in their judgement the subject ought
not to be proposed to the Council by the Apostolic
See, unless at the petition of the bishops.[1] This
advice of the theologians was unanimous. Thus the
schema as originally proposed contained a chapter
on the primacy, but nothing on the infallibility. An
additional chapter on the infallibility was, however,
drafted, in readiness to be added if called for.[2] Thus
there was no mention of the infallibility in the official
documents concerning the Council, and the Pope at
the beginning said its introduction would be left to

[1] Mansi, I (49), 668; *Lac* 1106.
[2] Mansi, III (51), 701; *Lac* 641; (below, Chap. XXI).

the bishops. But in view of heated controversies in most countries during the previous decade, and of the excitement of men's minds on the subject, it was perfectly certain that a large number of bishops would want to bring about a formal definition. The matter had, in truth, been in agitation ever since the proclamation of the Council in 1867. Manning tells how on that occasion he and Senestréy, Bishop of Ratisbon (Regensburg) in Bavaria, took a vow to promote the definition :

> On the eve of St. Peter's Day [June 28, 1867] I and the Bishop of Ratisbon were assisting at the throne of the Pope at the first vespers of St. Peter ; we then made the vow drawn up by P. Liberatore, an Italian Jesuit, to do all in our power to obtain the definition of papal infallibility. We undertook to recite every day certain prayers in Latin contained in a little book still in my possession. The formula of the vow with my signature is bound up in my copy of *Petri Privilegium*.[1]

These two, Manning and Senestréy, were true to their vow. From start to finish they stood shoulder to shoulder, straining every nerve to bring about the definition, and in the strongest terms that could be got through the Council, terms it will be seen stronger far than those actually passed.

We have seen in Ullathorne's letters that the infallibility was in the air from the start, and immediately on arrival in Rome the extremists on each side formed international committees to work for or against the definition. Manning in the reminiscences of 1887 tells the story :

> The public history of the Council I have given in the 'True Story'. The private history is known to few. Ratisbon, Carcassonne, Malines, Paderborn and I [Senestréy, Roullet de la Bouillerie, Dechamps, Martin, Manning] began

---

[1] Purcell, *Life of Manning*, II, 420.

meeting in order to watch and to counteract the French and the German bishops who were united in an international committee. We met at my rooms, and Ratisbon's and Paderborn's rooms, and finally at the Villa Caserta. One day the Opposition came and half filled the room. We had to adjourn. The international committee met often, and we met weekly to watch and counteract. When they went to Pius IX we went also. It was a running fight.[1]

After the first victory in the election of the deputation *de Fide* the infallibilist committee pressed onward in their campaign and set to work to organize a monster petition from the bishops that the infallibility question be brought forward at the Council. Senestréy's Diary tells the story.[2] On December 23 the inner circle met at the Villa Caserta : Manning, Dechamps, Senestréy, Martin, half a dozen more. It was agreed that a letter be prepared, to be circulated among the bishops, asking for signatures to a petition that the doctrine be defined at the Council. On 28th they met again and accepted the form of letter that had been prepared ; it was signed by sixteen bishops and was printed and issued on 30th, not to all the bishops, but to selected ones, who were asked to obtain as many signatures as they could, but to keep the thing secret. A few days later the letter was issued again, with over fifty signatures, and now was circulated generally without note of secrecy. As a fact, it got out at once into the newspapers ; Ullathorne says some English bishops first saw it in the papers. The actual proposition to be signed was couched in these terms :

The undersigned Fathers humbly and earnestly beg the holy œcumenical Council to decree clearly and in words that cannot be mistaken, that the authority of the Roman Pontiff is supreme, and therefore immune from error, when,

[1] Purcell, *Life of Manning*, II, 453.
[2] Mansi, V (53), 276 ; *Lac* 1696.

in matters of faith and morals, he lays down and enjoins (statuit et praecipit) what is to be believed and held, and what is to be rejected and condemned, by all the Faithful.

There was added to the letter a statement of the reasons why the proposition was opportune and necessary, and an appendix giving pronouncements of various recent provincial Synods—Cologne, Utrecht, Prague, Kalocsa (Hungary), Baltimore, Westminster, all since 1850—asserting the papal infallibility.[1]

The signing of the petition went on throughout January. 'I remember', says Manning, ' our anxiety while the signatures were coming in, hindered and delayed by intrigue and misrepresentation.'[2] Some bishops, as those of Southern Italy, preferred forms of their own. Finally, by the end of January about 380 signatures were attached to the main petition, and about 100 to the others. At the same time counter-petitions, that the subject be not introduced, were going round and secured about 140 signatures.[3] At the end of January all the petitions were put in at the Congregation *de postulatis*.

The lists of signatures to these petitions make it possible to see how the bishops of the different countries ranged themselves. The case of France stands apart : for the rest, it may be said, in general, that the definition was favoured in Catholic countries in which there was no other strongly organized religion; while the oppositions and hesitations came from those countries in which Catholicism stood face to face with predominant Protestantism, or, as in Eastern Europe, Hungary and the Slavonic provinces of Austria, with

---

[1] Mansi, III (51), 644; *Lac* 931, 1703; the document is given in full in English in Manning's *True Story of the Vatican Council*, 113-21.

[2] Purcell, *Manning*, II, 453.

[3] All these petitions and lists of signatures are given in Mansi, loc. cit., 650-86, and *Lac* 923-50.

CARDINAL MATHIEU,
Archbishop of Besançon

CARDINAL DE BONNECHOSE,
Archbishop of Rouen

the various Eastern Orthodox Churches : in these countries the bishops feared definitions that might, by creating fresh obstacles, retard the progress of the Church, by making reunion and conversions more difficult.

In detail, the Spanish bishops, both of Spain and of Spanish America, and those of South Italy (Papal States and Kingdom of Naples) supported the definition almost unanimously ; and the Belgian and Polish bishops (all but Lemberg), and the Swiss (all but St. Gall), quite unanimously. The French petition against the definition bore thirty-six signatures : among them the Archbishops of Paris, Rheims, Avignon, Albi, Sens, and among the bishops Dupanloup, Meignan of Chalons (afterwards Archbishop of Tours and Cardinal), Dupont des Loges of Metz, Ginoulhiac of Grenoble (promoted during the Council to the Archbishopric of Lyons, the primatial see of France). The leader of this group of the French episcopate was Cardinal Mathieu, Archbishop of Besançon. The leader of the moderate Ultramontanes among the French bishops was Cardinal Bonnechose, Archbishop of Rouen ; with him were the Archbishops of Tours, Toulouse, Cambrai, Rennes, and Lavigerie, the Archbishop of Algiers, later Cardinal. On the extreme Ultramontane wing were Pie of Poitiers, Plantier of Nîmes, and Wicart of Laval. The bishops of the French portion of Canada for the most part favoured the definition. To the French petition against the definition were joined four Orientals, and a separate Oriental petition in the same sense bore sixteen signatures : the Oriental bishops were about equally divided. The Archbishops of Milan and Turin and five other bishops of North Italy sent in their own petition against the definition.

But it was from Germany and Austria that the opposition was the weightiest : the archbishops of all the great sees of Germany and the Austrian Empire, including Hungary and the Slav peoples, the Cardinal Archbishops of Vienna and Prague, the Archbishops of Salzburg (Primate of Germany), of Esztergom (Primate of Hungary), of Kalocsa (Hungary), and with them all the Hungarian bishops; of Cologne, of Munich, of Olmütz, of Bamberg, and most of the bishops, the most distinguished being Ketteler of Mayence, Hefele of Rottenburg, and Strossmayer of Bosnia : in all a formidable list of close on fifty names. The Ultramontanes were hardly a dozen, but among them were Fessler, the Secretary of the Council, Senestréy of Ratisbon (Regensburg), Martin of Paderborn, Gasser of Brixen, the last three among the foremost champions of the infallibility ; and some Bavarian and Tyrolese bishops.

The case of the English-speaking bishops is for us of special interest. Of the thirteen English bishops all but two were at the Council, the absentees being Brown of Newport, the senior bishop, who stayed in England, and Goss of Liverpool, who started for Rome, but was held invalided at Cannes ; and there was Archbishop Errington, Wiseman's retired coadjutor. Besides Manning, only two signed the petition for the infallibility to be brought on, Cornthwaite of Beverley, an extremist of the Manning type, and Grant of Southwark, a moderate old-fashioned Ultramontane. Clifford of Clifton was the only diocesan bishop to throw in his lot heartily with the Minority ; but with him was Errington. The other seven, no doubt following Ullathorne's example, stood aloof from all extra-conciliar movements ; but some of them, as Vaughan of Plymouth, Amherst of Northampton, Turner of Salford, certainly inclined to the inopportunist position. A letter from Goss to Newman shows that he was a Gallican. The Benedictine Hankinson, Bishop of Port Louis, Mauritius, was a supporter of the definition.

Of the Irish bishops all but four were on the Ultra-montane side, Cardinal Cullen of Dublin and Arch-bishop Leahy of Cashel being prominent supporters of the definition ; the dissentients were the famous John MacHale, Archbishop of Tuam, Moriarty of Kerry, one of the leading spirits of the Minority, Furlong of Ferns, and Leahy of Dromore, a Dominican. The Australian bishops too, all Irish, were solid for the definition.

The English-speaking North-American bishops were greatly divided. Archbishop Spalding of Balti-more led on the side of the definition ; with him were the Archbishops of New Orleans and San Francisco ; and five other United States bishops sent in a separate petition for the infallibility to be brought on. But Archbishops McCloskey of New York, Purcell of Cincinnati, Kenrick of St. Louis, also Connolly of Halifax, Canada, and nineteen bishops of the United States signed the English-speaking inopportunist peti-tion, among them the very remarkable Bernard McQuad of Rochester, whose life has recently been published in three volumes.

On the text of the petition for the introduction of the question of the Pope's infallibility becoming public, Döllinger printed in the Augsburg *Allgemeine Zeitung* of January 21 a long signed article, characterized by Ollivier as ' virulent ' : [1]

No one from the origin of the Church to our day has believed in the infallibility of the Pope, that is, as he believes in the Holy Trinity. At most, some have believed it to be probable, or humanly certain. The innovation in faith and in doctrine would be a unique event, the like of which has not happened in eighteen centuries. It would reduce the testimony of the Church to the testimony of the Pope bearing witness to himself ; but eighteen hundred and forty years ago One greater than the Pope said one day : ' If I

[1] *Lac* 1473.

bear witness of myself, my witness is not true.' The condition of *ex cathedra* was unknown for centuries. Florence was not œcumenical. The whole thing is a plot of the Jesuits, skilfully engineered during a long period.

And a week later he said that he knew most of the German bishops, in particular his own Archbishop of Munich, were in agreement with his views.

This brought Ketteler of Mayence into the field, to protest against such an assertion, and against Döllinger's agitation against the Council and the Holy See and the Church herself : [1]

> I agree only with the Döllinger whose lessons formerly used to fill his pupils with enthusiasm and love for the Church and the Holy Apostolic See ; I have nothing in common with the Döllinger whom the enemies of the Church and of the Holy See are to-day loading with praises.

The Archbishops of Cologne and Munich and other bishops published similar protests, calling on their flocks to be loyal to Church and Council, whatever the outcome might be. Manning is certainly right in saying that the Minority bishops were compromised and handicapped by the disloyal agitation of Döllinger and Friedrich.

It will now be of interest to have Bishop Ullathorne's comments on the course of events inside and outside the Council during this phase :

> Jan. 8. I have formally declined uniting with any party representing extreme views. Still I believe that even these have their value, and compel reflection on important points that otherwise would escape sufficient attention. Of course I am talking of what passes outside the Council, not inside. There also is going on an agitation, variously viewed by various groups of prelates, on that subject about which all the world is talking. That it will be brought on

---

[1] *Lac* 1485.

is certain ; that it will lead to long and anxious discussion is equally certain ; that the temporal powers are doing their utmost in vain to stop it is a fact of which you may be assured ; that it will not be brought in by the Pope is also a determined fact. But I have seen a printed paper that is being very cautiously circulated in private, the object of which is to get a list of signatures for its introduction.

You would be amused to see how one gets sounded by first this prelate, then that, and how one has to fence for the purpose of keeping one's liberty intact for within the walls of the Council. For it is not so much the interior of the Council as the outside of it that is such a little world, bringing out the ways of many and different natures ; all, however, in earnest, all feeling a deep sense of responsibility, but some, one thinks, trying to manage their neighbour perhaps a little too much. Still, the general character of the episcopate is high-mindedness, straightforwardness, and deep conscientiousness.

Jan. 16. I have just been having a conversation with Cardinal Pitra [the Benedictine Cardinal of the French Congregation] on the position of things. He of course reflects the general sentiments of the Powers that be. There is a general satisfaction at the position of things in the Council ; a full expectation of a definition of the infallibility, of which not a word has yet been uttered in the Council, but which is so vividly agitated out of doors ; and a great, indeed an intense, desire to have it settled on the part of the higher Powers, thinking it will put an end to many internal controversies. I am quite disposed myself for a moderate declaration, well-balanced, provided something is said to strengthen the bishops in their own dioceses.

On January 20 Ullathorne wrote to Newman :

It has occurred to me that a letter from me would not be unacceptable to you. I therefore write before I get too much involved in the labours of the special deputation of discipline, to which I was, however unworthy, elected.

We have now got through all the preliminaries and formalities, and the Council is fairly at work, and my impression is that it will ultimately do a good work for the Church.

But large bodies move slowly, and the Roman Curia is unaccustomed to the craft of managing great assemblies engaged in discussion. They are also naturally timid of innovations, and cling to such traditions, especially those from Trent, as remain recorded. Now Trent at its fullest had but 200 prelates, whereas there are above 760 in the present Council. The difficulty of the aula as an auditorium has been tolerably mastered as far as ordinarily good voices are concerned, and as many of the speakers prefer reading from a paper, they can better manage their voices. I have myself so good a position that I hear everything with ease. Nor is there much, indeed I may say there is no real difficulty arising from difference of pronunciation. At least I find none, and hear but few in any case complaining. A little more usage will remove the last relics of that difficulty from all except those who may suffer from deafness.

There is no stiffness in the demeanour of the assembled Council ; and there is a good deal of coming and going in a quiet way without interference with the speaker, who addresses from an ambo from the lower end of the aula. An awning stretched from the ambo end over a third of the space detains the voice from ascending. In Congregation, as opposed to Session, when we have twice the length of space, the bishops are confronted, twenty lines to twenty opposite lines on tiers ; besides which the steps in the tribune and the whole space between the throne, the Presidents' tables, and the steps, are covered with seats filled by bishops. Thus it is one mass of many-coloured mantellettas, and episcopal faces, and a very lively scene ever in gentle waving motion, unless when some able speaker rivets attention. There has not hitherto been any visible hesitation or bungling in the use of the Latin language, even when reading was dispensed with.

We are under pontifical secrecy, provided for in the consecration oath, with respect to the matters brought before the Council, and with respect to what is said in their discussion. But everything else, such as who are voted for, who are the speakers, etc., go into the Roman papers before they reach you in your own journals. Some French journals, such as *La France* and *Le Français* have more, and more accurate, information of what passes than the English papers. The *Tablet* is far from accurate in many of its details.

As to the *Times*, until lately it was ridiculous and absurd in almost every statement. Its correspondent was evidently hoaxed of set purpose by the Roman wits. Both its ordinary correspondent, and even Mozley who was sent expressly, complained that other writers' statements were put in, in preference to theirs. Now, however, up to the last receipts, the *Times* has grown more sober and nearer the truth.

Thus far the Germans have exhibited the greatest solidity and closeness to the business in hand. The Hungarians have delighted by the fluent and pliable ease with which they use the Latin as a vernacular tongue. The French, with two very marked exceptions, have been rhetorical; but these two exceptions exhibited, the one close and solid learning, and the other very great tact and shrewdness in debate. The Northern Americans have been able and businesslike. The Italians have presented opposite qualities; some clever and to the point, others mere academical preachers. The Spaniards have been least successful, whether for judgement or handling the point in hand. I see a good deal of leading American prelates who all have a great affection and respect for you. Indeed I am at the American College frequently, for deputations from the English-speaking countries meet there periodically for the consideration of our disciplinary requirements.

You will hear a good deal of movements outside of the Council, and, indeed, I wish there was less of them; but they certainly began on what may be called the 'ultra' side, which naturally led to efforts at counter-organization. But everything will find its level, though this may require a little time. Many reputations will be marred and made in this Council, and the true metal, tried in the fire of patience, will come out at last. For my part, I decline all invitations to all reunions of a party character,—to all moves in fact, that can be construed into partisanship outside the Council, and have made my rule known that I will put hand to no petitions or propositions on this side or that.

I hear all sides, say my say when I think it prudent, and keep my course for the interior of the Council. The Pope said to most of the nations at their audience : ' You will find the Holy Ghost inside the Council, not outside of it.' Still, I allow that prelates must understand one another, and that each nation must confer on its own requirements, and there must be understandings come to as to joint action. I think, however, you will understand me.

Be assured of this, that Rome itself is learning a great deal about the state of the Church, and of the position of the faithful in their divers countries, and that the very freest speech is used, consistent with that mutual respect which the authorities of the Church owe to each other. One great result of the Council must necessarily be the widening of knowledge and experience on the part of Rome as well as on that of the universal episcopate. For the rest, even the strongest adversaries, in so far as questions of ecclesiastical polity are concerned, are full of kindness and courtesy towards each other, even to great edification.

This letter it was that called from Newman that one which, becoming public by a misadventure, caused so great a stir throughout the world. An account of the whole episode is given in the *Life of Ullathorne* (II, 58-64) and need not be repeated here ; but it seems necessary to include Newman's letter in any History of the Council ;—and all the more so in that Ullathorne's reply is full of interesting material :

Jan. 28. My dear Lord : I thank your Lordship very heartily for your most interesting and seasonable letter. Such letters, if they could be circulated, would do much to reassure the many minds which are at present distressed when they look towards Rome. Rome ought to be a name to lighten the heart at all times, and a Council's proper office is, when some great heresy or other evil impends, to inspire the faithful with hope and confidence ; but now we have the greatest meeting which ever has been, and that at Rome, infusing into us by the accredited organs of Rome and its partisans (such as the *Civiltà*, the *Armonia*, the *Univers*, and the *Tablet*) little else than fear and dismay.

When we are all at rest, and have no doubts, and—at least practically, not to say doctrinally—hold the Holy Father to be infallible, suddenly there is thunder in the clear sky, and we are told to prepare for something we know not what, to try our faith we know not how. No impending danger is to be averted, but a great difficulty is to be created. Is this the proper work for an œcumenical Council? As to myself personally, please God, I do not expect any trial at all; but I cannot help suffering with the various souls which are suffering, and I look with anxiety at the prospect of having to defend decisions which may not be difficult to my private judgement, but may be most difficult to maintain logically in face of historical facts. What have we done to be treated as the faithful never were treated before? When has definition of doctrine *de Fide* been a luxury of devotion, and not a stern painful necessity? Why should an aggressive insolent faction be allowed to 'make the heart of the just to mourn, whom the Lord hath not made sorrowful'? Why can't we be let alone, when we have pursued peace, and thought no evil? I assure you, my dear Lord, some of the truest minds are driven one way and another, and do not know where to rest their feet, one day determining to give up all theology as a bad job, and recklessly to believe henceforth almost that the Pope is impeccable; at another tempted to believe all the worst that a book like *Janus* says; others doubting about the capacity possessed by bishops, drawn from all corners of the earth, to judge what is fitting for European society, and then again angry with the Holy See for listening to the flattery of a clique of Jesuits, Redemptorists and converts.

Then, again, think of the store of pontifical scandals in the history of eighteen centuries which have partly been poured out and partly are still to come. What Murphy inflicted upon us in one way, M. Veuillot indirectly is bringing on us in another.

And then again, the blight which is falling upon the multitude of Anglican ritualists, etc., who themselves perhaps, at least their leaders, may never become Catholics, but who are leavening the various English denominations and parties (far beyond their own range) with principles and sentiments tending towards their ultimate absorption in the Catholic Church.

With these thoughts before me, I am continually asking myself whether I ought not to make my feelings public; but all I do is to pray those great early Doctors of the Church, whose intercession would decide the matter—Augustine and the rest—to avert so great a calamity. If it is God's Will that the Pope's infallibility should be defined, then is it His blessed Will to throw back 'the times and the moments' of that triumph which He has destined for His Kingdom; and I shall feel I have but to bow my head to His adorable, inscrutable Providence. You have not touched upon the subject yourself; but I think you will allow me to express to you feelings which for the most part I keep to myself.

Ullathorne replied :

Feb. 4. Your letter received to-day, and written with true tact, and deep feeling of the position created by the zealots, but repeats with force what many here are feeling, as well as yourself. But I think I may venture to say that the zealots are doomed to future confusion. Some are in fact beginning to find it already.

As the question of which you speak has not yet been even breathed within the Council Chamber, I may venture to give you some information as to its actual position outside of it.

Cardinal Bilio [President of the special deputation de Fide] informed an American archbishop, who informed me, only two days since, that although a schema de Summo Pontifice has been prepared, it had been decided to put it aside, and not to present it, in so far as that important question of the infallibility was concerned. But when Maret and Dupanloup came out so strongly in antagonism, then it was thought desirable to do something. This recent information takes us back to the starting point.

I, of course, do not forget that one of these prelates

was roused up by excesses on the other side, nor do I forget who roused him.[1]

When I reached Rome I found a fiery propagandist action in full play on the part of our friend [i.e. Manning] and certain others whose names are well known. This roused up counter-action. And that again stimulated the zealots. Meanwhile Rome watched and kept quiet. After a while Archbishop Manning's proposition and circular began to be criticized.[2] It was never shown to the English bishops, Archbishop Manning declaring to me that he kept away from us through delicacy. Some of us saw it first in the French papers or the *Times*. So soon as I saw it I pronounced that it did not incorporate the doctrine of infallibility at all. The ' suprema ideoque irreversibilis auctoritas ' was just our own constitutional doctrine : there being no tribunal above him, the King can do no wrong. The Neapolitans saw this, and their copy struck out the ' suprema ideoque ', and kept the rest. The Spaniards also and South Americans drew up their own. Thus the boasted signatures were appended to not one but different documents, not one of which, I believe, included the word ' infallible '.

On the opposite side many of the 150 signed Schwarzen-berg's document, or some other—there were three on the other side also,—with the sole view of enforcing modera-tion. It became well-known also that many who, like the Bishop of Poitiers [Pie] and myself, refused to sign any document, were disposed to moderation. The Americans [as Spalding of Baltimore and others] were very anxious to avoid the word ' infallible ', and drew up a document in which they rehearsed the former decrees in favour of the Pontificate, and added a censure on the Four Gallican Articles.

The Pope has refused to receive personally any of these presentations, referring them to the Congregation he has appointed to receive ' proponenda ' for the Council. He is

[1] He refers to Manning's pastoral and the controversy that arose out of it between him and Dupanloup.

[2] The petition for the introduction of the Infallibility, above, p. 203.

also reported to have said that he would be contented with a negative definition.

For my part, I have quietly and in private maintained that I should not oppose a calm and moderate definition, *provided* it was duly balanced by strengthening the authority of the episcopate ; provided also it was duly limited, so as to save us from enthusiastic and fanatical interpretations. And I have insisted on the importance of reviving the old canon in the Sexto, against laymen leading in theological writing and publishing.[1]

My personal position must necessarily call for my further explanation. One or two of the zealots made free with my name : I was a Gallican, I had signed the Remonstrance, etc. These false accusations roused me. I saw two cardinals and had a very plain talk with them, not merely about this, but about the entire position and views of the English bishops. This brought out to me in confidence that our position and relations, both in England and here, were being quite understood. Further it began to appear on all sides that the zealots were getting them here into an awkward position, which would not do. They are beginning to descend, and calmer and more prudential views are taking ascendancy. One cardinal assured me that, though in consequence of court intrigues and anti-papal writings, something must now come in, yet it would be proposed in such very moderate terms that it will not fail to meet the wishes of the moderate of all parties. And the American archbishop, before alluded to, told me but yesterday that he also had been assured by the cardinal who knew most of the matter, that the proposition would be most moderate. My general knowledge enables me to say that this, amongst other things, implies the omission of the word ' infallible ', and I apprehend also the limitation to some such terms as the obedience due to Pontifical decisions and their irreversibility.

I speak therefore of what is passing outside the Council. In a short time the question will come before it, and then my tongue will be tied. And of course, though I write this to you, I could not with propriety write so to others.

---

[1] Such cases as Ward and Veuillot.

But in your prudence I feel myself safe. Of this you may be quite assured, that the most active and politic agitation of strong measures is going down on all sides, and is beginning to be found inconvenient. The weather-wise, even among the praelati, are beginning to say, ' I don't sail in ——'s track ; he overdoes it '.

Be assured, my dear friend, that whatever mischief is doing outside by our own newspapers, to which so many of us are alive, moderation will be the upshot in the Council. If you could but see, as I see, schemata brought in, only to be pulled to pieces and sent out again, bleeding in every limb, to be reconstructed by the special deputations by the light given in the Council, you would realize how the general sense of the Fathers prevails over all party views and idiosyncracies.

You may have heard of this or that prelate being called to order. But in the rare instances in which this has occurred, there have been real excesses, and that beyond the point in hand, and the whole sense of the Council has gone with the Presidents. What the bishops universally feel, and want to get corrected, just as in the Council of Trent, is that often the time of the Council is abused by irrelevant matter. And the Presidents set us all an example of patience. The Pope spoke of you very kindly the other day.

God bless you and the brethren.

CHAPTER XII

QUESTIONS OF DISCIPLINE AND CANON LAW

It was on January 10 that the schema on Catholic doctrine was sent out from the Council to the deputation *de Fide* to be remodelled; and it was not until March 18 that the revision was presented at a General Congregation. The period was used for the treatment of matters of ecclesiastical discipline, practically the reform of the canon law. Twenty-eight schemata on points of discipline had been drawn up before the Council by the commission of canonists and theologians;[1] but only four came under discussion at the Council. The first two had been distributed on January 8; the discussion began on 14th. The first was on 'bishops, synods, and vicars general'; the second on 'the vacancy of episcopal sees'. The former was in seven chapters; the bishop's office, residence, visitation of diocese, visit *ad limina* (i.e. visit to Rome at stated intervals), provincial and diocesan synods, the vicar general, with Annotations.[2]

The general discussion of the two schemata 'as a whole' opened on January 14; it went on during seven Congregations, thirty-seven bishops taking part. On January 25 the two schemata were remitted for revision to the deputation *de Disciplina :* of this deputation Ullathorne was a member.

The course of the proceedings seems to show that

[1] They will be found in Mansi, V (53), 721-84.
[2] Mansi, II (50), 339-58 ; *Lac* 641-55.

218

public debate at a General Council was not a practical way of reforming the canon law. Only if, as seems to have been expected, the prepared schemata had been accepted with small discussion or amendment, could the thing have been possible. But the disciplinary schemata were subjected to the same fire of criticism as the dogmatic schema. Only a few outstanding features of the debates can be noticed, as illustrating the history and atmosphere of the Council. A pocket notebook of Ullathorne's survives in which he took pencil notes at the debates on discipline, being, as a member of the deputation, particularly concerned in them.

At the outset, January 14, the Cardinal President exhorted all speakers to study brevity, not wandering from the subject, nor repeating what had already been said.

The debate was opened by Cardinal Schwarzenberg, Archbishop of Prague : [1]

He wondered that the schema began with the bishops, not a word being said, unlike Trent, about the cardinals, or the Roman Curia, or the Roman Congregations ; though it is common knowledge that desires exist on these subjects. As to the bishops, only their duties and obligations are spoken of ; not a word is said on their status as successors of the Apostles, their office and dignity, jurisdiction and rights, and canonical position. Nor is anything said about the mode of election and appointment ; this seems greatly needed, as in most countries the nomination lies with the Government.[2]

Cardinal Mathieu, Archbishop of Besançon, and Simor, Archbishop of Esztergom, spoke in like strain : the latter raised a laugh by a protest against the expression ' Morbidae pecudes ' as neither Scriptural nor

---

[1] The debates Jan. 14-25 are in Mansi, II (50), 358-518.
[2] It is worthy of note that the points raised by Schwarzenberg are met in the Codex of Pius X.

patristic,—bishops are shepherds of 'oves', not of 'pecudes'.

On 14th two more disciplinary schemata were distributed.

The next day a Piedmontese bishop said that bishops are told, should exhortations fail, to apply correction : this is impossible in these days ; something should be found more consonant to the actual conditions of modern society.

Mgr. Darboy, the Archbishop of Paris, made a long and outspoken criticism of the schema and of the whole method of procedure. As a sample of the full freedom of speech used by the bishops and allowed without let or hindrance by the Presidents, it will not be amiss to give an outline : [1]

He called for a summary programme of the full business proposed to be transacted at the Council. Forty days had now been spent on particular questions brought forward without order or connexion. What were the evils to be cured, and what the remedies proposed ? They had hoped that a conspectus of the proposed work of the Council would be provided, not in an oratorical and diffuse form of words, but a short synopsis, that they might have before their minds what they were aiming at. If the principles were laid down the solution of particular and less important things would follow. But we are confusedly walking through a thicket of particulars and the vain and uncertain 'placita' of the schools. We are gravely discussing questions for canonists, and are being set to labour over all kinds of trivialities (puerilia).

Many had been fearing that the Vatican Council was going to attempt greater things than a sick society could bear. My fear is, lest having arrested the attention and the expectation of all, the Council be found unequal to the task it took in hand, in the judgement of those who make up that queen of the world, public opinion.

He turned to the schema : like Schwarzenberg and

---

[1] Mansi, II (50), 400.

others he complained that only the duties of bishops were spoken of, not their status, powers, jurisdiction, rights. It is neither logical, useful, or becoming to speak of the duties of bishops unless their rights have previously been asserted. And what a poor idea it is of a bishop's duties ! Residence, visitation of the diocese, visit *ad limina,* provincial and diocesan synods,—is this the whole duty of a bishop ! It seems as though the canonist who made the schema had looked out on the world from the recesses of a cavern or of a cell. He does indeed speak of the relations of bishops with princes and magistrates,—but how unhappily (infauste) does he touch on this question ! What ignorance of things, what want of care in words ! It looks as if they were written by a doctor of a royal court, who looks on religion as a department of the State. It regards a condition of things quite passed away in most countries. . . .

Finally, on the practice of making honorary vicars general, which the schema orders to be abolished at all costs : if such honorary titles are to be abolished, let the protonotaries and the innumerable honorary prelates at Rome be abolished also. These honorary titles are either desirable everywhere, or undesirable everywhere.

In conclusion : Let all the schemata to be brought forward be given to the bishops at once ; and let this schema ' de episcopis ' be sent out to the deputation to be emended, proper account being had of the rights and dignity of bishops ; and be reintroduced, corrected and augmented, no longer jejune and shapeless (informe), but such as may be approved by this venerable Council of so many and such great bishops.

It was a forcible and eloquent speech in good and easy Latin. Darboy was followed by Melchers, Archbishop of Cologne. He spoke against the tendency to over-centralization in the government of the Church : bishops' faculties should be increased, not given, ' ad quinquennium ' but ' durante officio ' ; bishops being ' Ordinaries ' ought not to need extraordinary faculties for dealing with constantly recurring matrimonial cases.

Here the President intervened: This being new matter, it could not be introduced at a General Congregation, but should be submitted to the Congregation *de postulatis*.

This, on January 19, was only the second intervention of the Presidents in the course of the debates. On the same day the President said to an Italian bishop: 'Right Reverend Father, I beg of you this one thing, that you do not wander from the point, but keep to the subject under discussion.' Ullathorne has a note: 'A display of rhetoric—cardinals and bishops laughing. President called him *ad rem*. He was coming to the point—went on as before, everybody laughing.' There was no further intervention on the part of the Presidents during the course of this debate, to January 25, though some of the speeches were of prodigious length, Strossmayer's running to thirteen columns of Mansi.

The debate over, and the two schemata remitted to the deputation, an analytic synopsis was prepared of all the criticisms and exceptions that had been made in the speeches or in papers privately submitted to the deputation.[1] The minutes of the deputation *de Disciplina* are not printed in either edition of the Acts of the Council; but it appears from Ullathorne's letters that several sessions were held over the amending of the schemata. The revised schema *de episcopis* never was brought before the Council; but it is given in Mansi (V (53), 721). In compliance with the general wish, a very ample statement is prefixed, setting forth the status, dignity, and rights of bishops:

Bishops hold the highest grade in the divinely instituted hierarchy, and so great is their dignity that in Holy Scripture they are decorated with the title of 'angels'. For, being placed by the Holy Ghost to rule the Church of God, they

[1] Mansi, II (50), 865-900.

are higher than priests; in the place of the Apostles, to whom they have succeeded in the episcopacy, they exercise a legation for Christ. Hence it pertains to them to feed the flock of Christ, to guard the deposit of Faith, and out of the plenitude of the priesthood, which they enjoy, to ordain the ministers of the Church. So great being the height of the episcopal order, let all, laity and especially clergy, yield to them all rightful honour, reverence, and obedience.

Out of the debate on the schema *de episcopis* arose, not one of the scenes, but one of the episodes of the Council. As it was one of the two occasions on which the Pope administered a personal rebuke to a bishop for things said at the Council, it will be well to tell the story, even at the cost of a small digression.[1] The affair had to do with the Oriental bishops. Not counting the four Patriarchs of the Latin rite, all Italians; or certain vicars apostolic of the Latin rite, as of Syria or Egypt, also Italians: there were at the Council just fifty genuine Oriental bishops, four of them Patriarchs. They were the bishops of the various Uniat Eastern Churches, of the Greek, Armenian, Syrian, Chaldean, and other rites. These Eastern Churches have ever been fearful of Latinization, clinging with jealous loyalty to their liturgies, traditions, customs, practices. So far as the liturgies were concerned, for all the indiscretions of some Latin missionaries, the Holy See has steadily safeguarded them; but certain customs and practices have not found the like favour, in particular the manner of appointing bishops and patriarchs. They were elected by clergy and people, and consecrated and installed without recurrence to the Holy See. The patriarchs entered on their jurisdiction at once, but asked for the Pope's ratification and took an oath of fidelity. The Council of Florence in the articles of Union had recognized

---

[1] See Mourret, 226-42; Granderath, II, Bk. ii, c. 5.

the position. But it was little in accord with the mind of Rome, and in 1867 a bull ' Reversurus ' was issued bringing the procedure into line with Western practice, and requiring papal confirmation before consecration. This bull had occasioned a schism among the Armenian Uniats, and very nearly another among the Chaldeans, averted with difficulty by Mgr. Audu, Patriarch of Babylon of the Chaldeans. In these circumstances the Oriental bishops came to the Council their minds full of forebodings of what might be in store for their privileges, customs, and even their rites. Audu became their spokesman, and he was the last speaker in the debate 'on bishops', January 25 : or rather his was the last speech, translated from Chaldaic into Latin, read by the Archbishop of Sens :

It would seem that a plan is afoot to establish one and the same discipline for the Western and the Eastern Churches, and to enact one and the same corpus of canon law for both. Perhaps the illustrious consultors thought that there is little or no difference between the laws, customs, rites of the two Churches. But in reality they differ as far as the rising of the sun is from its setting, as far as a convalescent sick man is from a robust warrior. Bishops, priests, people are, many of them, raw converts from Nestorianism ; churches, schools, seminaries are lacking ; in many places Christians are slaughtered or transported, and churches are destroyed. Yet are the Chaldeans wonderfully faithful to their Catholic religion. Judge then if it be possible to legislate for such a desolated church the same as for the flourishing churches of the West. In the things of Faith, whatever may be decreed by the Council will be accepted as a matter of course ; but concerning canons of discipline the like cannot be said. The Orientals are so tenacious of their ancient discipline that even small things cannot be changed without tumult and scandals and danger to souls. In view of the circumstances he urged that not all disciplinary canons can be applied indiscriminately to all the Churches ; that in each patriarchate any reformation to be attempted should be made in view of the actual conditions, to be considered by national synods ; and as the practical solution, he begged the Pope to allow the Oriental bishops to consider any disciplinary canons of the Council, and to compose a corpus of canon law for the Eastern Churches, combining these canons with the old canons and constitutions of those Churches, this new code to be submitted for approval to the Council.

At his consecration as Patriarch he had sworn to preserve and hand on intact all the privileges and all the rites of the patriarchate. Any changes in these things would make more difficult the return to Catholic unity of the separated Eastern Churches. When the Uniat bodies had been received back from schism to the bosom of the Catholic Church, it had been under the definite condition and pact that there would be no change in the canons, rites, prerogatives, constitutions, customs and rights of their Church. To violate this contract would be against justice, and a grave scandal alike to Uniats and to the separated.

Granderath and Mourret agree that there was nothing in this speech that need have offended the Pope ; and they think that had he waited until seeing the stenographer's report he would not have been greatly moved. But before he saw the report an account had been given to him immediately after the Congregation, no doubt by Cardinal Barnabò, Prefect of Propaganda, the prime mover in the effort to overrule the independent customs of the Oriental Churches, to whom Audu's speech must have been greatly displeasing. However it was, Audu was summoned that same evening to the Pope's presence and had a scolding : what the Pope said has not transpired, but he called on Audu under pain of deposition to sign there and then a paper undertaking to consecrate two bishops nominated by the Pope a couple of years previously, but whom he had not consecrated in face of the agitation called forth thereby. It was said that on leaving the Pope's presence he remarked to the Oriental bishops that he did not consider himself bound by the signature. The upshot was a schism in the Chaldean Church, lasting some years; and trouble went on between the patriarch and the Holy See over the consecration of bishops without the Pope's confirmation. After Audu's death, Leo XIII spoke of him as a 'bishop conspicuous for piety and religion' (Mourret, 235). For the rest, the Holy See has allowed the matter of the appointment of the patriarchs and bishops of the Oriental Uniat Churches to lie in abeyance (so Mourret, 241). It is worthy of note that canon 1 of the new Codex states that it is for the Latin Church alone, and does not apply to the Oriental Churches.[1]

The third disciplinary schema, on the Manner of Life of the clergy, 'de vita et honestate clericorum ',[2] distributed on January 14, was introduced at the General Congregation of January 25. The discussion went on through eight Congregations, thirty-eight speaking, till on February 8 the schema was remitted to the deputation *de Disciplina*. On the first day spoke the Cardinal Archbishop of Seville and the Primate of Hungary, who raised the question of the reform of the Breviary. Martin of Paderborn pleaded strongly for beards for the clergy, enforcing his argument by pointing to the bearded Oriental and Capuchin bishops. Verot of Savannah urged that it should be forbidden for clerics to hunt with guns, that 'there never may be exhibited to the faithful

---

[1] Granderath (loc. cit.) questions that the audience with the Pope was occasioned by Audu's speech, but was the sequel of events before the Council. The account in the text is Mourret's, based on Icard's Diary. Icard was likely to be well informed, being theologian of the Archbishop of Sens, the one who read out Audu's speech to the Council. Friedrich's account may be set aside as entirely tendentious and exaggerated.

[2] Mansi, II (50), 517-22; *Lac* 659.

people the disgraceful spectacle of a man of God going about the roads and fields shooting birds and beasts '. He spoke also of the breviary : some things in it cannot be read with gravity and reverence, as St. Augustine's explanation of the thirty-eight years the sick man at the pool of Bethsaida had been in his infirmity—' I must confess I can never read this without distraction '.

President : Let the Right Reverend speaker speak with greater reverence of the holy Fathers.

Verot : I do wish, Eminence, to speak with all reverence of the holy Fathers ; but ' aliquando bonus dormitat Homerus '. He went on : apocryphal stories and incongruous homilies—as St. Gregory's, that the end of the world is at hand—should be removed.

President : The subject of discussion is the Life of the Clergy ; the speaker has sufficiently expressed his desire for the reform of the breviary.

Verot : I would like to add something about the corrections of the breviary that have been made : the matter is of great importance.

President : If he does not speak of the Life of the Clergy, let him make way for another speaker.

Verot : I willingly obey ; although I think the matter of reciting the office with reverence is intimately connected with the Life of the Clergy.

Of the English bishops Clifford spoke : Many of the proposed regulations were not possible for general application. In regard to the breviary, he urged that provision be made for the weekly recitation of the whole Psalter.[1]

Haynald of Kalocsa, Hungary, spoke at great length (nine columns), especially on the reform of the breviary : it should not be tolerated that anything

---

[1] This desire has been realized in Pius X's reform of the breviary.

fabulous or false be contained in the great prayer-book of priests ; it is high time that the intentions of various Pontiffs in this matter be carried into effect.

The Bishop of Coutances spoke for so long that he exhausted the patience of the audience, and several began conversing with one another ; to whom he said : ' If you who are talking wish to mount into the ambo, you can do so.' Another bishop failed to hear the President's bell thrice calling him to order for wandering ; he apologized the next day. On February 8 the schema was remitted to the deputation, and the discussion began on the fourth schema, the proposal for a standard elementary catechism for the whole Church ; forty-one spoke thereon at six Congregations. Great divergence of opinion was manifested, especially on the proposal that Bellarmine's catechism, in use at Rome, should be the norm ; the German bishops were very adverse to the supplanting of Canisius' catechism by any other, it being in universal use throughout the German lands, and most excellent in itself. A Spanish bishop declared that as the Pope said : ' I lay before you a universal catechism for the Church of God, all we bishops should say " So be it, so be it," and nothing more. He who sitteth on the throne, surrounded by the four and twenty elders, is the Roman Pontiff surrounded by the bishops, who, as often as and along with him they decree something in faith or discipline, cast their crowns before the throne, saying, " Benediction and glory and wisdom and thanksgiving and honour to our God for ever and ever." And so when the supreme Pontiff says a catechism is necessary, let us cast down our crowns, and say ' : etc.

The debate ended February 22 ; on this day occurred one of the lesser scenes of the Council. Haynald was speaking and was criticizing severely the shortcomings of Bellarmine's catechism. His remarks

MGR. SIMOR,
Archbishop of Esztergom :
Primate of Hungary

MGR. HAYNALD,
Archbishop of Kalocsa, Hungary

called forth vehement expressions of disapproval. He went on : ' Someone had said that the " shadow of Peter " would heal the schemata. It was the sick that the shadow of Peter healed, and therefore those proclaimed the schemata to be sick and infirm who had recourse to the shadow of Peter to cure them (murmurs of indignation). To catechize the people is one of the great duties and rights of a bishop ; if a catechism is dictated to us, our sermons will next be dictated.' (A tumult of indignation ; voices rising from all sides hindered the speaker from being heard. The President called for silence by a gesture, and the speaker went on :) He had obtained from the Presidents permission to make an explanation in regard to his criticisms on the breviary, made in the previous debate, February 4 : he had not made an attack on the breviary itself, but had urged that it needed reform, certain blemishes being removed. ' If there was any offence in this, I have as accomplices the Fathers of the Council of Trent ; I have as accomplices the supreme Pontiffs who have effected reforms in the breviary ; I have as accomplices those great and pious men who cherish this same desire of mine. . . .'

Cardinal Capalti, one of the Presidents, interrupted : You have sufficiently declared your mind as to what you said on the emending of the breviary. Further words are quite useless and most annoying to the Council. Put an end to this already long enough speech, and give place to another speaker.

Haynald : I certainly would have finished my speech. . . .

Capalti : You have made your explanations, and that is enough about them. Anything further will only be boring (non inserviunt nisi ad taedium) ; therefore it is enough.

Haynald : I have used my right.

But he was interrupted again and again by the

bishops, who applauded Capalti's words, and on a definite sign he came down.

This closed the debate and the schema was remitted to the deputation on discipline. There was a break in the holding of General Congregations of a month's duration, from February 22 until March 18, during which time an effort was made to alter the arrangement of the aula and lessen the acoustic difficulties. It will be convenient to anticipate things and pursue to the end the matter of the catechism.

Four schemata on discipline had been discussed and sent to the deputation for amendment, and the deputation had been at work on them; but the Catechism was the only one that came on for further discussion at the General Congregations. The speeches had been analysed and scheduled,[1] and when the deputation met it was agreed unanimously that there should be a standard elementary catechism, and that it should be imposed universally as obligatory; also, that Bellarmine's be taken as the basis of the new catechism. The schema was in great part rewritten, and was distributed on April 25, the day after the Third Public Session.[2] The discussion on the revised form began on 29th. There still was much dissatisfaction: Cardinal Rauscher (whose speech was read for him by Hefele) still thought the idea undesirable and impracticable; it was most undesirable to supplant in the German lands the catechism of Canisius, which is quite as orthodox as Bellarmine's (murmurs of the Fathers; the speaker, ' Listen, kindly '). If such a catechism be made it should not be imposed as of obligation.

Verot urged that any vote taken now should be provisional, no final vote being given until the actual catechism be drawn up and laid before the Council.

The next day Vaughan of Plymouth made a short

---

[1] Mansi, II (50), 931-44.
[2] Mansi, III (51), 449-56; *Lac* 664.

speech : to his mind Bellarmine's, as an elementary catechism for children, was, of all known to him, the least adapted to the needs of our time, too diffuse in parts, and in others inadequate. Also, the proposed catechism should be submitted at the Council. 'Though nervous, he got through very well,' says Ullathorne.

Clifford followed with a conciliatory speech.

The emendations proposed were considered by the deputation. They principally centred round two points : the imposition of the catechism as of universal obligation, the bishops of Germany and Austria objecting to the suppression of the Canisius catechism ; [1] and the allowing the actual drawing up of the catechism to pass wholly from the control of the Council and the bishops into the hands of Roman theologians.

On May 4 the votes were taken on the emendations one by one, and nearly all were rejected by large majorities. The schema as a whole was then put to the vote. There voted : placet, 491 ; non-placet, 56 ; placet iuxta modum, 44 (i.e. with a reservation to be expressed in writing and put in with the vote). The reservations are scheduled, Mansi III (51), 514-34 ; they were dealt with by the spokesman of the deputation at the Congregation of May 13. And here the matter of an Elementary Catechism was dropped ; though ready for presentation, it was not brought on at a Public Session for the final voting and enactment. The fact was that the great debate on Church and Papacy had begun and was engrossing the entire attention of all, so that catechism and discipline had faded out of view.

In fact, the proposal of the catechism has remained inoperative, no move ever having been made since the

---

[1] St. Peter Canisius having since been canonized, and created a Doctor of the Church, the attitude of the German bishops would no doubt command greater consideration now than it did at the Council.

Council to give effect to the idea of a standard elementary catechism for the whole Church. The use of local catechisms has gone on, according to the mind of the Minority bishops at the Council.

Ullathorne's letters follow, dealing with this phase of the Council:

Jan. 20. Passing by your General [the Master General of the Dominicans] at the last Congregation, as I often have to do, a long speech was going on, he put out his hand smiling, and said, ' One has need of a good deal of patience '; so I whispered in his ear, ' Yes, I sometimes think of what is said in the Book of Maccabees, that the Romans hold possession of all things through their counsel and patience.' [1] He saw there was a meaning below the surface and laughed out. Of course these Roman cardinals with all their shrewdness are sitting patiently four hours a day, and taking every man's measure ; but on the other hand, they are also getting a good many lessons themselves. In that Congregation we had two of the most remarkable addresses yet delivered. And one could speak of the two million souls in his diocese [Darboy of Paris] ; the other of the 800 parishes in his, which it took him ten years to visit [Melchers of Cologne]. The ability and importance of one prelate [no doubt Darboy] hung all ears upon his lips from beginning to end, and there were shrewd hits too, though given with the velvet glove in all politeness, as well as a large survey of ecclesiastical polity, and of the position of the Church, and of reforms deemed to be needful. It is worthy of remark that it is the great men, of great sees, who are the first in taking large and comprehensive views, and who give up contracted notions with the least sparing hand.

Jan. 21. We have generally about two great men up amongst the speakers each day. To-day it was Bishop Ketteler of Mayence and the Bishop of Orleans. Both were able, each represented his country. The German close, solid, not throwing away a word, and saying many valuable

[1] 1 Mac. viii, 3.

things. The Frenchman eloquent, rhetorical, yet saying some very good things, and treating one important point fully. He was the only man yet to whom many bishops, including leading men, paid the compliment of crowding down in the middle, and there standing as close as they could to hear him more perfectly. He told me he had lost one eye and the other is very weak. It was much observed that his recent adversary in polemical warfare, Archbishop Manning, stood in front of all the listeners who had left their places for the purpose of hearing better.

We had a new schema delivered to-day on the Church, quite a volume. I suppose we shall complete the first discussions on the first two schemata on discipline to-morrow, when they will be handed over to the special deputation for reconstruction.

The same date. We are now fairly launched into work, hold three General Congregations a week, and have had some very able speakers as well as some muffs. We have before us two long schemata *de Fide*, and four *de Disciplina*. The first *de Fide* is sent after long discussion to its special deputation. The two first *de Disciplina* will have had, I hope, all the first stage of discussion finished to-morrow, when our special deputation will begin its work. These two deputations will have no easy time of it. And in the end I suspect ours will be the hardest worked.

I have been quite well for a long time until to-day, but I suppose this little touch of the old complaint will soon pass. I observed to-day in the Council that a good many bishops were ill, and hanging about the doors. You can always get a cup of good brodo [broth], or a glass of wine, by going into the adjoining chapel, where, entering a door at the base of the plinth, you find a nice room, with a little kitchen adjoining, all carpeted round, etc., with chairs and a sofa ; and, as in the tea room of the House of Commons, the enquiry of the next comer is, Who is on his legs, and what is he saying ? Is it not odd to find all this in the internal base courts of St. Peter's ?

Jan. 22. Since writing the above, another day, and another sitting of the General Congregation has passed. We hoped to finish our present subject to-day, but there are still four speakers, so we shall have to go in for it again on Monday, this being Saturday. And then for our work.

It is extraordinary how weak the men show themselves in discussion, who are unhabituated to public assemblies. They don't feel their audience, or the tone, tact, or method requisite for securing the interest and attention of a large assembly of 'periti'. It is the grandest opportunity for really able men, and we generally get about two in the course of a sitting. The Germans and Hungarians beat the Spaniards and Italians hollow. The latter have had the bad training of academical discourses.

The same date. Just returned from General Congregation. All had hoped the discussion would have ended to-day on the two schemata, but we had some muffs in place of speakers, and that means, soft, nonsensical, muffy length. One speaker alone [a Peruvian bishop] awakened a deep interest, narrating the troubles and difficulties of his distant church in illustration of points in question. I stood by the ambo and watched the slow effect by which he gradually subdued the impatient and the restless wits, until he fairly conquered them almost to tears, as at the close he himself wept from his heart.[1] A Council is like all the great assemblies in this respect, that many speakers fail to catch hold of the tone and mode that suits them. In this respect the prelates of our constitutional countries show their great superiority.

After all, this Council ought to be a very good thing for the souls of the bishops; for severed from the ordinary distractions of governing a diocese, one is entirely occupied with truth, with law, with the policy of the Holy Ghost. If anyone occupies himself too much with things outside the Council, it is his own fault. In some respects I look upon this Council as a prolonged retreat, devoted to the divine Head of the Church and the Holy Ghost.

Jan. 24. I feel very strongly inspired to say something in the Council, which if well received, would be of great

---

[1] 'He spoke with great emotion and touched the Fathers with so great sorrow that they acclaimed him as he came down from the ambo' (note of a bishop).

importance for the clergy, and the sanctity of the Church for all time to come, and I expect the opportunity will present itself before many days are past. It is something on which I have thought much and long, if I can only so put it that others may see it in the same light. I write this letter and finish it to-day, hoping it will get in time for you to pray for my intention. [He seems not to have carried out this idea.]

We five bishops here [at the English College] are very happy together, three of them also have their secretaries. Bishop Vaughan is both my next door neighbour and constant companion, as we have our carriage and servant in common. We are very well provided in these respects. The other three bishops are Grant, Turner and Cornthwaite, and the Bishop of Shrewsbury will be here from England in another fortnight.

The more I see of this Council, the more sure I feel that great things will come out of it. It will give much light both to Catholics and to those who are seeking the Church. And there is due consideration shown for the sad condition of those who are in a state of blindness. As to discipline also, very valuable principles will be cleared up, and sound regulations based upon them. Then the discussions are enlightening all parties, and each portion of the Church is teaching the rest. Even the party warfare outside the Council is doing its valuable office of guiding things by its diagonal action into the ways of caution and moderation. All will come right, and begins to look like coming right. No extreme party will prevail. *Virtus in medio.* Even the intense curiosity pervading the exterior world touching the Council, and the agitation and exaggeration of the world's journals, are preparing the world itself for receiving the work of the Council, when it shall at last appear, in its true colours, in such a way as to make the deepest impression on human minds. No Council will have ever given such clear expositions of Catholic principles, or have dispelled so many erroneous impressions as to the real spirit of the Catholic Church.

It appears in the *Unità Cattolica*, as we had previously heard from rumour, that a Wallachian, known here as a

spy of the Italian Government, was actually caught trying
to enter the Council in the dress of a Bishop. The Assignatori di posti know the bishops so well, take the list of
those present daily, and stand in a group daily, watching
all whilst entering, that it would not be easy for a wrong
person to get in and not be found out. When we come
out in a great stream, with our papers and schemata under
our arms, cardinals, patriarchs and prelates of all ranks
mingled together, and streaming off in coloured lines to the
doors, it is curious to mark the eagerness of the spectators,
gentlemen, ladies, reporters, and others, all peering into our
faces, and at the covers of our books, as if trying to penetrate
the mysteries of the Council.

Feb. 2. There is talk now of a break up of the Council
at the end of May, to be resumed in the end of autumn.
The Pope is anxious to get business faster on, but that
will be difficult with so large a body. Meanwhile some
bishops are getting leave of absence, which the Council
has to vote; some from pressing business, others from
infirmity.

Feb. 4. It is quite true that a Council presents a large
field for observation, not of individuals only, but of national
idiosyncracies. Nations come out here, all men of one
tongue and one climate, with a distinctness from each other
that perfectly individualizes them. For example: the
Orientals have sweet and clear voices, with a certain rich-
ness, especially the young and middle-aged, the older voices
growing thinner. Their movements and gestures are quiet
and gentle, full of dignity and self-possession. For instance,
there is an Armenian archbishop, with grave but youthful
features, very regular and sweet, with his coal-black hair
parted *à la Nazarène*, and peaked beard, who has been twice
in the ambo; and his entire presence, front face, profile,
gentle gesture, and sweet full voice, earnest without effort—
his whole man, in short, so irresistibly strikes me as exactly
like our ideal of Our Lord, just as He is painted in a certain
old picture at Oscott, even to the very costume, that I have
been wonderfully captivated with this type from the plains
from which the Hebrews sprang. Then there was a

Pomeranian, who gave such an interesting and pathetic account of the difficulties of religion in his country as the basis and reason of his argument ; and he spoke so bravely, so much like a martyr in spirit and in fact, that, as he ended, there burst out an unusual applause, even to clapping and bravos, which were ruled not to occur again, as unsuited to a Council and a church.

Strossmayer now sits just under me : he is a warmhearted, affectionate Croat, as eloquent as he is warm, but apt to get over-vehement.   We have taken quite an affection for each other.   On one side of me sits the Bishop of Pegu, in Burmah, learned in Buddhism ; and beyond him the Bishop of Hobart Town, Van Diemen's Land.   On the other side sits the Bishop of Vancouver's Island, and next him the Bishop of the Sandwich Islands, all speaking English.   Behind me is the Bishop of Ivrea, in North Italy, who says that his predecessor ordained St. Patrick, and that he has the body of an Irish Saint in his Cathedral. Behind them sit the Archbishops of Baltimore and New York ; behind them Archbishop Errington ; and, at the top seat, the new Primate of Ireland, who has just got the pallium [MacGettigan of Armagh].   If I go out at one end of the bench I come in contact with Bishop Serra, a Spaniard, and Long, an Australian bishop.   If I go out at the other end nearer the cardinals, I come upon a bunch of Americans. But one gets to know half the bishops of the Council, to be on talking terms.

About this time rumours went about that Ullathorne had thrown in his lot with the Minority and had signed the petition against the introduction of the infallibility. Odo Russell, the agent in Rome of the British Government, in close touch with the rest of the diplomatic corps in Rome, said this in a letter to Manning,[1] and the *Times* correspondent put it into his Roman news. The following letter of Ullathorne was printed in *The Times* of February 11 :

---

[1] Purcell, *Manning*, II, 439.

I must ask you to allow me to state in your journal (1) that I am no Gallican; (2) that I have joined no party outside the Council, or with reference to the Council; (3) that I have signed no document drawn up by any person or party whatsoever; (4) that I neither contemplate secession from the Council in any contingency that could arise, nor do I know of anyone who does. Finally, that I am contented with the position of affairs in the Council.

Feb. 8. He wrote to Dr. Northcote: Yesterday I despatched a letter to the *Times*, not sorry that its Roman correspondent gave me the opportunity; as both here and in England rumour, and the trick of parties, has been free and unjust in the use of my name. It has been for some time said that I took part with, and signed the petition of the anti-papal party, as it may be called, for want of an accurate designation. On the contrary I have been exercising quietly a moderating influence. The Pope himself believed it, but now has been able to see with his own eyes that it is not true. Of course, as I told you before I left England, the outside of the Council is an arena of policy and intrigue, and moderate men are disliked by the extremes of both parties. Still I am quite satisfied with the position, and I know from most authentic sources that moderation will prevail.

I have not spoken. I prepared, but delayed in consequence of the diarrhœa, which is now quite gone, and left me well. After that, the Council got so wearied with long and prosy speakers, that I said the time was passed for the present. Then the debate still went on, and the great mass of prelates felt their time was being wasted, and as my views were of a high order, I felt they could not come in, and be taken up by exhausted bishops 800 strong in electric impatience. But I had qualms in silence, so I consulted a friend, and he said, ' Don't do it now, you will have another occasion '; and I acquiesced. But to-day, light flashed up anew in the debate, and to-morrow I shall have a good chance for one of my three points in the special deputation of Discipline, which sits for the first time. About the *one* question, which has really occupied all minds, I think I can tell you with confidence, for it has not yet entered the

Council, that it will be settled in so moderate a way as to satisfy all the prelates. Conflict out of doors has prepared for great moderation within, and this I say upon certain private knowledge, from three distinct but thoroughly informed sources.

After one scheme more has been discussed we shall approach that subject. You know it regards the prerogative of the Sovereign Pontiff. I could not have said this much had it been already before the Council.

Feb. 12. . . . Since writing the above, I have had to write a Pastoral, and we have had the first meeting of the deputation of Discipline. We are now waiting for the printing of the substance of thirty-six speeches, which themselves fill a large volume, before we go on with the work of reconstruction, to go again before the General Congregation. This is a Saturday, a free day, so you will get your letter.

Feb. 16. The Bishop of Shrewsbury is just arrived, giving better accounts of Bishop Goss, who is at Cannes. Bishop Grant was taken out of the Council the day before yesterday in a most precarious and suffering condition. He still lies in bed, but is easier. His case is a very anxious one, as it might at any time become mortal. He has suffered more torture for the previous two days than he ever did in England or here before. Up to this he has appeared to be gradually improving.

I think the number of bishops dead since the Council began is now 10, and others are seriously ill. Of course many are old men. I am quite well, unusually so.

The Council moves slowly on. We have had speaking, or enrolled to speak, twenty-eight bishops on one single point, the number speaking in one day varying from four to seven. After our present schema is finished, we shall come to the *great point*, and then the interest will grow intense. But all is prepared for moderate measures. I have just been having an hour's talk with the celebrated Bishop of Poitiers [Pie] on the position of affairs. He is a leader in the special deputation *de Fide*, and was very busy with the work of reconstruction of a schema that the General Congregation had sent out, mangled and pulled

to pieces. What I said in the letter to the *Times* I repeat ;
I am quite satisfied with the position of affairs. If we are
not doing as much in the time as Rome anticipated, we are
doing more. All sides are learning great lessons for future
use.

During this same time Bishop Amherst also wrote
home :

Jan. 21. I never read anything so absurd as the accounts
of the Council in the *Times* and other English papers. They
don't know what to write and are obliged to invent. Nothing
can be more quiet, orderly, and cordial, than the relations
of the bishops at all the meetings, and the liberty of speech
is perfect, anyone saying just what he pleases on the subjects
in question. In fact, unless people in England know things
for certain from other sources, they may put down all they
read as *lies*. All is going on in perfect order, and the
questions before us are being thoroughly discussed.

Feb. 1. As to the Council, all I can say is that it goes
on vigorously and calmly. There has not been the semblance of a *scene*, as some of the papers make out. Dupanloup
did not touch upon the infallibility question in his speech,
and as to liberty of speech, that is entire. Men are never
called to order unless they wander from the subject and
waste time ; and that has only happened once or twice.

I hear the *Standard* has said something silly about me
and Clifford, and wants to make out that I signed a petition
against the definition. I authorize you to contradict this
in toto if you hear it mentioned. There is no use in writing
to the paper to contradict it, they would only have something
still more stupid next time.

Feb. 4. The Purification was a great day in St. Peter's.
The Pope blessed the candles but did not distribute them
to all the bishops on account of time ; and only eighteen,
besides cardinals and patriarchs, wore cope and mitre and
went in procession. Still it was very grand, the church full
of people, among whom I saw several English uniforms ;
Scott-Murray was very grand in red and silver as a Knight
of Malta.

Dr. Clifford made a great speech yesterday in the Council, which seems to have created quite a sensation ; he spoke for nearly an hour, and it was certainly one of the events of the Synod.

Clifford had made his studies in Rome and spoke Latin fluently and well. The speech of Feb. 3 was on 'The Life of the Clergy'. He urged that many of the regulations proposed would be impracticable in Protestant countries : he advocated a reform of the Breviary, especially a weekly recitation of the whole psalter. The only part of the speech at all sensational was the end, wherein he pointed out that the practice of sending all schemata out of the Council to the deputations, to be reconstructed, was counter to the prescriptions of the 'Multiplices', by which only points of special difficulty should be remitted to the deputations, but the emending of the schemata should be the work of the body of bishops in Congregation. 'A General Council (it is of Catholic faith) can be convoked only by the Pope, and to him it belongs to lay down the method by which the business is to be conducted. If we can speak at this Council, if our decrees are to have any force, it can only be in so far as they accord with what is laid down in the "Multiplices". No one of us has the right of proposing, discussing, or ordaining things in a different way from what is laid down in that constitution. To do so is to expose to doubt the validity and authority of our acts.'

Strong and clear doctrine from a Minority bishop. (See Mansi, II (50), 602-9.)

Feb. 10. The Pope is wonderfully well, and I don't know how he manages to get through all he has to do. He says he is eighty, but is as active as a man of sixty in perfect health. A number of French people nearly pulled him to pieces at one of the great audiences. The guards were obliged to surround him and hold up his arms above their heads to get him out of the crush and scramble. Mr. Danvers-Clarke and his wife were there and they describe the scene as inconceivable. It was all affection, but the Pope was obliged to say : ' Save me from my friends.' An American lady called out to the Pope to 'speak up', but I don't think she meant anything uncivil.

Feb. 24. The story about a false bishop is a good one for those who like sensational tales. Not one of us has heard of such an adventurer, excepting through the English papers. Such a thing is simply impossible, just as much so as a false peer getting into the House of Lords. What will they say next ? As far as I am concerned, not one word of what the Protestant papers say is true, but as yet I have not thought it worth while to contradict what they said.

We spent Shrove Tuesday at Frascati and enjoyed ourselves. Mrs. Furse gave us an English dinner : roast beef and boiled turkey, but forgot the pancakes.

CHAPTER XIII

DISSATISFACTIONS WITH PROCEDURE

AFTER the Congregation of February 22 there was a month's break in the holding of General Congregations, until March 18. During the interval a further endeavour was made to rearrange the Council-hall and improve the acoustic conditions, still unsatisfactory. This, however, was not the reason for the suspension of Congregations; the real reason was that the work of the Council had come to a standstill, the deputations *de Fide* and *de Disciplina* being congested with the work remitted to them by the Council. The General Congregations had done nothing but pull to pieces the schemata laid before them, and hand them over to the deputations to be recast. The deputation *de Fide* had had in its hands since the middle of January the Constitution on Catholic Faith, and was still engaged upon it; the deputation on discipline now had four schemata to revise. It was felt there was no use in piling up more work for the deputations until that in hand had been cleared. A universal sense prevailed that the Council so far had been a failure. No positive result had yet been achieved, not a single decree or canon enacted: 'per totam noctem laborantes nihil cepimus' was heard on all sides—after three months' work we have got nothing !—only endless speechifying and destructive criticism.

The general dissatisfaction found expression in a number of representations addressed to the Presidents and to the Holy Father himself.[1] Senestréy of Ratisbon in particular put in a long statement : the speakers speak as orators, and the speeches are rhetorical efforts, diffuse, vague, obscure, not to the point ; there is no real debate or discussion on the questions at issue, no co-ordination between the speeches, each one treating of a fresh aspect of the subject out of all relation to what has gone before ; only those who unite a loud voice to fluency in Latin, and have no shame in consuming time, can get a hearing. He proposed remedies : that a time-limit of a quarter of an hour be set for the speeches ; that some of the theologians should be present at the Congregations to reply at once to questions and difficulties at the call of the Presidents.

These petitions were referred to the Congregation *de postulatis*, which formulated a series of proposals to be submitted to the Presidents, who in turn communicated with the Pope. As the result the Presidents at the end of the Congregation of February 22 promulgated by order of the Pope a decree supplementing and modifying the procedure established by the decree ' Multiplices ' at the beginning of the Council. These new regulations raised a great storm among the Minority bishops, as unduly interfering with freedom of debate, and even opening out questionings of the proper liberty of the Council and the validity of its acts. This, then, will be a suitable place to take in hand and weigh the objections and grievances urged by the Minority against the general conduct of the Council.

The grievances went back to the original Regulations promulgated at the outset in the decree ' Multiplices '. In all things the Pope kept to himself the complete mastery. Things which at Trent had been

---

[1] Mansi, III (51), 4-9.

left in the hands of the Fathers—settlement of claims to take part in the Council, appointment of officials, regulation of procedure, etc.—were all now fixed by the personal act of the Pope. Such things were not vital; but one thing, left indeterminate at Trent, the right of proposing questions, 'ius proponendi', was in the eyes of many vital. It was now laid down unequivocally that the right and duty of proposing the matters to be treated of at the Council belongs exclusively to the Pope and the Apostolic See. The bishops were invited and exhorted to suggest freely anything for deliberation that they thought would be for the general good of the Church. But such proposals or postulations must be submitted to a special Congregation, nominated by the Pope, for dealing with such postulates, to consider them and report its advice to the Pope, with whom the decision would lie as to whether the thing be brought forward at the Council or not. On January 2 was addressed to the Holy Father a respectful but firm protest, claiming that it was a right, not a concession, for any bishop to bring forward at the Council anything he believed in conscience to be for the good of the Church; and objecting to such proposals being subject to the control of the Congregation *de postulatis*.[1] It bore the signatures of twenty-five archbishops and bishops of Germany, Austria, and Hungary, headed by Cardinal Schwarzenberg, and the single other signature of Archbishop Kenrick of St. Louis, U.S.A. The Pope's answer was that he could not admit that any prejudice to the rights of the bishops was done by the regulation, which he therefore adhered to.

It has to be remembered that the Vatican Council, though an œcumenical Council, was also a deliberative body for the transaction of business, and therefore

---

[1] Mansi, II (50), 52; *Lac* 917.

some method of controlling the agenda was a matter of practical necessity. That it should be allowable for every bishop to bring forward anything he thought to be for the good of the Church, was an idea plainly impossible, so that there was need of some control. So Ullathorne thought : in the letter of January 1 he said : 'Some such provision [as the Congregation *de postulatis*] is needful, to prevent the time and patience of the Fathers being consumed by all sorts of things, fit or unfit, being introduced.'

It is worthy of note that the procedure of the Council, its machinery, was in the main that suggested by Hefele, himself a leading spirit of the Minority ; and in particular the Congregation *de postulatis* was his idea. No one could express more forcibly than he did in his Report the need of such a control : [1]

It would be impossible that every bishop could bring forward at the General Congregations as many propositions as he wished : all order of discussion would be thrown into confusion ; a wide door would be thrown open to petulance of spirits ; endless superfluous matters would be brought forward ; disputes would arise ; and everything would be interminably protracted, so that there would be no end.

And when it is realized that the postulations for subjects to be brought on, submitted by the bishops to the Congregation *de postulatis*, run to 330 columns of Mansi (V (53), 331-662), and that they range freely over the entire field of faith, morals, discipline, canon law, relations of Church and State, and practical devotional life, it will easily be seen that some control of the kind was necessary : otherwise, in order to deal with a programme so immense, would the Council have had to go on in permanent session from that day to this, and, at the rate at which it did its work, would not yet have finished.

[1] Mansi, I (49), 534 ; *Lac* 1089.

The Congregation *de postulatis* worked assiduously on the great miscellaneous mass of material laid before it up to the end of April; then it divided itself into four sub-committees to try to cope with its task. The prorogation of the Council made impossible the introduction of any of this fresh matter.

The supplementary regulations promulgated on February 22 were intended to quicken and make more businesslike and less cumbrous the procedure of the Council; yet against them very vigorous protests were made.

The main provisions of the new decree were as follows : [1]

When a schema was distributed, a period was fixed by the Presidents during which such bishops as wished should write their criticisms and suggestions, all to be submitted to the appropriate deputation. The deputation would take all into consideration and recast the schema in the light of the various comments ; and the recast schema along with a summary of all the suggestions should be printed and circulated. After a reasonable time for examination the matter would be brought before the General Congregation and submitted to a discussion, first of the schema as a whole, and then of each of its parts. All proposed amendments were to be scheduled by the deputation and circulated in print, the deputation by its spokesman recommending the adoption or rejection of each. The amendments were then to be voted for one by one, the votes being given by the bishops standing up from their seats. The deputation should incorporate in the text the amendments adopted. Then the schema was voted on as a whole by 'placet', 'non-placet', or 'placet iuxta modum', each one who gave this latter vote submitting in writing the amendments he desired. These amendments were considered again by the deputation, and subjected to yet another voting of the Congregation. Only then was the schema proposed at a Public Session, to be finally voted on by 'placet' or 'non-

---

[1] Mansi, III (51), 13 ; *Lac* 67.

placet', 'iuxta modum' being now excluded; and, if so be, to be confirmed and enacted by the Pope.

There was provision for ' closure ' : if a discussion was being unduly prolonged when the matter had been sufficiently exhausted, the Presidents, at a request in writing from ten bishops, might ask the Congregation if it was the wish that the debate should go on ; and if a majority voted, by standing up, in favour of ending the debate, the Presidents might apply the closure.

The following letter written on the very day, February 22, shows Ullathorne's approval of the new regulations :

To-day has seen a great turning-point in the history of the Council. We have been long crying out for more and better regulations in the management both of the discussions and the general business of the Council. Private and public representations have been given incessantly. Amongst others, I went to one of the Presidents and both pointed out the evils existing and suggested remedies. Others did the same, and the last schema discussed has been so long in hand, we have been so wearied with endless repetitions of the same things, and with long diversions from the point, that bishops were getting positively sick of the whole business. But Rome, with its usual wisdom and its shrewd penetration, was carefully noting and considering everything. And to-day, after a more tedious discussion than usual had brought the subject in its first state to an end, we were all wakened up by the publication of a code of new regulations, which were, several of them, loudly applauded as, one after another, they were read out, and then given us in print. A list of the whole of the schemata yet to come was also distributed, and six new schemata put in hand. After that, we all went out with unusually light steps and smiling faces, that must have whetted the curiosity of any newspaper correspondents that might be on the look-out for signs and tokens of what had been doing.

Half an hour before, we had been trying to get a prelate down from the ambo, who we thought was talking to no purpose, by crying all over the aula : ' Satis, descende '.

But he seemed to think we were crying ' Satis bene ', for the more we called out, the more earnestly he went on, plunging from one pit of untimeliness into another. So, through sheer stolidity, he went on and finished, and our innocent revenge was to give him some hearty laughter when he came down.[1] It is extraordinary how men, not trained or used to the habits of public assemblies, lose hold of the Council after a few sentences, whilst others keep hold of everybody's attention on to the last words of their address. The two classes who best succeed in holding attention are those accustomed to public meetings, and those who have been theological professors. A Spaniard the other day completely redeemed the reputation of his nation by the brevity, point, wit, solidity and truth of his arguments and replies. But then he had been a practised theological professor.

The new rules throw very heavy and constant work on the special deputations, and I see that ours will have far the most work, as not less than twenty-eight schemata, in the course of the Council, will come to us.

We now expect that we have a holiday until the beginning of Lent, but we are to have special notice of the next General Congregation, so we know not when it will be, though no one expects work until after Ash Wednesday, beyond their private studies.

This letter implies that the regulations were very generally welcomed ; yet the Minority bishops were greatly moved by certain features in them, and soon various protests went in, one from thirty French bishops, one from twenty Italians, Orientals, and others, two from thirty-six Germans, Austrians, and Hungarians, and later one from four Americans ; ninety in all.[2] The chief object of protest was the closure : it was claimed that every bishop, as witness to the Faith, has the right not merely to vote, but to set forth the grounds on which his vote is based,

---

[1] This must refer to the Haynald episode (p. 229).
[2] Mansi, III (51), 18 ; *Lac* 958.

should he desire to do so. Such a theoretical claim, if acted on by all or nearly all the 700 Fathers, would have led to endless repetitions and have made the Council impossible. It was, on one side, a deliberative assembly, and was bound to some extent to fall under the laws found necessary for the conduct of business in all deliberative assemblies. As a matter of fact, though often called on to do so, the Presidents applied the closure only once, June 3, and, as will be seen, Ullathorne considered their action to have been justified and proper.

The method of voting by standing up was also objected to, as an innovation, and as being 'contagious', not securing the full responsibility of an individual vote by voice; it was urged that at least each canon under anathema should be separately voted on vocally. It has to be realized that the individual voting 'placet' etc., by 600 was a long business; we have it from Ullathorne that it took two hours, or at least one and a half, to take such a vote, each name being read out and the vote recorded; it might have been possible to shorten the process, but hardly to less than an hour, ten a minute. It was evident that the hundreds of amendments could be dealt with only by some quick method. Standing up is not more contagious than show of hands, which is not considered to impair the responsibility or the freedom of a meeting.

More important, a protest was made against the principle that questions should be decided by a majority; it was urged that the practice followed in œcumenical Councils should be adhered to, and dogmas of Faith be defined not by a numerical majority, but by a moral unanimity; a principle so fully accepted by Pius IV that at Trent, when an important question of dogma was being dealt with, he said 'he wished to define nothing but what should be decreed by the unanimous consent of the Fathers'. And, so vital was the point thought to be, these bishops declared, that if it were not conceded 'their conscience would be weighed down with an intolerable burden, and they would fear that the character of the Council might be called in question and its authority undermined, as lacking liberty'.

Over this matter of moral unanimity a great controversy broke out; pamphlets were circulated on both sides, and the thing kept cropping up continually until the end of the Council. Bishop Fessler, the Secretary, was commissioned to make a report. He was a learned man, who had been professor at Vienna University of Church history and canon law. There was really not much evidence available. At some Councils, as Constantinople I, unanimity was obtained only by the abstention of a number of dissidents. The only fact that really told with force in favour of the theory of moral unanimity was the action of Pius IV, and this might well be held to have been a counsel of prudence, not the assertion of a law.[1]

On this point Ollivier is able to point out that

Up to the Vatican Council Ultramontanes and Gallicans agreed in rejecting this unreasonable pretension, and in recognizing that even at Councils a majority ought to prevail. Bellarmine teaches: 'That is a true decree of a Council which is made by the majority, for otherwise no decree would be legitimate, there being always some dissentients.' And the Cardinal of Luzerne, one of the lights of pure Gallicanism, approves this doctrine: 'Unanimity is not necessary for the decision; it is the majority that makes it.'[2]

Apart from the aforesaid objections, which were considered by those who made them to touch matters

---

[1] Granderath gives a summary of the pamphlet controversy, III, Bk. i, c. 4.

[2] *L'Église et l'État au Concile du Vatican*, II, 74.

of principle vitally affecting the very essentials of the Council, a variety of proposals for the better conduct of business were made, some of which certainly were reasonable enough. One was that the prepared schemata should all be given to the bishops at once, and not be let out in driblets, so that they might know from the beginning the full work before them and the inter-relations between the various items : it often happened that a criticism was met by the assurance that the point was dealt with in a schema not yet circulated. This request, reasonable in itself, was met by the reply that there were obvious reasons against it : it must be supposed that the danger was meant of schemata getting prematurely into the public press, as some did, thereby causing no small mischief : the secrecy of the Council was badly kept.

Another proposal was that each bishop should be able to go to the Congregation *de postulatis* or the deputations, to explain and defend his proposals or amendments. This again seems reasonable,—until we reflect that it was quite unworkable : if the hundreds of amendments were to be thus discussed with their proposers, the work of the deputations would have been endless and hopeless. Again, in view of the difficulty of any kind of close discussion at the Congregations, it was suggested that commissions of the bishops of the different nations should be set up, to thresh things out at meetings of a manageable size at which real discussion would be possible ; and then one or two bishops be appointed as spokesmen for the public debate at the Congregations. It was answered that this might be done privately, but no such arrangement would be admitted as part of the authorized machinery of the Council.

Another suggestion was made to meet in part the inconvenience arising from the bad acoustic properties of the Council-hall, so bad that, at any rate at first, the speakers were unintelligible and even inaudible in large tracts of the hall. It was suggested that the stenographic reports of all the speeches should be printed and circulated day by day; or at least that every bishop who wished could have his speech printed and circulated. This again seems reasonable, until we look at the reports in Mansi; if this great volume of oratory had come out day by day bishops and deputations would have been snowed under. That a bishop might not have his speech printed fell under a general regulation, that nothing concerning the Council might be printed in Rome itself by any bishop whomsoever; such things might be printed elsewhere, and many were printed at Naples or Paris, and might be brought to Rome; but each bishop had to see to the circulation of his own productions; the Roman Post Office would not undertake the delivery of such literature. These restrictions did not in fact impede the free circulation of a great quantity of controversial literature; but they were vexatious, and certainly tended to foster in the Minority bishops a sense of irritation, a sense that they could get no hearing even when their representations were reasonable enough. There was no disposition on part of Presidents or Pope to conciliate or meet them in any degree.

It is worthy of note that M. Ollivier, viewing things from the independent standpoint of a statesman practised in parliamentary routine, makes a telling defence and justification of the Pope's Regulations for procedure, and of the actual conduct of business at the Council.[1]

[1] *L'Église et l'État au Concile du Vatican*, II, 67-77.

CHAPTER XIV

ATMOSPHERE OF THE COUNCIL

HAVING spoken in the foregoing chapter of the dissatisfactions felt by many with the rules of procedure laid down by the Pope, we may now fittingly speak of what may be called the ' atmosphere of the Council ', the mentality of the different parties, and in particular the nature of the proceedings, a point on which there has been very violent controversy.

At the middle of February Dr. Ullathorne wrote the usual Lenten pastoral letter, to be read in all the churches of his diocese of Birmingham, and he spoke to his people of the Council :

Given at Rome outside the Aurelian Gate this 10th day of February 1870

Much will you have heard through the newspapers respecting the proceedings of this great Council, and much that is either altogether untrue, or that is the very opposite to the truth, or that is so distorted from the facts, that it no longer has the likeness of truth upon it. . . . Yet how can it be otherwise ? For as to what comes before the Council, and as to what is said in discussion by its members, all who are within the Council are bound to solemn secrecy ; whilst outside the Council, the society gathered together from all quarters of the world is a prey to ever-changing rumours, guesses, and imaginations of what is passing within the forbidden doors. About those entrance-doors, and in the great nave of St. Peter's, a gazing crowd, including the correspondents of the newspapers,

254

alive with excited curiosity, and left a prey to their imaginations, get their minds disposed to take fire with fancy at every word they hear dropped, so that out of the smallest materials they build up imaginary scenes and speeches, and fill the minds of the outer world with airy inventions of what is passing within the Council and amongst its members. Thus schemes are said to be under discussion which are not under discussion ; designs are attributed to the Council of which the Council knows nothing ; and bishops are invested with views and notions, and are described as taking this or that course of action, which are utterly unbefitting their characters, and are often in direct opposition to their real sentiments.

Large bodies move slowly, and the Church acts with great deliberation, prudence, and moderation. As to the agitation respecting the Council which moves the outer world, we only mark in it, how much the solemn assembly of God's Church weighs on the minds of men ; how it stirs them with hopes and with fears ; and how portentous to the heart of man is the power of the Church. One cannot but see already that its work, like the work of its divine Master, will be for the resurrection and the fall of many.

Within the Council itself, we may say that it unites order with reverence ; dignity with apostolic freedom ; and the keenest sense of responsibility with an untiring patience and charity.

These words present the picture of a dignified, orderly, religious assembly, strangely at variance with the picture popularly accepted, at any rate in England, which is one of intrigue, violence, and unseemly behaviour of every kind : on my telling a friend I was at work on the Vatican Council, the comment came pat : ' I have always understood it was a regular beargarden.' It might be said that what Ullathorne wrote in the pastoral was what a prudent and loyal bishop would write in a public letter to his flock, and should be taken as representing his official, not his real, mind. But we have seen, and we shall go on seeing, that the tenor of his private letters, in so far as the proceedings inside the Council-chamber were concerned, was from start to finish steadily in the same sense as the pastoral.

Here it is necessary to deal with another set of letters from Rome during the Council, presenting a very different picture from Ullathorne's,—the letters mainly responsible for the popular ideas of the conduct of the Council. These are the famous *Letters from Rome* of 'Quirinus'.[1] They are sixty-nine in number, published in the Augsburg *Allgemeine Zeitung* during the whole course of the Council. It is known that the writer was Döllinger; but they were made up from materials supplied to him from Rome by three correspondents, closely in touch with the principal Minority bishops and with the embassies of the Catholic Governments, and so were (presumably) well informed on what was going on. Two of them can be identified: Dr. Friedrich and Lord Acton. Of Acton's activities more will be said in the sequel. Friedrich was in Rome in a twofold capacity: he was theologian to Cardinal Hohenlohe, brother of Prince Hohenlohe, the Bavarian Foreign Minister; and he was an official agent of the Bavarian Government, attached to the Bavarian embassy at Rome. As Council theologian to the Cardinal he saw all the documents of the Council, and was conversant with everything that took place: the bishops' theologians were admitted to all the Council secrets. But more than once Quirinus scouts the notion that the secrecy imposed on all members of the Council had any binding force; and so in his letters everything is freely laid bare—the contents of the schemata, reports of speeches, all the incidents. Thus, by this breach of confidence, the Letters of Quirinus contained a quantity

---

[1] The English translation (Rivingtons, 1870) makes a volume of over 800 pages.

of information nowhere else to be found, and that could not well be controlled, until the publication of the full Acta in the continuation of Mansi during these last half-dozen years. It was this circumstance that enabled the English translator to claim in 1870, ' that this collection of letters is the best authority for the history of the Vatican Council.' They were first in the field and they have held the field ever since, at any rate in England. For instance, in so popular a controversial book as Dr. Salmon's *Infallibility*, the account of the Vatican Council, told with all the raciness of which Salmon was master, is really based wholly on Quirinus. But now, thanks to the publication of the Acts, it is possible to test the accuracy of the picture presented in the Letters, and it is incumbent on any historian of the Council to take this task in hand.

Quirinus is bitterly hostile to the Council; his letters are frankly and undisguisedly partisan and one-sided, without pretence of any kind of impartial estimation ; in them are manifest the spirit and the hand of ' Janus ' : the Council is the outcome of a carefully laid plot on part of Pope, Curia, and Jesuits, to bring about the complete subjugation of the bishops and the whole Church to the Roman Curia : the official reason given for its convocation, ' to find a remedy for the religious and social disorders of the times ', was a blind ; the true objective, designed all along, was nothing else than the definition of the Pope's infallibility : that once secured, the Pope had only to proceed by decrees to re-enact and re-enforce Syllabus, ' Unam Sanctam ' of Boniface VIII, deposing power, papal domination of Innocent III and Hildebrand, and so assert the complete subjection of State to Church even in the temporal order, thereby bringing about irreconcilable and disastrous conflict between the Church and modern society as constituted in all civilized countries, to the irreparable injury of religion.

Such was the alarmist campaign of Quirinus and his associates. It has been proved a baseless panic by the logic of facts during the sixty years since the Council. But it has to be recognized that wild statements of over-enthusiastic papalists at the time did give some colour to such fears.

What concerns us, however, more nearly is the picture Quirinus presents of the happenings in the Council and of the mind of the Minority bishops. His picture is one of the central authority crushing a minority by mere force of numbers, and having recourse to all the expedients by which a government with an obedient majority at its beck can browbeat and muzzle and render impotent a minority opposition. To such an extent were these methods of coercion used, that finally the Minority protested that the Council was not free. Such is Quirinus' picture : and the question is, How far is it a true picture of the Council itself, and of the mind of the Minority bishops ?

And herein, to my mind, lies the value of Dr. Ullathorne's letters, as a counterpoise to those of Quirinus ; being the only set of letters known to me hitherto published from the inside of the Council, by one who actually took part throughout ; a shrewd observer of sound practical judgement, a non-party man who stood for moderation, and kept himself austerely aloof from all agitations and movements and petitions and protests that were going on outside the Council. His is probably the most impartial, and therefore the truest, impression obtainable of the atmosphere and character of the Council.

It may be that his very aloofness from the movements afoot outside the Council-chamber, though he was well aware of all that was going on, tends to give to his impressions an undue optimism, for his letters

are steadily optimistic in tone. And it has to be recognized that Ullathorne's picture is more optimistic
than that of the abbé Mourret, reflecting the Diary of
M. Icard. Icard was in Rome at the Council as theologian of Mgr. Bernadou, Archbishop of Sens. He
was at the time Director or Superior of the Seminary
of St. Sulpice in Paris, and had been during forty years
professor there of theology and canon law. A number of the French bishops had received their training
and had made their theological studies at St. Sulpice
during these years, and they looked on Icard as their
old teacher and spiritual father and valued friend.
Thus they flocked around him in Rome, and he was
deeply in the confidence of the leading French bishops
of both parties, as Darboy, Dupanloup, Pie. Though
Bernadou was a moderate inopportunist, Icard himself had always taught a clear but moderate and
strictly theological Ultramontanism. He will figure
largely in the sequel, for his influence was great and
extended over wider circles than the French bishops ;
it was always exercised on the side of moderation and
conciliation.

The leading French bishops sought his advice at
every turn, or listened to it willingly when proffered ;
the Cardinal Presidents consulted him : so that he was
one of the most influential forces—an always pacificatory influence—behind the scenes. Through his relations with so many of the French bishops Icard was
thrown into the thick of the fight in a way that
Ullathorne in his aloofness was not. Thus the picture
of the Council drawn by Mourret, chiefly from Icard's
Diary, is one of stress and strain, certainly less pleasing
than Ullathorne's.

Although up to Easter the great dividing line of
the Papacy had not yet been broached inside the
Council, outside, the keen controversy was in full
course, indeed, had been from the outset, and the

two great parties, Majority and Minority, had been definitely formed. And Mourret declares that all the earlier discussions and debates were carried on under the shadow of the ' Great Question ' that everyone knew was lurking below the horizon and was surely destined to emerge. And so the earlier proceedings of the Council, even the discussions on quite neutral questions, as the Catechism, were overclouded and vitiated by an atmosphere of misunderstanding and mistrust between the bishops of either side. The month of marking time, during which the General Congregations were suspended, will be a suitable point at which to take stock of the state of affairs, and to try to form a just estimation of the forces ranged on either side.

It would be just as wrong-headed to view the Majority, with Quirinus (and Salmon), as a block of fanatical, ignorant, cowardly men, ' abject sycophants ' (Quirinus), weakly yielding to pressure from above, afraid to stand by their real convictions, and voting down their opponents by sheer force of numbers ; as it would be to view the Minority as factious, disloyal, anti-papal, half-Catholic. Far otherwise was it : the Minority numbered among its members many of the foremost and finest bishops of the Church, and not a few of the leaders were afterwards raised to the Cardinalate by Leo XIII, nay, by Pius IX himself.

Long before the introduction of the actual papacy debate, in fact from the very beginning, the existence of a Minority out of touch with the management of the Council and the conduct of affairs made itself felt. One of the Cardinal Presidents said to Icard at an early date that there was ' an Opposition '. Certainly the Minority had definite complaints causing dissatisfaction and friction—it is of the nature of a minority to have dissatisfactions on the conduct of the majority.

It will be well to hear them, even as expressed by Quirinus.

(1) The first was the matter of the acoustic properties of the Council-hall. As at first arranged many, perhaps most, of the bishops could not hear what was said by the speakers. This we have heard from Ullathorne, as also the various proposals to hold the Congregations elsewhere, as in the Sistine or the Quirinal; we have also heard from him the alterations made in the attempts to improve things in the aula. He was quite satisfied with the result, but he tells us he had a good place: his notebook shows that he could hear quite well from January 14 to February 22; he specially notes one speaker as inaudible. On the other hand, Darboy declared still on January 19 that he could hear or understand hardly anything from his place.

The allegation made by Quirinus more than once, that it was done on purpose by those managing the Council, in order to stifle discussion and muzzle the bishops, is too foolish to call for comment. As a fact, part of the reason of the month's break in the holding of Congregations after February 22, was to allow of another effort being made to improve matters. The Archbishop of Cambrai at a later stage assured his clergy that anyone who spoke clearly could be heard.[1] One of the cardinals was reported as saying he had heard nothing at all all the time. It is to be remembered that many of the bishops were very old men; it would be impossible to provide a hall seating 700, in which old men could hear well. It may safely be said, that unless the great body of bishops had heard fairly well, there would not have been 600 of them in regular attendance at the lengthy Congregations.

(2) One principal complaint of the Minority was

[1] *Lac* 1410.

the number of non-diocesan bishops who took part in the Council. As this figures so largely in Quirinus and in Salmon, and in other hostile writings, it is right to go into the matter exactly. Says Quirinus : 'It has become evident that the strength of the Romanist party lies in the number of titular bishops selected by the Pope, and vicars apostolic or missionary bishops' (Dec. 29; p. 118). At the end of Mansi, V (53), is a catalogue of all those entitled to take part in the Council, 1000 in number. Of these 750 actually were there. The longest roll-call was that of the Second Public Session, January 6, when close on 750 responded. Of these 64 were not bishops at all : viz. 23 cardinals in Curia and 41 superiors of Religious Orders. It is possible to distinguish the non-diocesan bishops, because they are marked 'in partibus infidelium', and when any one of them was a vicar apostolic, etc., the fact is entered. There were just 100 non-diocesan bishops, and of these 57 were vicars apostolic.[1] The statement of Quirinus, repeated by Salmon, that 'the bishops i.p.i. were persons having no flocks, or only having them in expectation, and representing in fact nothing and nobody, and can therefore bear no testimony to the faith of their churches, which have no existence,' is quite extraordinarily out of touch with fact so far as the great majority of vicars apostolic were concerned. For instance, at that date the Catholic hierarchy had not yet been set up in India, and there were twenty vicariates : thus vicars apostolic of Calcutta, Madras, Bombay, and of other districts of India with large Catholic communities, were at the Council : the vicariate of Jaffna, Ceylon, counted 60,000 Catholics. The Scottish bishops and the Dutch were still but vicars apostolic ; parts of North America were still ecclesiastically unorganized,

[1] Salmon's 300 !

so that Bishop Gibbons sat as vicar apostolic of North Carolina; similarly British Guiana and British Columbia were vicariates. And the bishops of the great mission fields of China, Japan, other parts of Asia and Africa were all vicars apostolic. But the greater number of the vicars apostolic were exercising true episcopal jurisdiction and functions over important Catholic communities. Moreover, nine of the bishops *i.p.i.* were coadjutors or auxiliaries to diocesan bishops. This leaves just 36 merely titular bishops without any kind of jurisdiction—officials in the Curia or members of the papal diplomatic service, and a few retired bishops, like Dr. Errington. To sum up in round numbers: of the 750 present on January 6, 580 were diocesan bishops with full status as ordinaries; 60 were vicars apostolic exercising episcopal jurisdiction, often in large and important districts; 10 were coadjutors; 36 were mere titulars; 64 were not bishops. An analysis of the roll-call at the Third Session, April 24, yields a similar result.

It thus appears how misleading is the suggestion that the Council was flooded with titulars and packed by the Pope for the purpose of carrying the infallibility.

(3) Akin to this was the complaint of 'the Pope's boarders', which looms so large in Quirinus and Salmon. The fact was that the Pope offered hospitality to bishops from missionary lands or from poor dioceses, maintaining them at his own cost. The insinuation made freely that this interfered with the liberty of those who received the Pope's hospitality, and that it was of the nature of a bribe or intimidation, seems unworthy of all credence. Quirinus says there were three hundred such 'Pope's pensioners', all safe votes, and that they were costing the Pope £1000 a day: Ullathorne gives the figure at £200 a day that the Council was costing the Pope, a more likely amount. Quirinus' words are: 'The main strength

of the infallibilist legion consists of the 300 papal boarders who go through thick and thin in singing to the tune of their entertainer' (Jan. 30; p. 173).

(4) Another ground of complaint, especially in German circles antagonistic to the Council, and loudly voiced by Quirinus, was the small number of German bishops as compared with those of other countries, especially Italy. Salmon says fourteen—the real number was nineteen. This of course means the bishops of what became the German Empire, and did not include the Austrians and Hungarians. Italy had over 250 bishoprics—of course not all attended the Council. There is a tacit suggestion that this extraordinary preponderance of Italians was somehow manœuvred with a view to the Council. The idea is wholly false. The cause was historical and had its roots in the distant past. In Italy in the early Middle Ages every Roman municipal town, no matter how small, was a bishopric, so that the ecclesiastical map of Central Italy is a network of bishops' sees.[1] In the German lands, on the contrary, the dioceses tended often to follow the political divisions of the country : Rottenburg was the one diocese embracing all Württemberg, Freiburg all Baden. And the great Prince-bishoprics were of immense extent : the Archbishop of Cologne had more Catholic subjects than all the sixteen English and Scottish bishops together. Nor was Germany the only country underrepresented : Belgium was in the like case, with only six sees, whereof Malines is as big as the great German dioceses. The enormous preponderance of Italian bishops had been a problem at earlier Councils : at Constance it gave rise to the plan of voting by nations, so that the small number of French or English bishops carried the same weight as the overwhelming number of Italians.

[1] One of the articles of the recent Concordat provides for a diminution of the number of dioceses in Italy.

Though the under-representation of the German Catholics at the Vatican Council was made a great grievance at the time of the Council, it does not appear that there has since then been any move in the direction of dividing the German dioceses and so making more bishops. The grievance was a real one, but it had nothing to say to the Council. The remedy would seem to lie in the hands of the German bishops. The Holy See shows itself not averse to the policy of dividing dioceses, on reason being shown. The thirteen English dioceses of 1870 are now eighteen. But in their postulata of things to be brought before the Council, the German bishops did ask for a subdivision of the great German dioceses.

(5) A curious proposal was put forward, that a bishop's vote should carry weight proportionate to the number of his flock, after the manner of voting at the Trades' Unions Congress; so that the Archbishop of Cologne could outvote all the sixty bishops of the Papal States as reduced in 1870. It was calculated that in this way the Minority could outvote the Majority at the Council, having in addition to the German and Austrian dioceses, such great dioceses as Milan and Paris. The fact may be doubted; but certainly such a method of voting was unknown to any ancient Council. The idea of ' representation ' did not come in. It is notorious that at the first œcumenical Councils the Western Church was, it may be said, wholly unrepresented, except for the papal legates.

(6) Akin to this was Döllinger's contention that bishops were only mandatories of their dioceses, and had to give not their own mind but that of their flock. Of this unheard-of idea it suffices to say that it would have compelled many of the French Minority bishops to vote Ultramontane (cf. Ollivier, op. cit., II, 238).

(7) Quirinus and Salmon make great play with the

'eighteen empty red hats' that were being dangled before the eyes of wavering bishops as bribes. This grotesque idea is refuted by the fact that for three years after the Council there was no creation of cardinals. Then in the creation of 1873 was Régnier, Archbishop of Cambrai, a strong supporter of the definition, and the Archbishop of Valencia; but of the Opposition, Simor, Archbishop of Esztergom. Dechamps and Manning had to wait until 1875 for their Hats. In the first creation of Leo XIII, 1879, along with Pie of Poitiers were Haynald and Fürstenberg, prime leaders of the Opposition; and of those who, though not members of Council, had taken part in the controversy, Newman on one side and Hergenröther on the other. At later dates Leo raised to the purple Meignan and Foulon, both foremost inopportunists. And it is on record that but for the political objections of the Austrian Government, he would have done the same for Strossmayer. So little is it the case that the line of action taken at the Council influenced the bestowal of red hats.

It seemed well at this point to make it clear that Salmon's picture of the Council, the one best known in English circles, is a travesty of the facts. As has been said, it is wholly based on Quirinus. It may be that Quirinus repeats, but surely by a loud-speaker, things said in moments of excitement and irritation by Minority bishops—feelings and party spirit ran high, and wild sayings were by no means confined to one side. Quirinus reflects the mentality of Friedrich and Döllinger, who were frankly working to wreck the Council by every means, and sought to represent the Minority bishops as being of the same mind as themselves. It will appear with a superabundance of evidence later on that such a representation of the mind even of the most determined bishops of the Minority is an entirely false picture. Certain grievances they had, and expressed very strongly in formal protests, concerning the regulations and manner of conducting the discussions of the Council, and the freedom of debate : this matter of the freedom of the Council will be dealt with more conveniently at a later stage (Chap. XXVI).

On some of these objections M. Ollivier, ' incroyant ' though he was, seems to reach a higher and more religious level than some Catholic critics : [1]

In a Council there are not Italians, or Frenchmen, or Germans ; there are bishops, all equal, because their competence comes from the sacred character conferred by consecration. Why, in the judgement of a question of faith, should the bishop of a great city weigh more than the bishop of a small town ? If detachment, heroism, the practice of apostolic virtues, give the spirit a greater aptitude for laying hold of truth, why should the vote of vicars apostolic, habituated to sacrifice and ready for martyrdom, carry less weight than that of the wealthy bishops of Austria and Hungary ? Is it not unworthy to suppose that the apostolic liberty of such confessors of the Faith can be destroyed by the necessity in which their meritorious poverty places them, of accepting from the Pope during their stay in Rome a roof and a bit of bread ?

It may be said with much truth that the uneasiness felt by many bishops was due to reasons deeper than the questions of theology raised by the proposed defining of the Pope's infallibility : other things were haunting men's minds, motiving the attitude of those more or less in opposition. There was solicitude as to the maintenance of the position of bishops as Successors of the Apostles, holding their authority, once instituted in their dioceses, by divine right. As one bishop put it, there was a fear lest, having come to the Council as princes of the Church, they would go back

[1] Op cit., II, 71.

to the dioceses satraps of a central autocrat.[1]   Again,
many Ullathorne among them, felt alarm at the prospect of a vague indeterminate infallibility, capable of
being extended almost indefinitely, as Ward was doing.
Such fears are illustrated by a representation of some
American bishops, that it would be impossible for them
to persuade their Irish congregations to accept as infallible the act whereby Adrian IV handed over Ireland to English dominion.[2]   The notion seems to us
a most ludicrous ; but it does show the ideas in the
minds even of bishops during the Council, as to the
limits to which the infallibility might be stretched.
Then the bishops of the democratic countries were
afraid of the tendencies of the Syllabus of 1864, as fore-
boding a possible reassertion of the claims of the
medieval and renaissance Popes over civil governments ; among the French bishops these politico-
religious questions of Church and State were the
cause of deep-seated anxieties : abbé Gay, Pie's theologian, was probably right in saying that when these
questions came on, there would be more acute controversy over them than over the infallibility.   Lastly,
there was the jealousy, as old as St. Bernard,[3] at the
ever-growing tendency towards centralization and con-
centration of the government of the Church in Rome,
and the feeling that bishops should have a freer hand
and fuller authority in the ordinary government of
their dioceses.

Such considerations go far to account for the mentality of the Minority bishops.

[1] So Bishop Goss of Liverpool.
[2] *Lac* 1375.   [3] *De Consideratione.*

CHAPTER XV

THE CONSTITUTION ON CATHOLIC FAITH

It was on March 1, after seven weeks' work, that Martin of Paderborn laid before the deputation *de Fide* the result of his labours. He had divided the schema into two parts, the first dealing with fundamentals— God the Creator, revelation, faith, faith and reason, with a Proem prefixed; the second with particular doctrines of Christian belief. The revised schema is given in Mansi, V (53), 164; *Lac* 1628. The First Part was gradually hammered into the shape enacted in the ' dogmatic constitution on Catholic Faith '; the Second never came before the Council. In the First Part the first eleven chapters of the original schema were compressed into four and almost halved in length, but a long Proem was prefixed—Gay tells us that it was written by him. The deputation at once set to work discussing and emending the reformed draft with great thoroughness. The schedule of proposed amendments takes up thirteen columns of Mansi. At the first session, on the Proem alone, fifty-six amendments, great and small, many merely stylistic, were proposed by members of the deputation. At the next session Martin took up these amendments, accepted some, and persuaded the deputation to reject most. And so at the succeeding sessions the deputation worked through the four chapters of the constitution and the canons. In this way, after eight sessions, it was on March 11 passed for press and for presentation to the Council.

On 14th the new text was circulated among the bishops, accompanied by a brief report on the part of the deputation, explaining how they had endeavoured to meet the general wish of the Fathers as manifested at the previous discussions.[1]

At the General Congregation of March 18 the discussion was opened by Archbishop Simor of Esztergom, Primate of Hungary, who in the name of the deputation made a report on the revised schema;[2] his speech was greatly appreciated on all hands, and is lauded by Ullathorne in a letter of 20th as 'a masterpiece of clear exposition and beautiful easy latinity'. Then commenced the discussion of the reformed scheme as a whole. This was finished in two sessions, seven speaking, the reception given to the new schema being on the whole favourable. No more desiring to speak, at that same session was commenced the debate on the Proem. And now, March 22, occurred the one real ' scene ' of the Council. Strossmayer was speaking (Mansi, III (51), 72):

> The Proem ascribes to Protestantism all the errors of the day,—rationalism, pantheism, materialism, atheism ; but all these errors existed long before Protestantism. And there are among Protestants many grave men who are a great help to Catholics in opposing these errors, as in former times Leibnitz, in our day Guizot, whose refutation of Renan I would like to be in the hands of all (murmurs). I believe that there is in the midst of Protestantism a great crowd of men in Germany, England, and America, who love our Lord Jesus Christ and deserve to have applied to them those words of Augustine, ' They err indeed, but they err in good faith (murmurs) : they are heretics, heretics ; but no one holds them for heretics.'
>
> The President, Cardinal de Angelis : ' I pray you, Rt. Rev. Father, to refrain from words that cause scandal to some Fathers.' Strossmayer went on in the same sense

---

[1] Mansi, III (51), 31 ; *Lac* 69. [2] Mansi, l.c., 42 ; *Lac* 80.

MGR. STROSSMAYER,
Bishop of Bosnia

MGR. VEROT,
Bishop of Savannah, U.S.A.

with words not caught by the stenographers; but he was cut short by Cardinal Capalti, one of the Presidents, who said it was not question of Protestants but of Protestantism, not of the persons but of the heresy; modern errors do arise from the principle of Protestantism, private judgement; therefore it is not against charity to say that these monsters of error are derived from Protestantism.

Strossmayer: I thank your Eminence for this instruction; but your argument does not convince me that all these errors are to be attributed to Protestants. I believe that there exists in Protestantism not merely one or two, but a crowd of men who still love Jesus Christ (murmurs).

Cardinal Capalti: I beg that you stick to what the schema says. There is no mention in it of Protestants, but only of the sects condemned at Trent. Therefore it seems to me there is no offence given to Protestants. And so I beg you to desist from such speech, which I must frankly say offends the ears of very many bishops.

Strossmayer: I finish. But I know that there are many living amidst Protestants, who with all their heart desire that there be not anything put into the schema that may be a check to divine grace working among them.

Capalti: It seems to me, I must say, that your animadversions have no foundation in the schema, that could make Protestants put forward their hatred of the Catholic Church.

Strossmayer: I finish; but against one observation of your Eminence I must say just one word . . .

Capalti tried to speak, but immediately, Fathers on all sides murmuring, Strossmayer said: I attribute this to the deplorable conditions of this Council (an uproar of indignation made it almost impossible to hear what he said). He went on: I make another observation, short, very short, but which I hold touches the essence of things, and so moves my conscience that I can by no means keep silence. In the recent Regulation it is laid down that questions are to be settled by majority of votes. Against this some bishops have put in a statement, asking if the ancient rule of moral unanimity . . .

The speaker's words were made inaudible by the renewed and increased murmur of general indignation.

Capalti : This does not belong to the present discussion.
Vehement applause : the speaker tried to go on : most of
the Fathers shouted him down ; they almost raged (obstre-
punt, vix non fremunt) ; many called on him to come down.

Strossmayer : Your Eminence certainly should pardon
me. I respect the rights of the Presidents. I certainly, if
that former eternal and immutable rule of a morally unanimous consent . . .

The speaker's voice was drowned in the uproar of indignation. He said : I protest against every interruption,
I . . .

Fathers rising called out : We protest against you.

Strossmayer : I protest against any interruption.

The First President rang his bell again and again.

The Fathers generally : We wish him to come down ;
let him come down.

Strossmayer : I protest against . . . and he began to
come down. The indignant Fathers left their seats, all
murmuring different things. Some said, 'These people
don't want the infallibility of the Pope ; is this man infallible himself ! '

Others : ' He is Lucifer, anathema, anathema ! ' Others :
' He is another Luther, let him be cast out ! ' And all cried
out : ' Come down, come down.' But he kept on saying :
' I protest, I protest ', and came down.

This certainly was ' a scene ', the like of which
occurs from time to time in all parliaments, even the
House of Commons—no doubt peculiarly regrettable
in a General Council. However, it was the single real
scene of the Vatican Council, no such thing happening
again, even at times of severest strain.

When it is looked into, the Presidents may, I think,
be absolved from blame. Strossmayer was clearly out
of order in bringing in the matter of ' moral unanimity ':
it seems that, no answer having been given to the
remonstrance of the Minority bishops nearly a month
before, he was determined to bring the thing forward
publicly. Capalti's interventions seem in proper form ;

there is no sign of loss of temper or undue heat in his words. The fault seems to lie with the bishops, of whom, as Granderath acknowledges, greater calm and dignity might have been expected. It is doubtful how many took part in the disturbance; the report seems to imply nearly all; but even Quirinus says it is doubtful that more than two hundred took part, and that the greater number disapproved (p. 388). As Granderath says, bishops living in Protestant countries would be able to understand and sympathize with Strossmayer's words; but those of the Catholic countries looked on Protestants in the same light as old-fashioned ' black ' Protestants of Ulster looked on Catholics.

The next day the Council met in chastened mood; and when Meignan of Chalons in clear but calm words pressed Strossmayer's plea that the Proem should not seem to say that pantheism, materialism, and the other errors of the day are derived from Protestantism; or that Protestantism leads by a necessary connexion to atheism, he was listened to without interruption or sign of disapproval. The debate on the Proem ended that day, the President saying that the amendments would be printed and circulated at the next Congregation. This was done the following day, 24th.[1] Meantime a revision of the Proem was in hand for the deputation. At its meeting on 25th, Bilio said that most of the amendments, being stylistic, or not touching the substance, could be dealt with in the revision without being put to the vote; only in regard to two or three was it necessary to take a formal vote. At the General Congregation on 26th Simor again spoke in behalf of the deputation:[2] the Proem was undergoing revision, account being had of all the observations made upon it; only three amendments touched

---

[1] Mansi, III (51), 123; *Lac* 88. [2] Mansi, l.c., 127; *Lac* 91.

the substance so as to call for a vote. Of these the most important was, that to the words ' episcopis nobiscum sedentibus et iudicantibus' should be added ' et definientibus', this being an assertion of the position of the bishops at the Council. Simor pointed out that the clause was founded on the text, ' ye shall sit on twelve thrones judging the twelve tribes of Israel ' ; the word ' judging ' was to be taken in its fullest sense, as including ' defining', and the Acts of the Council were fully the act of the whole episcopate. Moreover, ' those of us who are alive at the end of the Council will subscribe the Acts " Ego definiens subscripsi " ' ;— little did he think that not one would be alive to subscribe the Acts at the close of the Council, for it has not yet been done !—and so he concluded : ' Absolutely nothing is taken from the rights of the bishops ' (' Bene ! bravo ! '). It is to be noted that before this date Simor was acting with the Minority. This amendment, as well as the two others singled out for a formal vote, had been made by Whelan of Wheeling, U.S.A. ; he now declared himself satisfied and withdrew them, so that no amendment had to be voted on ; and the President said the Proem would be brought forward as soon as the deputation had finished the revision. This it did next day, 27th, when the revised text was ' read, examined, discussed, corrected, finally approved ' and sent to the printer. On 28th it was distributed among the Fathers ; and at the General Congregation on 29th the Proem was accepted unanimously by the 620 Fathers present.

It is of great interest to compare the two forms of the Proem, that proposed by the deputation *de Fide* on March 18 and that passed on 29th,[1] the latter being identical, but for a couple of stylistic improvements, with the form enacted at the Public Session of April 24

---

[1] Mansi, III (51), 31 and 178 ; *Lac* 69 and 96.

(see Appendix, Vol. II). The first thing that springs to the eye is that Strossmayer's protest had borne fruit : the passage definitely attributing to Protestantism the rejection of Christ and consequent widespread pantheism, materialism and atheism, has been cut out; moreover the general style has been greatly toned down, a number of needlessly offensive expressions being removed: as *impio ausu, opinionum monstra, impiissima doctrina, mysterium iniquitatis, impia pestis :* the only such expression remaining being *pantheismi, materialismi et atheismi barathrum.* It is curious that all these changes were but a return to the text originally presented to the deputation by Martin; how the offending words came in does not appear, for they are not among the amendments proposed at the deputation on March 1 and 2, and there is no notice of further amendments having been proposed. There can be no question that not only in calmness and dignity of tone, but also in point of latinity, the Proem was vastly improved by the criticism and discussion to which it had been subjected.

Meantime the discussion on the four chapters and the canons of the schema was going on. These being concerned with such fundamental beliefs as God and creation, revelation, faith, faith and reason, gave rise to discussions on points of speculative theology, wherein certainly the highly trained theological mind and the keen intellectual force of many of the bishops came conspicuously into play. Not only had systems openly antagonistic to Christian belief, such as pantheism and materialism, to be condemned, but also certain theories that had been broached in recent times in Catholic circles had to be ruled out. The most prominent of these was the system known as ' Traditionalism ', associated with de Lammenais, which held that the human reason is unable of itself to attain to a knowledge of God, but depends on a primitive revelation to our

First Parents, handed on to mankind throughout the ages. What was called 'mitigated traditionalism' found a number of supporters among the French and Belgian bishops, and gave rise to keen debates of a high order ; thus one speech took the case of Aristotle and showed that by the working of pure reason he had attained to the idea of God. The Council finally declared that 'the one true God, the Creator, can be known certainly by the natural light of the human reason', thus asserting the rights of the human intellect and the validity of its operations.

The course of the four chapters of the Constitution was the same as that of the Proem. The text of each of them as proposed by the deputation *de Fide* was in turn debated at Congregations from March 22 till April 6 ; the amendments to each chapter were scheduled and printed—to chapter I were 47, to II were 62, to III were 122, to IV were 50 ; they were commented on individually at successive Congregations by selected members of the deputation ; then they were put to the vote one by one ; finally the revised text of each chapter was passed as amended. There were in all fifteen General Congregations, at which just one hundred speeches were delivered. Then took place on April 12 what may be called the trial voting, at which the text of the Constitution as a whole was voted on in the shape in which its five parts had severally been passed. This time the vote was not taken by standing and sitting, but each one recorded his vote aloud when called upon by name. The result was that 510 voted 'placet' and 85 'placet iuxta modum', i.e. with a reservation ; this was like voting for the second reading of a bill with the intention of moving an amendment at the committee stage. There were no 'non placets'. Each one who voted 'placet iuxta modum' had to submit in writing the amendments he desired, along with the reasons for them ;

these when scheduled in order, line by line of the text, mounted up to 148, and make quite interesting reading for any theologian. One of the reservations complained of the latinity : The style is harsh, not good Latin, redolent of Germanism, and should be corrected, so that the decrees may commend themselves even by an irreprehensible form of language : and an improved form for the opening of the Proem is suggested, which however was not adopted. Some of the bishops had a craze for rewriting the texts ; the Spanish bishop of Urgel rewrote, it may be said literally, every chapter, decree, canon, that came before the Council. All the amendments were again considered by the deputation : a large number were in effect a call to reconsider points already voted on at General Congregations ; these the deputation ruled out, as also points merely stylistic. So on April 19 the spokesman of the deputation—as we should say, the minister in charge of the bill—made a long relation at the Congregation on all the amendments, the upshot of which was that the deputation recommended the accepting of two and the rejecting of the rest. The two were put to the vote and carried almost unanimously ; but in regard to the rest, no opportunity of challenging or even discussing the verdict of the deputation was given : of course, the majority of ' placets ' at the voting of April 12 had been overwhelming. On 20th the deputation put a few final touches to the text.[1]

One of the two amendments admitted at the eleventh hour was due to Ullathorne. We shall hear him speak of it in his letters, but a record of the facts

[1] The whole material of the debates and discussions on the Constitution on Catholic Faith are in Mansi, III (51), 31-426, and V (53), 159-225 ; *Lac* 69-246, and 1647-77. Granderath summarizes the outstanding features of it all. It will be found of no small theological and philosophical interest.

will be of interest as a sample of the procedure of the
Council in a particular case. The first chapter of the
Constitution as proposed by the deputation opened
with the words : ' Sancta Romana Catholica Ecclesia.'
When this chapter came under debate on March 24
Ullathorne moved

that the word ' Romana ' be placed after ' Catholica ', that
we may not seem to encourage in any way the tendencies
of those who wish to qualify the word ' Catholic ' by the
word ' Roman '. English Protestants wish to appropriate
the name of Catholic, which occurs in the Apostles' Creed,
and to dispute our exclusive right to it.   They pretend that
the Catholic Church is divided into three parts : the Romano-
Catholic community, the Anglo-Catholic community, and
the Graeco-Catholic community.   Officials and Government work persistently to familiarize men's minds with this
idea.   In the new laws, in the debates in parliament, in
public speeches, in the press, and in private conversation,
they give to us, and our Church, the name ' Roman Catholic '.
They cannot bear that we call ourselves simply ' Catholics ',
and that we call ourselves not a part of the Church, but the
entire Church.   They demand that we call ourselves Roman
Catholic bishops, so that the name ' Catholic bishops ' may
be used also by the Anglican bishops.   A society was
formed some time ago to propagate the doctrine of a Church
divided into three Branches.   If now the Vatican Council
names the Church, not ' Catholic and Roman ', but ' Roman
Catholic ', the Puseyites will draw thence an argument in
favour of their theory of the three Branches, and the
Government will spread it abroad that, overcome by the
truth, we finally recognize our Church as only a part of
the true Church.

His amendment was : that instead of ' Roman
Catholic Church ' be read ' Catholic and Roman
Church ' ; or that, at least, a comma be placed be-
tween ' Roman ' and ' Catholic '.

Clifford followed in support, advocating a return

to the simple form of the Apostles' Creed, 'The holy Catholic Church'.

The deputation *de Fide* on March 27 rejected these suggestions unanimously ; and their spokesman at the General Congregation of 29th expounded the reasons why the deputation adhered to the form : 'Sancta Romana Catholica Ecclesia' ; he said, however, they were prepared to accept the comma between 'Romana' and 'Catholica'. Clifford's amendment was thrown out by a large majority, and so was Ullathorne's suggested transposition of the two words. But on the question of the comma, the voting by standing up was so uncertain, that the scrutators were preparing to take a formal count ; until several Fathers declared they did not well understand the significance of the comma, and asked the Presidents to postpone the voting till the next day. On the next day the spokesman made a special relation on the comma all by itself, saying that having maturely considered the question in sight of God, and having consulted a number of Fathers, he had come to the conclusion that the reasons alleged by the English bishops were invalid,—their point would be dealt with in the schema on the Church ; —and consequently he recommended the Fathers to delete the comma ; which they did.

When, however, the schema came up again on April 12 to be voted on as a whole, no fewer than thirty-five of the 148 amendments of those who voted 'placet iuxta modum' were, one way or another, backing Ullathorne. The spokesman of the deputation *de Fide* said that one or two of its members had objected to any change being made, but that the great majority thought the representations of the English and American bishops should be met, and the formula 'Holy Catholic Apostolic Roman Church' adopted by the Fathers. When put to the vote the amendment was carried almost unanimously ; and so the first words of the actual dogmatic decrees of the Vatican Council are due to Ullathorne's intervention; it is of interest to note that a small number of bishops were, on occasion, able to make their view prevail over that of the deputation.

The Minority bishops, especially the leaders, were most desirous that the Constitution on Catholic Faith might be passed without dissentient voice at the Public Session. But another dissatisfaction loomed big among the ' iuxta modum ' reservations; thirty-eight objections were lodged against the two concluding paragraphs that follow the canons. They may be seen in the Constitution at the end of Vol. II. The first calls on all the Faithful, especially pastors, to guard the Church from the errors here condemned : the second lays down that not only must heretical pravity be shunned, but also errors which more or less approach to it; therefore the duty is inculcated of keeping (servandi) those decrees of the Holy See by which such evil opinions are proscribed and prohibited. These paragraphs originally stood at the end of the entire Constitution on Catholic Faith; but when the Constitution was divided into two parts, and only the first part was brought before the Council, they were transferred to the end of this part following the canons, and so stood in the revised schema distributed March 14. They seem to have attracted little attention : at the discussions only one bishop, a Piedmontese, questioned the desirability of their being in this place; it would seem, he urged, that there would be a like reason for repeating them at the end of each Constitution enacted. This seems to have impressed the deputation, and on April 8 the spokesman, Pie of Poitiers, announced that the deputation had come to the view that this conclusion had better be restored to its original place at the end of the complete Constitution; this was agreed to almost unanimously. The next day, however, the deputation changed its mind, and a notice was issued that the question of this conclusion would be put to the vote again at the ensuing Congregation. The going back on a point already settled by a vote called forth a protest from nine prominent Minority bishops. But on April 12 Pie explained that, the text of the Constitution having got into the public press, postponing the conclusion would be taken as retracting it, and thereby would give countenance to the error that only formally defined truths have to be accepted. On his recommendation the Fathers acquiesced in the retention of the conclusion. When the fourth chapter was put to the vote as a whole, along with its canons and the conclusion, only one or two stood up to vote against it.

There then followed the trial voting by ' placet ', etc., on the entire Constitution. As has been recorded, there were no ' non placets '; but in the ' iuxta modum ' reservations now no fewer than thirty-eight Minority bishops objected to the conclusion. The objection seems to have been mainly against the procedure whereby it had been reintroduced : so for instance Clifford, ' the procedure was irregular '. But the matter raised a good deal of excited feeling in the Minority, and on April 18 forty-four bishops sent a memorial to the Presidents, representing their strong desire that the Constitution should be passed unanimously at the coming Public Session, but expressing their fear that this would not be if the conclusion were retained, and if the opening words ' Romana Catholica Ecclesia ' were not altered. The letter was signed by Schwarzenberg, Rauscher, the Archbishops of Munich and Cologne, of Paris and Rheims, and a number of French, German, and Hungarian bishops ; of English-speaking bishops were Kenrick of St. Louis, Domenec of Pittsburg, Fitzgerald of Little Rock, and Errington and Clifford.

At the Congregation the next day, April 19, Gasser of Brixen as spokesman of the deputation, in dealing with the reservations, announced that the deputation adopted and recommended the form ' Sancta Catholica Apostolica Romana Ecclesia ' ; but in regard to the conclusion he said the deputation considered it most necessary to guard against the idea that opinions not explicitly condemned in the canons were thereby left open for free discussion in the schools ; but he pointed out that the theological question as to the dogmatic force of decrees of the Holy See was not touched in any way by the words of the conclusion. So the matter was not put to the vote again.

The Minority bishops had now to decide what line they would follow. None of them had any objection to the substance of the Constitution or of the canons, which was all fundamental Catholic belief; any hesitations were about subsidiary points, e.g. the desirability of promulgating so many canons with anathema. Schwarzenberg and Rauscher now exercised their influence to the utmost to secure a unanimous ' placet ', and Clifford is specially mentioned as active in the endeavour to bring about this result.[1] The outcome of it was that Strossmayer absented himself from the Public Session, but all the other leaders of the Minority gave their ' placet '.

And so, when the Public Session of Low Sunday, April 24, was held, the 667 Fathers present gave a unanimous ' placet ' to the Constitution, thus with immense labour and discussion brought into its final shape. Ullathorne's letter describing the scene will be given in its place (p. 298). When the voting, which took an hour and a half, was over, Fessler, the Secretary, ascended the pontifical throne and announced the result to the Pope : ' Most Holy Father, the decrees

---

[1] Granderath, II, Bk. ii, c. 12, p. 472.

and canons have pleased all the Fathers without exception.' Then the Pope arose : 'The decrees and canons just read have pleased all the Fathers without dissentient, and We, with the approval of the Sacred Council, define them as read, and confirm them by apostolic authority.' He then made a fervent allocution :

You see, beloved brethren, what a good and pleasant thing it is to walk in agreement in the house of God. So walk always. And as our Lord Jesus Christ to-day gave His peace to His Apostles, so I, His unworthy Vicar, in His name give you peace. Peace, as you know, drives out fear. Peace, as you know, shuts the ears to words without knowledge. Ah ! may this peace accompany you all the days of your life ; may this peace be your consolation in life ; may this peace be your refuge in death ; and may it be your everlasting joy in heaven.

He intoned the 'Te Deum,' gave his solemn blessing, and with the publication of the indulgence the Third Public Session ended.[1]

[1] Acta of Third Session, Mansi, III (51), 427; *Lac* 247. The Constitution on Catholic Faith, 'Dei Filius', is given in full below, Appendix, Vol. II.

CHAPTER XVI

DR. ULLATHORNE'S LETTERS, MARCH AND APRIL

It has seemed best to give together in sequence Dr. Ullathorne's letters of March and April, up to the Third Session, April 24, so as not to break the course of the narrative of events at the Council. But for the understanding of some allusions of the letters a simple framework of facts and dates must be supplied.

The second dogmatic schema, ' de Ecclesia Christi ', had been distributed to the bishops on January 21. It was a lengthy document of fifteen chapters and twenty-one canons, followed by still more lengthy annotations : this schema will have to be dealt with in the next chapter. Under the regulations promulgated on February 22, the Fathers were given ten days to write such comments as they wished on the first ten chapters, the portion concerned with the theology of the Church, up to, but excluding, the chapter on the Papacy. The comments, which were voluminous, had to be lodged with the deputation *de Fide* by March 4. On March 6 the announcement was made that the question of the Pope's infallibility would be brought on, and the formula prepared by the theologians in case it should be needed was distributed, and the bishops had until 25th to write their animadversions and lodge them with the deputation *de Fide*.

The letters may now speak for themselves.

March 1. Our new Rules for managing the Council were in the papers, so you will see them. As we have had ten days to write on the first part of the schema ' de Ecclesia ', to help the special deputation to reform it before it comes on for discussion, we have had a great time. I believe we meet again in General Congregation next Tuesday, when we shall probably have *the question* brought on to write upon. But the schema, or rather addition to schema which contains the proposition, already we know prepared, is not yet put into our hands. We soon expect to have the first schema *de Fide* returned to us from the special deputation *de Fide*, recast in form and reformed in language ; and then will come the last discussion upon it. I hear the Pope calculates on a Session to promulgate decrees on the 25th inst. But I doubt if we shall have very much ready. We of the deputation of discipline are still waiting for printed matter from the discussions. I know that the first schema *de Fide* has been very much changed in consequence of the discussions. The second schema *de Fide* has already beed printed three times before the bishops have touched it, ann will be again before it is discussed, upon the written suggestions sent in to the special deputation. General Councils are tedious things, except for the ever varying incidents that are occurring in what I may call the policy of its management.

March 6. My last news is, that all things are marching on the path of moderation, and the zealots are being tamed down, as much as they may, to prudence. The definition is being moderated so that it may have nothing in it that is new or startling even in form.

The Pope has had more than one cry over his troubles, although he bears himself bravely in public. Amongst other things, the conflicts in the Catholic papers and the imprudent letters of some bishops have given him distress. Then political affairs are anything but reassuring. A protracted Council can scarcely be thought of. And one hears that the Revolution has laid its plans throughout Europe. Then the position of things in France is critical. In short the Pope is in his hour of trial. Still, one trusts that God will come in to his help. It cannot be pleasant that strong protests have gone in on the part of a considerable body of bishops against some of the new rules. I think they will work well, and that they ought to have had a fair trial, and perhaps will have still.

March 8. The Pope paid us a visit yesterday, chiefly to visit Dr. Grant, who, though now free of fever, is still very weak, and takes nothing but a little broth, and a sip of brandy and water. We had only five minutes' notice, and only three bishops were at home. We received him at the door, and he lingered along the corridors of the first and second story, chatting and making himself agreeable. There are fourteen portraits of British cardinals in the corridor on second story, from Wolsey to Cullen, and he stopped before them, and asked about those he did not know, telling himself of Pole, how he converted Frammingo (*sic*) from Socinianism ; and of the Cardinal Duke of York, how he went a voyage, I think to Malta, but being sick midway took the royal resolution to leave the ship directly, a proof that he was more an Italian than an Englishman. Of course we laughed at the Stuart's expense, which was only courteous to the Pope. Seeing Cardinal Howard in a black mozzetta, he asked me if he was a Benedictine, which was more complimentary to me than to the Dominican cardinal, about whom he evidently knew but little. However I told him that he was not only a Dominican, but had built this College at his own cost. Before the last of the series he exclaimed, ' Povero Wolsey '.

Throwing off his red cloak, his Holiness entered the room of the sick bishop and stayed some twelve minutes, and we waited outside. Bishop Grant said he was very kind. He then returned, lingering and stopping to chat. He talked of ' povero Giorgio ', meaning Talbot.

March 15. We have just received the first schema *de Fide*, as recast by the special deputation, and the new discussion on it begins on the 18th inst. The papers prepared from the discussions for the deputation on discipline are also just ready. Cardinal Capalti tells me they are voluminous, and so our special deputation will now have close and hard work. The deputation *de Fide* has been working daily, Sunday included. Henceforth work will be continuous.

Dr. Northcote is writing out our joint Latin translation of my 'Votum de Summo Pontifice', which goes in to-morrow, the last of the ten days allowed for writing on the great question. [Dr. Northcote had joined the Bishop in Rome as his theologian.]

March 20. We had a General Congregation on Thursday for discussing the reformed schema on Catholic Faith. The Congregation showed that we are not yet sufficiently protected from talkers who give no light, although the exposition of what had been done for the schema by the special deputation, revising it in the light of the previous discussion, by the Primate of Hungary [Simor], was a masterpiece of clear exposition and beautiful easy latinity. We broke up an hour earlier than usual, as on the Fridays in Lent the Pope comes down to St. Peter's to pray. We waited, with a crowd of strangers, for half an hour in St. Peter's, and then the Pope came down. He went and kissed the foot of St. Peter, and prayed with his head against it, and then went to the priedieu prepared for him, in front of the Confession of St. Peter, as it is called. The relics had been placed on the High Altar. After praying a quarter of an hour, the cardinals kneeling behind him, and the bishops all down the two sides of the nave, and the crowd behind them, some kneeling, some standing and staring, amongst whom many of our countrymen and women, the Pope arose and departed. Then there was a general melting away.

We shall have another General Congregation on Tuesday. Our deputation of discipline met for real work yesterday, and in three hours got through a good deal of work. The Pope wishes to have a Session to promulgate the first Chapters of Decrees on Faith and on Discipline as soon as they are ready, and it is to be hoped that in a few weeks that will be done.

A cardinal called on me yesterday, who kindly gave me a survey of the existing state of diplomatic relations with respect to the Council. They are considered to be in a better condition than externally they look. The French Ambassador is gone to Paris, well informed, and in satisfactory dispositions, to explain to the Emperor. Prussia is moderate. The Austrian minister von Beust is troublesome, but will not prevail. Some of the Munich professors, who have been already censured for unsound doctrine, are likely to give trouble, and these are active. Here the chief concern of the Roman Court is the energetic opposition of the Bishop of Orleans.

I am still satisfied with the prospect of affairs in the Council. If there is positive fanaticism on the part of some leaders on one side, the resolute opposition on the other will bring things to their proper temper and moderation. All that belongs to parties gets cleared away by the time anything is reprinted for the second discussion. The Council will do much for the Church, and a good deal of what with time has become useless lumber will be cleared out of the canons. But the Council will not print its work this year. And if we disperse, there will never be as many bishops united together again for a second year.

I sometimes think it may end this way, the decrees of faith and a part of those on discipline be got through, and the bishops be called upon to write on the next from their sees, and the Pope publish the remainder of the decrees of discipline. For a break-up, and a recall, would, I feel convinced, exhibit a much smaller Council.

A good many bishops are getting leave to depart now, on one ground or another. And it would be a serious thing for the bishops to be absent from their sees when the decrees of the first year had got out into the world.

On March 13 died Montalembert. The two sections which Ollivier, an intimate friend, consecrates to him are a worthy tribute.[1] It is pleasing to know that the *Univers*, forgetting past animosities, appeared in mourning the next day, and said : ' M. de Montalembert has been, of all the laymen of our time, the one who has given to the Church the greatest and most devoted services.' In his last days he threw himself with vehemence into the party of opposition to the infalli-

[1] *L'Église et l'État au Concile du Vatican*, I, 449-58 ; II, 172-5.

bility. A friend asked him what he would do, supposing it were defined by the Council united with the Pope ? He said calmly, ' Eh bien, tout simplement je croirai.' In the following letter Ullathorne refers to a matter that gave rise to much comment :

March 21. There has been a great sensation here about a Requiem Mass for Montalembert. Being a Roman Patrician, he was entitled to a Requiem at the Capitol in the Ara Caeli, attended by the Senate and Patricians. An anonymous circular was sent round exhorting people to attend. It was shown to the Pope, and fearing a demonstration— for you know poor Montalembert published a very strong letter against the definition, and about ' making an idol in the Vatican ', a little before he died [1]—the Pope prohibited it. And although, alarmed at the sensation the prohibition would make, Cardinal Antonelli, the Governor of Rome and head of the police, entreated the Pope to yield, he stood firm. But the next moment the Pope went out to a church where a Mass was said for Montalembert, and assisted at it. The whole affair caused great excitement. The Bishop of Orleans was also refused leave to preach his panegyric.[2]

March 24. The last three days in the Council have been given to most thorough work, at the rate of some ten speeches a day. As it has been the last revising of the schema on Catholic Faith after its reconstruction by the deputation *de Fide* subsequent to its first discussion, everyone has felt the importance of weighing not only every sentence but every word. This has been done with great learning, ability, and conscientiousness, and with a solid method, devoid of rhetoric. The work has shown how much philosophical and theological learning the Church possesses in the episcopate, and I doubt if any previous Council has exhibited as much. The three days have been a great treat. But you will get some notion of the result when I tell you that the mere list of printed amendments

[1] Letter of Feb. 28 : *Lac* 1385 ; Ollivier, II, 63.

[2] This seems to be inaccurate ; there was no question of a sermon by Dupanloup.

proposed upon about six pages of matter fill more than twice that number of pages, and everyone of them will have to be put to the votes of the Council one after another ; and yet this is only with reference to the Proem and first chapter of the first schema, and is the result of discussions upon a document already reformed throughout upon a long previous discussion.

You may be interested to know that I made, or rather read, my first speech to-day in the General Congregation. It was in advocacy of an amendment about which the English bishops were anxious and which no one else seemed likely to take up ; and being both delicate and difficult to be understood by the bishops who had never lived in a Protestant country like ours, I felt it required some tact to secure an attentive hearing until the sense of a question altogether new to the majority was fairly brought out. Thank God I was heard with perfect silence and attention, all parties saw the importance of the point, and bishops of all parties and nations congratulated me on the success of the exposition. But the whole speech only filled a sheet of note-paper.

March 25. I had made all arrangements for going to the Minerva, where the Pope assists at High Mass with the cardinals and the bishops on this holiday of obligation in Rome [Lady Day, the feast of the Annunciation B.V.M.], and where he blesses the Golden Rose ; when I remembered that a whole volume of amendments had to be studied upon the first schema, for voting in the Congregation to-morrow morning ; so while Dr. Northcote is making his preliminary notes on them as theologian, I continue this letter. All the bishops here are at similar work, and I suspect the Pope will have but few of them to attend at the Mass. I have not yet been again at the Exhibition, the mornings being so occupied between General Congregations, special deputations, and the studies for them.

The reporting for the Council is a curious process, as every word whether spoken or read is taken down. There are twelve young men picked from the different colleges who have been trained, and who have their working room behind the Council partition. You see two of them at work on a moveable table where they stand, each has a narrow long sheet of paper. One writes one half of a line, speaks the finishing word of his half line, which the other takes up, and finishing his half line speaks the final word, which the first takes up; this continues for four minutes and a half, when two other reporters arrive, who take up the last word being written by their predecessors, and write on for another four and a half minutes, when they give place to another pair of stenographers, and so on to the end of the session. When each two retire with what they have written, they put the two pages of half lines together, and it takes them 40 minutes to reduce to ordinary writing what they had obtained in four and a half minutes. The bishops bear testimony to the accuracy of their work. Two of the shorthand writers are from our college,[1] and we take them daily to their work in our carriage, but they are generally at work until two hours after we return. Whilst this is going on at one end of the aula, close to the Presidents, the secretaries and their assistants are at work at the other. They chronicle the history of the Council, examine letters sent in, and draw up documents for the Presidents, and watch over the general management of the Council. The Chief Secretary is Bishop Fessler, an Austrian Bishop, chosen not only for his capacity, but for his enduring power of working sixteen hours a day constantly; an amiable man who is generally popular. The under secretary is a Roman prelate, Mgr. Jacobini, Secretary of the Oriental Propaganda, whose duty it also is to read from the ambo all notices, documents, and lists of bishops going to speak, that they may be heard by all, after being given out officially by the chief President, Cardinal de Angelis, who is a tall and venerable old man with white locks, and one who has suffered imprisonment at the hands of the Italian Government for his staunch adhesion to canonical principles. Whilst all this is going on, the ' assignatori di posti ' in their violet robes are going from bench to bench, taking down the names of all the bishops and others present by

---

[1] One was Samuel Allen, afterwards Bishop of Shrewsbury. The stenographers had been specially practised in the various pronunciations of Latin, the French, Spanish, etc.

right in the Council, which is done every day : first, to record the names of all present on that day ; secondly, to secure that there is no intruder. But as they know everybody, they have not to enquire. Another precaution against intrusion is this. Within the entrance door stand half a dozen ' bussolanti ', marking the bishops by sight as they come in. Thus, even in this vast assembly, it is impossible for a stranger to get amongst them. If a new bishop arrives, he is presented either to one of the Presidents or to the Secretary, and has to go through the process of having his place assigned him. And then there is his number conspicuous in large figures at the back of his seat. The President's bell, a beautiful piece of workmanship, made by two priests, brothers, expressly for the use of the Council, is the instrument that calls general attention whether for an announcement, or, as sometimes happens, I will put it delicately, when a bishop who is speaking gets distracted from the point.

According to the new rules, when a schema has undergone reconstruction in the special deputation in consequence of a first discussion, at the discussion again of the reformed schema any member of that special deputation can rise, after leave given, and reply to any speaker in defence of the text proposed. This was done yesterday with great applause, when one of the special deputation *de Fide* arose to correct the views taken by one of the most able speakers of the assembly. But there was one truly grand and awful scene yesterday, when in reply to some previous speakers, who had argued on philosophical, theological, and prudential principles, against the anathematizing of certain false philosophical schools, an Italian Bishop [Gastaldi, Bishop of Saluzzo, Piedmont], long a priest in the Birmingham diocese, arose and ascended to the height of his argument with a scientific force and a vehemence of eloquence which caused the great majority of the Council to thunder out in one voice together the words ' Anathema, Anathema '. It was just after the speaker had capped the climax of his reasoning by exclaiming that we were bound to take into our hands the vindication of God, and to bear our testimony to His judgements.

During the last three Congregations one's soul has been literally bathed in theological light. And, as a rule, the listening assembly has been very silently conscious that it was giving the last touches to decrees of Faith that could never again be changed, and that were to stand, and to which the Church must stand, all days, even to the end of the world.

Still there is the usual rising and going out, after each speaker comes down from the ambo, beginning about an hour and a half after the opening of discussion, and so there are commonly knots of bishops in the adjoining chapels, used as lobbies, and each as big as a large church, some discussing, others saying Office, others stretching their legs by a walk. After about four hours, as the speakers cease, those who have long sat begin to get restless, and some rise, hoping the President will take the hint. This he sometimes seems to do, and closes the assembly by announcing that the hour is late, and that the next Congregation will be on such a day. But if he announces another Right Rev. speaker from the ambo, down they drop in patient resignation on their seats, and a general smile goes round those 700 faces. But the final words of dismissal are not out of the mouth of the President before the streaming away begins, the great mass of purple robes, variegated by the regulars and the red robes of the cardinals, presses on to the three doors of exit, in one close mass, the youngest, who are in the lowest benches, having the advantage of the venerable seniors ; and out pours the living flood, bowing, smiling, exchanging remarks to each other, pouring between the yellow red and black striped neck-frilled Swiss Guards, who keep the way open with their erect figures and shining long-poled battle-axes of the middle ages. Down the avenue the Fathers stream, some stopping to kiss the foot of St. Peter, all stopping to kneel and say a prayer before the Blessed Sacrament, passing the line of curious spectators from the Council doors to the holy water vase.

April 1. We finished the discussion of the part of the schema for the coming session this morning, but there will be two days yet for voting on as many chapters. On

Sunday *our* deputation meets, to settle the final form on the decree about the Catechism. What it is I must not say.

I am stopping in this afternoon in company with a fire and a cold. We have had no warm weather yet, and there is still snow on the mountains.

The Congregation 'pro postulatis' have had many sittings, but they say there is so much to do that they see not how many new propositions can be introduced. The deputation *de Fide* meets every evening, when at work in the General Congregation in the morning, and sits about three hours, up to 9 p.m. Whether it is the climate, or what, I do not know, but everyone gets tired and feels exhausted for the day after the four hours' session in the morning.

April 4. We are working hard in Council, but shall not be ready for Session before Easter. The work in its last stage is wonderfully different from the first schema. It is like the ox brought down to a few pounds of solid and compact meat.

We are all pleased with the result of this morning's work in the Council. The deputation *de Fide* has so met the sense of the bishops in their amendments, that they have got almost every vote on each point to be voted on. Points on which there was great anxiety have been modified so as to produce universal content. In Easter week we shall have a Session, and pass the first Decrees.

April 13. In General Congregation to-day we voted the first chapters by 'placet'. It took exactly two hours. Each bishop's name was given in turn from the ambo, and he rose as his name was uttered, and said 'placet', or 'placet ad modum', in the latter case putting in a paper containing his objection and its reason. Now for 'womanly curiosity'! My 'ad modum' had a following, and it was pronounced last night that it will be reconsidered in special deputation this evening. There was no other of any importance. The crowd in the nave must have been puzzled with hearing in the distance the incessant call of 'placet' like guns going off in file firing. For the stentorian voice of an official repeated each 'placet', and the milder voices of the prelates sounded like the reverberation between each shot of sound. So it went on for two full hours. 598 votes were given, and nearly 100 were absent.

April 17, Easter Sunday. Alleluia. Such an Easter was never seen in Rome before. The High Mass of the Pope was a marvellous function. St. Peter's so packed that one of our secretaries declared he could not get his hand down to his pocket, which was pretty near a literal story all over the huge building. The Pope was in great voice and vigour. The 800 mitres filled the two sides of the long tribune between the high altar and St. Peter's chair. The solemn stillness of the heretofore surging multitude, as the sublime trumpets in the dome after the grounding of arms by the troops announced the moment of consecration, was most thrilling to the senses. You get some little notion of the proportion of things when I mention that merely on the altar steps the dignitaries here and there in attendance on the Holy Father, though it was a mere spot in the vast whole, and they were comparatively scattered on the steps, numbered eighty.

When we moved out of St. Peter's for the grand blessing to the City and the World, everyone seemed to be seized with astonishment, the great piazza, the square beyond, and the streets right down to the bridge of St. Angelo, a mile in length, was one close mass of human heads. Never was such a spectacle seen in Rome. It was an utterly indescribable scene. There was of course a large body of troops, both horse and foot, but they seemed swallowed up in the countless mass. The vineyards on the right on the rising ground, the housetops, every place was covered. What would dear Mother Margaret have said, had she witnessed it all from the elevated position where I stood above the colonnade, taking it all in, Pope and all, at one and the same moment. The Pope's voice was as clear as ever, and we could hear every word of the absolutions as he uttered them; and when he rose and exalted his arms and voice, and the multitude went down on their knees, it was thrilling beyond expression. Then as he ceased, came up the roar of cheers, the roar of cannon, the clang of all the bells of all the Roman churches, almost drowning the martial sounds of all the military bands collected in the centre between the

two great fountains throwing their waters up into the vacant
air above the pavement of human heads. Next to me stood
the First Lord of the British Admiralty, Mr. Childers, who
went down with great reverence for the blessing, and was
very much struck with the unprecedented spectacle.

Bishop Amherst described the scene :

On Easter Day the Pope as usual sang the High Mass,
but, *not* as usual, was surrounded by seven hundred bishops
in copes and mitres. The blessing from the Loggia of
St. Peter's after Mass was the grandest thing I ever saw.
They calculate the crowd at 100,000. I, with about a
hundred bishops, was on the roof of the colonnade, where
Mgr. Pacca had covered a large space with an awning and
divided it into boxes. In the one furthest from the church
were royal and grand-ducal personages ; in the next,
bishops ; next, ambassadors ; next, Roman princes and
princesses. We could see the whole piazza and were on a
level with the Pope. The dead silence just before the blessing was given was the thing that struck me most. The
instant the blessing was given there was a tremendous cry
of ' Viva Pio Nono ! ' the clattering of bells, firing of
cannon and playing of military bands.

Then the moving of the enormous crowd away by the
different streets was most curious to see, and the way in
which order was kept for the carriages by the dragoons was
admirable : not the least confusion, though the streets are
narrow. In the evening the whole church and colonnade
were illuminated. When the change of lights took place
the church looked like a mountain of fire.

Also Dr. Northcote :

I must add a line about the Blessing this morning, which
was the most magnificent sight I ever saw. St. Peter's was
crammed. The scene of the Blessing was indescribable.
Nobody can say how many were present, and in every con-
ceivable costume : above 100,000 it is said. The mass of
people was unbroken from the piazza in every direction as
far as eye could reach. Spite of the myriads of people
present, all seemed to hold their breath and keep perfect

silence whilst the Pope gave the Blessing, which could be heard everywhere. He can never expect to see such a scene again, nor any of us, I suppose. The gala costumes of men and horses and carriages—the 7 or 8000 troops in the piazza, the hundreds of bishops, etc. etc.

Dr. Ullathorne wrote:

April 19, Easter Tuesday. Alleluia. My amendment is carried, Deo gratias! It has been a fight. Now for womanly curiosity. It was only the transposition of two words, but of great importance in English-speaking countries.

To Canon Estcourt the same day:

To-day in General Congregation my amendment was carried unanimously, two only rising against it : after it had been first proposed and voted, the votes left uncounted ; the substance of the question retracted and shelved ; and then voted against in another form by the ' placet ', except about forty who stood by me ; and then protested against on the score of informality ; then reopened by private correspondence ; then taken up anew and unanimously approved by the special deputation ; then to-day finally voted. The first to congratulate me was a cardinal, who rose from his place to do so from the distance by bows and waves of his hand, and pointing me out to his red-robed neighbours. The next was poor Strossmayer, and so much of it threatened me, that so soon as the Congregation rose I got away as fast as I could. It was the only amendment accepted by the Congregation and passed at the final voting, out of a large number proposed, except one other ; and mine was to boot a retractation of a former vote, while the other was but a new addition of a word. But many Americans voted with me, and I owed the reopening and working of the question in Council to the Archbishop of Baltimore [Spalding]. I shall I hope be able to show some day what a mess it has saved us from, in England especially. Our Archbishop behaved well in the last act in the special deputation.

The Session for the decrees *de Fide Catholica* will be on Sunday. We present nothing from our deputation, why, I cannot understand, for we had a schema ready for the final discussion [that on the Catechism].

The original schema of eighteen chapters *de Fide* is reduced to nine, of which four are complete for the Session, the other five, under a new heading, awaiting the second discussion. Twelve chapters of the schema *de Ecclesia* have been written upon and 130 documents have gone in long ago, but no summary of them has yet been circulated, and of course no discussion has taken place. But the special deputation has had prodigious labour, day and night, and certainly has shown great consideration to every movement made in the Council. The papers on the four chapters *de Fide*, and the frequently reprinted forms of them, will make a good folio vol., independent of the debates.

The talk now is of a suspension at end of June, and a resumption after the hot weather.

Low Sunday, April 24. Now for the Public Session of to-day, the third, but the first at which Decrees were passed. It lasted from 9 to 1.30. The Mass was of the Holy Ghost, and all the prelates were in red copes, looking like the army of the Church militant. The aula was used to its full extent, all screens being removed, so that all the acts were public, even the reading of the Decrees, which are now the property of the world, and the giving of the ' placets '.

I need not again describe to you the appearance of the aula at a Session, or the circle of cardinals round the apse, the inner circle of patriarchs, the long protracted lines of bishops in red copes and white mitres, interspersed with orientals in their many coloured robes and crowns, for they all seem to have a taste for Joseph's coat, and the officials at their tables between. Eight rows ascended on one side, eight on the other, face to face with a considerable space of green cloth covering the marble floor between. The altar is at the entrance and the pontifical throne at the opposite end, in centre of the apse. The Old Fathers in pictures of the old Councils look down on all, and the great dome forms a feature of the scene above, although considerably beyond the Council.

The Mass was sung. Then the Pope entered and the usual prayers were said and sung, including the 'Adsumus', the Litany, the 'Veni Creator', etc.

Then a bishop with a clear full voice read the Decrees seated in the ambo, and all sat listening, until the last of the anathemas was concluded. Then began the voting, which took an hour and a half. First the cardinals, then the prelates in their rank and according to their age in office, down to the generals of Orders. As each one's title was read, he uttered his 'placet', which was repeated by an official near him, then in a loud voice by one near the Pope, then re-echoed by one near the ambo, that the officials might record the vote. Those who were absent had 'abest' called out, instead of 'placet' after the name, with the same loud repetitions at the two ends of the aula. When all was done, and how long it seemed, the Secretary and protonotaries reported to the Pope that all, none excepted, who were present had given the 'placet'. Thereupon, the Pope declared his confirmation of the Decrees. He then arose, and poured out a short spontaneous address of peace and joy to the bishops. He was deeply moved and spoke in tones vibrating from his heart of the peace which unites the Church, of the peace which carries us through all trials, of the peace which makes us strong against all adversaries, of the peace and joy in believing which he prayed for us all in life and death, of the peace and joy of the Holy Ghost. And the bishops answered 'Amen', much touched, and some would have applauded, but others hushed them into silence. And upon this scene gazed a long array of retired Royalties from the boxes on one side, and the ambassadors on the other; and above them, from two opposite galleries the theologians. The crowd in the Church could of course neither see much or know much of what was passing.

Then the Pope rose once more to give the Benediction and Indulgence, and uprose the 'Te Deum', intoned by the Pope, chanted by the choir and the bishops alternately; the prayer; and the first important Session is concluded. When will the last conclude? As the Decrees are now public, you will probably soon see them. There is a preface and four chapters: on God, on Revelation, on Faith, and on

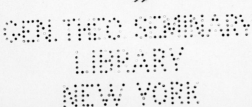

Faith and Reason, to which are added nineteen canons with an anathema to each.

The decrees now passed were four times the length in the original schema, and besides being reduced in quantity, they are very different in wording and in style. Almost every word has had its special discussion, and consequent modification. It is so compact, that each sentence, however short, strikes at one or more errors or heresies, and the uninitiated will require a guide through them. Hermesianism, false ontologism, and traditionalism are amongst the errors struck at, besides pantheism in its various forms, materialism, and the other modern infidelities. There are still five chapters more to come on the Mysteries of Faith, and then the great decree on the Church in a large number of chapters. All the errors of the age will be taken hold of in succession. There, I have told you all I can do. But I have just heard that the number who voted this morning was 667. A few kept away rather than say ' non placet ' on some point or term they wished to see modified, or on some point of rule, or supposed right of rule, in the discussion. Including the sick, perhaps forty were proclaimed absent ; besides whom a not inconsiderable number of prelates have got leave to return to their dioceses previously to the Session, on the score of health or of pressing affairs.

END OF VOL. I

H.C.A.R.C

DATE DUE

JUL 1 4 '89			
SEP 24			